Unwilling Mothers, Unwanted Babies

Law and Society Series
W. Wesley Pue, General Editor

The Law and Society Series explores law as a socially embedded phenomenon. It is premised on the understanding that the conventional division of law from society creates false dichotomies in thinking, scholarship, educational practice, and social life. Books in the series treat law and society as mutually constitutive and seek to bridge scholarship emerging from interdisciplinary engagement of law with disciplines such as politics, social theory, history, political economy, and gender studies.

A list of the books in this series appears at the end of this book.

Kirsten Johnson Kramar

Unwilling Mothers, Unwanted Babies:
Infanticide in Canada

UBCPress · Vancouver · Toronto

Learning Resources
Centre

12813133

15 14 13 12 11 10 09 08 07 06 05   5 4 3 2 1

Printed in Canada on acid-free paper

Library and Archives Canada Cataloguing in Publication

Unwilling mothers, unwanted babies : infanticide in Canada / Kirsten Johnson
Kramar.

(Law and society)
Includes bibliographical references and index.
ISBN 0-7748-1176-5

1. Infanticide – Canada. 2. Infanticide – Canada – History. 3. Sociological
jurisprudence. I. Title. II. Series: Law and society series (Vancouver, B.C.)

KE8910.J64 2005   345.71'02523   C2005-901815-1   KF9309.J64 2005

Canadä

UBC Press gratefully acknowledges the financial support for our publishing program
of the Government of Canada through the Book Publishing Industry Development
Program (BPIDP), and of the Canada Council for the Arts, and the British Columbia
Arts Council.

This book has been published with the help of a grant from the Canadian Federation
for the Humanities and Social Sciences, through the Aid to Scholarly Publications
Programme, using funds provided by the Social Sciences and Humanities Research
Council of Canada.

Printed and bound in Canada by Friesens
Set in Stone by Artegraphica Design Co. Ltd.
Copy editor: Joanne Richardson
Proofreader: Gail Copeland
Indexer: Heather Ebbs

UBC Press
The University of British Columbia
2029 West Mall
Vancouver, BC V6T 1Z2
604-822-5959 / Fax: 604-822-6083
www.ubcpress.ca

For Mieka

Contents

Acknowledgments

I have benefited immensely from the generosity of friends and colleagues who have supported my efforts to write this book. I am especially grateful to my friend William Watson who is forever willing to offer intellectual guidance, inspiration, and, always, laughter. I also wish to thank my friends, colleagues, and professors at the Centre of Criminology who very enthusiastically assisted my efforts to write a book on a wee criminal law spanning 100 years of criminal justice history. Special appreciation goes to Mariana Valverde who has provided ongoing support, especially as my dissertation supervisor, during the earlier incarnation of this work. I am also very grateful for the support of Carolyn Strange when I was a graduate student – thank you for the pony! Many thanks are also due to Professors Tony Doob, Philip Stenning, and Bernard Dickens who were always willing and able to answer technical questions. The staff at the Centre of Criminology Library helped immensely with the original research; thanks to Monica Bristol, Tom Findlay, and Andrea Shier for tirelessly tracking down source materials.

There are a number of dear friends and newly acquired colleagues who have been, in different sorts of ways, very supportive of my intellectual achievements. They deserve acknowledgment for their support: Elizabeth Comack, Constance Backhouse, Barry Edginton, Fiona Green, Peter Levesque, Renisa Mawani, Michelle Webber, Jo Van Every, and especially Kimberley White.

Finally, a special thank you to Wes Pue for his tireless commitment to nurturing Canadian law and society scholars and to those at UBC Press who worked with me on the manuscript: Randy Schmidt, Holly Keller, Ann Macklem, and Joanne Richardson.

Unwilling Mothers, Unwanted Babies

Introduction

In March 2002 a fifteen-year-old gave birth unassisted on the bathroom floor of her parents' home in Brampton, Ontario. Shortly thereafter she killed the newborn baby. The adolescent mother hid her pregnancy from family and friends and continued to attend Grade 10 at her Roman Catholic high school. She and her boyfriend had been sexually active since they were fourteen but did not use birth control. The Grade 9 curriculum at their high school had taught them to "protect and promote chastity" without providing any formal access to information about birth control or abortion, although there was evidence to suggest they knew where they could obtain both. She hid her pregnancy from her family and killed the baby at birth to protect herself and her family from the shame of her pregnancy. Family, friends, teachers, and classmates may have suspected the girl's pregnancy but apparently failed to get involved. They tacitly accepted the girl's denial, attributing her weight gain to overeating and teenage development. Just weeks prior to the birth, the girl was seen by a doctor who had no idea that she was in her third trimester. The coroner's autopsy concluded that the baby girl, named Destiny post-mortem, lived for two hours, having apparently died from one of the multiple stab wounds to her neck. At the time, the Brampton teen, whose identity is protected under the Canadian *Young Offenders Act*, was charged with second degree murder and held in a youth detention centre to await a bail hearing. The detective in charge of the case indicated that the police did not feel that "the components of the charge of infanticide were there" but declined to elaborate any further.[1] We are informed by the news reporter that, at the sentencing hearing almost one year later, the court was "torn between horror and mercy in teen mother's stabbing of baby daughter."[2] The adolescent woman pled guilty to infanticide and was sentenced to two years probation, 100 hours of community service, therapy, and sex education counselling.[3] According to the judge, the girl "was operating on a disturbed mind, if not full denial of pregnancy, suffering from psychological and emotional disturbance."[4]

The details of this case are like those of many other killings of newborn babies that have occurred over the past 100 years in Canada. Typically, a sexually active adolescent woman finds herself pregnant and conceals her pregnancy and subsequent delivery. Sometimes the women kill their newly born babies because they have been raped or otherwise coerced into sex by male employers, relatives, co-workers, or boyfriends. The women usually conceal and/or deny their pregnancies, give birth alone, and then dispose of the body of the baby in an outhouse, garbage bin, closet, field, or stream, where it is eventually discovered by the authorities. Once discovered, the coroner conducts an autopsy to determine cause of death and, on the basis of a finding of live-birth, the authorities lay a charge of murder or some lesser charge. For example, in 1926, Vera Fish, aged twenty-two years, was initially indicted on two counts of concealment of birth in Halton County in Ontario, following the discovery of an infant in a river. Fish was single and her pregnancy had been public, so the community suspected her of wanting to kill the illegitimate baby. When confronted, Fish confessed to having given birth to a baby girl but not to the baby boy discovered in the river near her apartment. During the investigation the burnt body of another baby was discovered in the oven at Fish's home. The coroner's autopsy indicated that the body of the infant was "burnt and roasted" but that one lung floated, suggesting that the baby had been "born alive." The authorities were unable to secure an indictment for murder from a grand jury. Fish was then charged with two counts of "concealment of birth" – one count for the baby found in the river and the second for the baby found in her oven. She eventually pled guilty to concealing the birth of the infant girl found dead in her oven.[5] Despite the very different times at which these events occurred, the two cases – one in Brampton and one in Halton County – share certain key similarities; in both cases we see a shameful pregnancy, the mother killing her newborn baby, and the court accepting a conviction lower than murder or manslaughter and offering a lenient disposition.

At the time of Vera Fish's conviction, the charges available in these kinds of cases were murder, manslaughter, concealment of birth (concealing body of child, now s. 243), and neglect to obtain assistance in childbirth (now s. 242), with the last two providing the more lenient options.[6] The provision for a charge of infanticide, the eventual conviction in the 2002 case, and an awkward and much criticized quasi-medico-legal category, was adopted by the Canadian Parliament in 1948. Before the enactment of the infanticide provision, the charges of "concealment" and "neglect" were frequently used in cases of suspected maternal neonaticide.[7] The authorities in the early twentieth century tended to resort to these charges when they failed to secure indictments for murder. Sometimes, when the authorities achieved an indictment for murder the case would eventually be disposed of by way of plea bargain for one of the auxiliary charges in order to ensure a conviction and to avoid taking the matter to trial, where their chances of success were poor. The difficulties of proving live-birth on medical evidence and of proving wilful intent in many of these cases, along with juror sympathy for adolescent women facing the death penalty, confounded the possibility of homicide convictions at trial, and Crown attorneys resorted to these auxiliary charges as a means of providing some kind of criminal law response. The auxiliary charges were much more likely to result in successful convictions than were the primary charges.

As of 1948, authorities could also rely on the law of infanticide. Section 233 of the *Criminal Code of Canada*, the infanticide provision, reads: "233. Infanticide – A female person commits infanticide when by a wilful act or omission she causes the death of her newly-born child, if at the time of the act or omission she is not fully recovered from the effects of giving birth to the child and by reason thereof or the effect of lactation consequent on the birth of the child her mind is then disturbed."[8]

The pre-existing charges available to be brought in cases of suspected maternal neonaticide being retained, the infanticide provision became, then, merely *one* of a range of potential options, intended specifically to address cases where women were suspected of killing their babies at birth. The infanticide provision was explicitly intended to provide the opportunity in these cases for a homicide conviction, which is less serious than a murder or manslaughter conviction; it stands with "concealment" and "neglect" as a less serious conviction but with murder and manslaughter as a culpable homicide.[9] Like "neglect," the infanticide charge is both formally gender-specific and restricted to cases where the relationship between perpetrator and victim is the biological relationship of mother and child. In practice, "concealment" almost always operates in the same way. The range of available charges is integrated through a scheme of "lesser included" offences; triers of fact can substitute findings of manslaughter or infanticide in cases where the Crown fails to prove murder (s. 662(3)) and concealment of birth where charges of murder or infanticide are not proven (s. 662(4)).[10] The integration of infanticide and concealment in this scheme maximizes the possibility of a jury returning a conviction for a *Criminal Code* offence in cases of women suspected of killing their newly born babies.[11]

Feminist scholarship, in older and contemporary versions, has often placed infanticide as well as the offences of "concealment" and "neglect," within the context of a range of laws that regulate (hetero)sexuality and reproduction rather than infant homicide. Consistently criticized in these analyses is the medicalization of infant killing integral to contemporary infanticide law. Much of the late twentieth-century critical scholarship on the law governing the killing of newly born babies by their biological mothers treats infanticide law as an expression of repressive state power, grounded in the intrinsically exploitative reproductive and productive relations governing women. According to Carol Smart's earlier critiques (1989, 1992), English infanticide laws from the seventeenth to the twentieth centuries regulated both illegitimacy and single motherhood – these being special challenges to the capitalist-patriarchal consolidation of the heterosexual monogamous family form. Her analysis of the state's regulation of women's sexuality locates infanticide law within the broader legal framework of nineteenth-century acts governing reproduction and sexual relations (e.g., infanticide, abortion, birth control, baby farming, illegitimacy, sodomy, prostitution, age of consent, and marriage). These laws were aimed at regulating so-called sexual deviance and trumpeted the prevention of immorality among the "dangerous classes" and the preservation of racial purity (Valverde 1991).[12] According to Smart (1992, 17), the seventeenth-century English infanticide law and its harsh punishment framework (typically, death by hanging) functioned to regulate, through detection, prosecution, and punishment, "the sexual and reproductive behaviour of a woman who had no man to support her."[13] By the end of the nineteenth century in England jurors' tacit understanding of the economics of infanticide eased the punishment framework for infanticide, which, by then, was rarely dealt with by way of hanging (17). Poverty, the result of capitalist industrialization, was both the mitigation for, and explanatory model of, infanticide.[14] Smart argues further that the established economic rationale for infanticide gave way to a modern medical rationale that linked infanticide to insanity and to the womb. Thus, infanticide law offers one of the most explicit examples of the medicalization of deviance in criminal law.[15]

Smart's analysis exemplifies the use of the text of the contemporary infanticide law as an illustration for the broader feminist critique of the medicalization of women's deviance. This broader critique problematizes the merging of law and medicine, viewing its development as part and parcel of the capitalist patriarchal structure within which juridical categories like infanticide can be used to control women (Smart 1992; Showalter 1985; Edwards 1984). This was achieved by a patriarchal medical profession through oppressive bio-psychological ideas expressed in legal categories like infanticide, which define women's deviance in relation to bodily difference or defect. According to this feminist critique of the medicalization of deviance, infanticide law has negative effects because it accounts for the causes of women's deviance in bio-psychological terms (pregnancy, childbirth, and lactation) rather than locating the causes of women's deviance in an oppressive patriarchal social structure (O'Donovan 1984; Osborne 1987; Smart 1989, 1995).[16]

I am able to show that this analysis does not fit well with the development of the Canadian infanticide provision, which was a pragmatic, even artful, solution to the problem of securing convictions faced by the prosecuting authorities. The *Hansard* record demonstrates that, from the perspective of government, the problem was that the then existing legal framework was being applied in an entirely ad hoc manner. This was *legally* problematic since it allowed far too much discretion on the part of individual agents of the state, with disparate outcomes for individual women charged with the various offences. Ironically, the legislators' apparent concern was "fairness" and "justice" through the even application of law, although they did not express the problem in quite this manner.[17] The parliamentary debates among legislators, all of whom were trained as lawyers, illustrate that "conceal-ment" was understood to be an entirely unsatisfactory response to the crime of infanticide. The concern articulated in the House of Commons was with the crime of maternal neonaticide and its prosecution. It was described as impossible to prosecute as "murder" since juries were unable or unwilling to sentence women to death. The various ways in which the crime was being dealt with interfered with the proper application of legal doctrine.

The immediate, practical purpose of the Canadian infanticide law was not to police the boundaries of gender relations but, rather, to provide a favourable legal solution to the problem of convicting women for the mur-der of their newborns in a manner consistent with lay and scientific knowl-edge. The issue was not whether these women should be punished for failing to conform to ideological standards governing femininity and motherhood; the issue was framed in terms of providing a measured appropriate response to the killing of babies in a manner that recognized women's unique expe-riences of pregnancy, childbirth, and lactation. Although this is not obvi-ous from a purely textual reading of the infanticide provision itself, both the mothers and the killed babies were understood in and by lay and scien-tific thinking, and in English law in the form of the infanticide provision, to be the victims of social injustice.[18] The coercive sexual relations between single women and their male "seducers" – men who failed to meet their social obligations dictated by prevailing rules of propriety – was the sub-stance of the humanitarian sentiment operationalized by infanticide law. In this sense, the new "medicalized" infanticide provision was more an at-tempt to gently redirect juror sympathy toward significant conviction than to reorganize the discourse around infant killing. As a consequence of the failure of fathers to meet their socially ascribed obligations to both mother and child, the issue of holding women legally responsible under the *Crimi-nal Code* framework for culpable homicide was, from the perspective of le-gal practitioners, uniquely vexatious. When the women sometimes confessed to murder, they were invariably sentenced to death, but the public's ada-mant opposition to the punishment eventually resulted in their release from prison on a ticket of leave (although not before they spent a considerable number of years in federal prison).

Subsequent to the socialist-feminist critiques, the less functionalist analyses have understood infanticide law as an essential component of a disciplinary society in which "woman" is constituted as a legal subject. These analyses rely on Foucauldian insights to argue that the law influences the formation of the category "bad mother," which interpolates ideological notions of proper motherhood. Now we see infanticide law, along with the other laws regulating (hetero)sex and reproduction, constituting specific action categories rather than expressing and/or consolidating capitalist and patriarchal power relations. In this critique, the economism drops away and infanticide law operates to help reproduce expert knowledge governing femininity and motherhood, which includes the constitution of deviant women in legal discourse as diseased, dangerous, and hysterical. With this Foucauldian turn, ideas about respectable femininity and motherhood articulated in and through legal text and trial get inside the minds and bodies of women, directing/motivating action in a particular manner. Here, regulation is more complex than in the economistic feminist approach. It is achieved through the inculcation of individual self-governance, accomplished partly through the infanticide law, which delineates a boundary between "bad" and "good" mother – with the bad mother being self-evidently deserving of punishment.

In her later work, Smart (1995) adopts this style. She abandons seeing infanticide law as inextricably linked to the furtherance of capitalism and patriarchy, and highlights the broader symbolic effects of contemporary infanticide law, which is still seen as regulating single women and constructing an exploitative medico-legal category. The infanticide law continues to be depicted as problematical insofar as it expresses a medicalized model of women's deviance. At both the practical and the symbolic levels, infanticide law is still conceived of as a reaction by the authorities to women's refusal to conform to a particular set of established patriarchal discourses that govern reproduction and mothering. This reaction by the authorities is linked to women's failure to conform to the dominant standards of femininity insofar as a woman who kills her newly born baby rejects her immediate responsibility to that infant. However, for Smart, the infanticide law is less about the act of killing babies and the prosecutions of women suspected in the deaths of babies, and more about the regulation and control of women's sexuality. The bio-psychological causation model built into the text of infanticide law is, thus, seemingly a paradigmatic example of the easy alliance between two dominant discourses: infanticide law illustrates how patriarchal law and medicine are deployed to secure conformity and to promote moral self-governance among women. Consequently, the trials of the single women accused of infanticide are an important means of communicating hegemonic ideals and regulatory aims (Smart 1992). In this model the regulation of women through medical knowledge, expressed as diminished responsibility on the basis of pregnancy, childbirth, and lactation, works by delimiting and describing single motherhood in negative terms. It is the discourse itself, rather than the economic system, that determines how single women are understood and how they will behave as a consequence of these negative ideas about women's deviance. Legal regulation works at both the practical and symbolic levels to control women.

Along with the problems inherent in the continuing adherence to the anti-medicalization line, which I have already identified, this Anglo-Foucauldian feminist critique of infanticide offers an analysis of the text of the infanticide law without interrogating the discursive basis of the text as articulated by the medical experts. In fact, the psychiatric theory upon which the apparently reductionist bio-psychiatric mitigation of infanticide is based turns out to be surprisingly "sociological." The experts believed that the straightened social and economic circumstances of many young and not-so-young mothers, combined with the physical stresses identified in the statute, produce mild mental disturbance.

The treatment of the reproductive morality implicit in the medicalized infanticide provision, especially when considered in relation to pre-existing juror sympathies, is also problematic. The Anglo-Foucauldian model suggests that, from the perspective of government, infanticide was an example of unrestrained sexual immorality. However, the immorality of infanticide was ambiguous. Single women who killed illegitimate babies to conceal their illicit sexual activity were acting out of the very sense of morality that the purity campaigns sought to inculcate. That the illegitimate babies did not survive to complicate paternal responsibility may also have explained juror reluctance to punish women harshly. Therefore, these killings were arguably *consistent* with the broader aims of the sexual purity movements because killed illegitimate babies could not disrupt lines of inheritance. More broadly, the women who killed their newly born illegitimate babies were understood to be *conforming* to ideological notions governing motherhood and femininity since they killed their babies to hide the shame of their ex-nuptial sexual activity and to protect the infant from living a life stigmatized by illegitimacy. In Canada the killing of these babies was sometimes openly backed by the women's lovers, families, and friends, who wanted to avoid stigma for themselves and the babies. In this very important sense, the women were seen in contradictory terms, at once virtuous and misguided in their actions.

Given that the trial is presumably an important means of communicating the ideas that Anglo-Foucauldian feminists identify in the statute, it is surprising that little attention is paid to the processes by which cases of women who kill their newly born babies come to trial. In practice, many cases of maternal neonaticide had very little impact in terms of communicating ideological notions about motherhood and medicalized notions of deviance. To begin with, in Canada, it was discovered very shortly after the adoption of the infanticide provision that the Crown could not meet its evidentiary burden with respect to the mental element. Following an amendment to the infanticide law in 1955, the only element required to be proven "beyond a reasonable doubt" is that the act or omission was wilful.[19] Section 663 of the *Criminal Code* prevents an acquittal on a charge of infanticide if the Crown *fails to meet its burden of proof* with respect to the psychological evidence of disturbance of mind:

> 663. No acquittal unless act or omission not wilful – Where a female person is charged with infanticide and the evidence establishes that she caused the death of her child but does not establish that, at the time of the act or omission by which she caused the death of the child,
>
> (a) she was not fully recovered from the effects of giving birth to the child or from the effect of lactation consequent on the birth of the child, and
> (b) the balance of her mind was, at the time, disturbed by reason of the effect of giving birth to the child or of the effect of lactation consequent on the birth of the child,
>
> She may be convicted unless the evidence establishes that the act or omission was not wilful.[20]

Thus, in the absence of proven psychological disturbance, a conviction for infanticide may still be secured as long as the Crown meets its burden and establishes that the act was wilful. The authorities are not required to establish the mental disturbance element; it is merely "read-in" from the killing of the infant and the charge of infanticide itself.[21] So here we see an extraordinary situation where a woman's ability to think and act rationally at the time of the killing – notwithstanding her mind being supposedly weakened by gestation, parturition, and lactation – allows her to be found guilty of the crime of infanticide. The infanticide law and its qualifying clause *is* a unique quasi-medico-legal category for which a controversial psychological rationale has been effectively abandoned as a formal legal requirement, yet its odd reliance on the supporting psychological knowledge has the effect of *preventing* vengeance toward "unmarried mothers" on the basis of gender and motherhood. This is because the law is based on the English version, where infanticide diminishes the punishment for manslaughter. In the Canadian version, the law is written as a diminished capacity provision but stands alone as a separate charge.

The idea that infanticide trials communicated negative ideas about single women fails to account for the many married and widowed women who killed their babies and were tried for infanticide, and it makes no mention of the means of communication of these ideas to delimit the broader effects on the social body. Overall, the relevant details of these cases have often been kept tightly within the legal arena. This "silencing" of the cases pre-dates the medicalized concept and continues after its adoption. Grand jury deliberations were conducted in secret and typically concluded without issuing a "true bill." In Ontario, during the early part of the twentieth century, most cases were disposed of by way of concealment or neglect indictments, with only some resulting in convictions. In these situations the issue at bar was usually about either women's *intent* to conceal the birth or neglect to obtain medical assistance rather than women's diminished mental state consequent upon pregnancy, childbirth, or lactation. Discussions at bar sometimes addressed the question of marital status but, typically, for the purposes of mitigation rather than retribution. For the vast majority of cases of mothers who killed their babies there were no trials. However, of the many women who were tried for killing their newly born babies, some confessed to killing while others pled not guilty. In situations where the women pled not guilty, the issues at bar dealt with the very difficult forensic question of live-birth. Even today, the scientific evidence adduced at trials cannot establish "beyond a reasonable doubt" that an infant, born outside of a hospital without medical assistance, is live-born. Therefore, the question of the communication of a medicalized notion of deviance through infanticide law is doubly diluted since, apart from the elimination of the need for psychological evidence, these cases rarely went to trial in Canada.

Once the infanticide law was adopted in 1948 it became an additional charge rather than a replacement for murder or the lesser auxiliary charges. Again, the communication of the now supposedly medicalized notions of deviance are limited because very few cases where infanticide was the actual charge went to trial. In any case, the organization of legal facts and various lay and expert knowledge produced a discourse around the killing of newly born babies by their mothers that perceived the women's actions as the product of the stress on the body and mind caused by socioeconomic hardship. Toward the end of the twentieth century, postpartum depression and/or postpartum psychosis developed into a dominant justification for women who kill their newly born babies. However, these situations are typically associated with the deaths of older children (over six months). It has been established that onset of postpartum depression occurs around the sixth month postpartum, when the hormone levels associated with pregnancy drop significantly. Typically, women who kill their babies during this phase suffer from psychotic delusions about the baby (often believing her/him to be the devil or going to hell) and suffer from hallucinations.[22]

It is, then, in many ways misleading to apply the broad notion that this particular "patriarchal" law is a sound example of the socially effective medicalization of women's crime. The approach laid out here moves beyond both the socialist-feminist and the Anglo-Foucauldian critiques, both of which firmly connect the medical aspects of the text of the infanticide law to the oppression/regulation of women. Infanticide law should be understood within a *legal* context as something quite different from the medicalization of women's deviance or the constitution and regulation of "bad" mothers *through this category*. The history of the passage of the law and its prosecution reveals that legislators had little concern for the medical knowledge underwriting the law. The discursive base of the law, as articulated by the English experts in mental medicine, understood infanticide as a product of exhaustion and stress on working-class women, and categories like "lactational insanity" and "exhaustion psychosis" were developed to provide both medical diagnoses and plain socioeconomic explanations for infant murders. Experts in mental medicine made no attempts to bind medicine to law or to control, regulate, or punish the women in their institutions. The women were in their care for very brief recovery periods and were then discharged. These were the very women who, in socialist-feminist and Foucauldian terms, failed to conform to ideological standards governing femininity or motherhood. Laymen empanelled on juries refused to indict women for murder when they killed their newly born babies because the death penalty was too harsh a punishment for a crime firmly connected to an unjust *legal* system in which women themselves were held wholly (individually) accountable for the product of illicit sexual activity, be it coerced or consensual. Then, when the "infanticidal" mitigation framework gets taken up in law, and thereby becomes highly individualized and focused on rationality and intentionality, its practical effect was to make convictions difficult to secure – until its biomedical teeth were pulled in the 1955 amendment.

While the killing of newly born babies can be modelled as a kind of political resistance to enforced motherhood as a result of a range of straightened circumstances, including rape, lack of fertility control, illegitimacy, and poverty, it is also a potential homicide of a live-born human being. In Western culture the killing of a live-born human being demands a formal legal response. Infanticide law is thus distinct from other laws, such as those prohibiting sodomy, prostitution, abortion, birth control, and obscenity, that have historically been used to govern sexuality and reproduction. Lumping infanticide law together with these other laws is conceptually problematic since infanticide is not an event we can now imagine failing to receive a criminal law response in Canada. Certainly, the killing of newborn babies by their mothers has not been universally constructed as a moral, legal, or quasi-legal violation, a fact that is well documented by anthropological literature, which casts a very telling light on the narrow Western conceptualization of the killing of newborn babies as a crime requiring a retributive response, even if only for the purposes of general deterrence.

Within differing cultural and historical contexts, the deaths of babies (of certain kinds) has been tolerated, understood in relation to the social conditions under which women mother. In part, this tolerance of infant death, both by the mothers themselves and the authorities, is connected to disparate valuations of infants and their differing relations in and to global economies. This literature is best exemplified by the ethnographic research of Scheper-Hughes (1985, 1987, 1992); and Scheper-Hughes and Sargent (1998). It illustrates that when acts and omissions, which would be viewed in the West as maternal apathy and neglect resulting in death, occur within the context of "environment[s] hostile to the survival and well-being of mothers and infants" (1987, 3), they are rarely constructed as requiring moral censure or punishment. In Western culture, where the standard of living is generally quite high, the killing of newly born babies by their mothers is ideologically taboo. Infanticide law is part of a much wider cultural formation that disallows the killing of live-born babies. To assert that infanticide law constructs the categories of "bad" and "good" mother around the notion that killing babies is wrong cedes far too much power to an ill-conceived and poorly operating law. This idea already exists as a formidable component of the broader culture. And that the formal legal response has typically been especially forgiving is perhaps perplexing from both the socialist-feminist and Anglo-Foucauldian feminist perspectives. After all, for both, criminal law is conceptualized, albeit somewhat differently, as a negative expression of power. That the law *diminishes* responsibility for the killing of babies by their biological mothers in relation to all other kinds of murder committed by both men and women demands an examination of the broader disciplinary effects of the rationale of diminishing women's responsibility for murder within the context described by Smart.[23]

In the English context, infanticide law has more recently been understood as creating a special category of mother-murderer whose responsibility is diminished by an understanding of women's troubles – an understanding rooted in liberal humanitarian sensibilities about the feminine class experience. These notions are taken up in and by law and are reconstructed to "fit" the legal ideology of the abstract rational individual who is the subject of law. And, as Ward (1999, 174) has argued, again in the English context, infanticide law *reconstructs* medical knowledge to fit the individualistic needs of law. More specifically, infanticide law provides an illustration of the tension between the abstract individualism of criminal law and the recognition of social and emotional pressures on human subjectivity and agency in lay and medical discourse. According to this critique, the English act, 1938 (a version of which was adopted in Canadian law), provides a working example of how "criminal law doctrine addresses itself to an autonomous juridical subject, the lay and medical narratives ... often depict a very different, much less autonomous subject" (Ward 2002,

269). It is argued here, along with Ward and others, that the mitigation for baby killing achieved by infanticide law is linked to gender in that the criminal justice system is not inclined to treat violent women as rational autonomous agents. According to Allen (1987, 93), women are more often treated as the "victims of circumstances, social or economic pressures, of violent men or violent emotions; she may indeed be much like other women, and have similarly pressing responsibilities in such feminine domains as motherhood and the family; she may indeed be a generally harmless creature who poses little threat outside the immediate – and perhaps exceptional – circumstances of a single crime. Furthermore, the recognition of these factors may quite genuinely enlighten many aspects of the case, and their acknowledgement is by no means necessarily oppressive or illegitimate."

In terms of the dominant mitigating discursive frameworks, it has been argued that women defendants have been viewed by the courts as "sad," "mad," and "bad" (Ward 1999, 2002; Wilczynski 1991, 1997a, 1997b). But this debate about how the courts have variously constructed women defendants misses the broader point that these three interconnected discourses are an integral feature of the criminal trial process. The acknowledgment of extenuating circumstances is a feature of *most* criminal trials. During the sentencing phase, evidence of social or psychological constraint on human subjectivity is usually introduced by defence counsel to reduce the punishment, while evidence of enhanced culpability is emphasized by the Crown to secure a conviction and appropriate punishment. The courts quite properly take into account a broad range of social and psychological variables when sentencing both men and women, and it is within this context that the mitigation framework offered by the infanticide law speaks directly to women's difficulties with pregnancy, childbirth, lactation, and mothering. In other words, the immediate (and perhaps disciplinary) effects of the infanticide law are positive insofar as that law abandons formal legal equality and abstract individualism in favour of a contextually located legal defence to murder. This provides a counterpoint to the argument that law is distinct and separate from the external reality of crime and that its categories are independently constructed. The law does not exist in a separate universe parallel to the one outside of the courtroom doors: it very immediately and easily takes up the medically authorized humanitarian mitigation model and moulds it into the language and form required in law.

In practice, the question of whether or not the infanticide category is used to control women turns out to be much more complicated than is suggested by the contemporary Anglo-Foucauldian feminist critique. This is not to say that there is nothing to the broad Anglo-Foucauldian and feminist claim that this bio-psychological category is used to control women. However, the question we might consider is this: how much controlling of women as a group does it do? The most consistent observable fact of this research is that the Crown wants to maximize its legal control over deviant women and that it pushes for a quasi-medical notion when it thinks it can accomplish this. It is important to note that its aims are pragmatic – it believes that the infanticide law would achieve the simple goal of gaining convictions for homicide. The state very readily picked up on the medical vocabulary written into English law, indeed adopting it in a rather cavalier manner, but when we get to present-day prosecutions, we see that it is able to drop the medical vocabulary because it believes it can get a harsher response another way. Therefore, we should not think of the criminal law here only as the moral governance of women as a group because these cases are very obviously about the arrest, prosecution, and conviction of individual women. The law does not just govern diffusely, it also governs immediately and directly. It is important to make a clear distinction between the law governing individuals directly and the diffuse effects of that law on society as a whole because, theoretically, we might not have the same prescription at these two very different levels of analysis. The development and application of contemporary infanticide law is probably a much better example of the latter than of the former. I argue that it is quite far fetched to see infanticide law as a coherent component of a system of governance with significant effects being articulated into the social body. Ironically, I believe that the socio-legal feminist critique of medicalization has done much more to articulate a medicalized notion of infanticide into the social body than has the infanticide law. After all, if we *are* being governed through this medico-legal category, then we must also include in our critical analyses of these processes the broader effects of the feminist critics who advanced the idea that infanticide law oppresses women because it is based on regressive ideas about women's mental capacity wrought by reproduction (and the feminist critique has become a much more generally broadcast discourse than has the infanticide doctrine itself). Instead, we must understand that infanticide law was an end run around the death penalty and that it diminishes responsibility for a crime very firmly located within a sociological or cultural understanding of these women's experiences of broader patriarchal oppression. That it governs immediately and directly an especially vulnerable group of adolescent women should not escape our notice.

In the prevailing punitive climate, the legitimacy of diminished responsibility is disappearing and, with it, the use of the infanticide law as a legal response. This can be linked to a broad range of law reforms affecting the formal legal status of women and, particularly, of women's reproductive freedom (especially the greatly increased availability of contraception and abortion and the destigmatization of illegitimacy). In the early part of the twentieth century, before the enactment of the infanticide provision, both the Canadian authorities and the public had a more complex understanding of the vagaries of life for single working-class mothers than they appear to have today. In the early twentieth century, people sympathized with the everyday hardships faced by single women with illegitimate babies, and they understood that there were extreme economic and emotional hardships connected to raising babies for single working-class mothers. The view that the women were victims of social circumstance was, of course, realistic given the social, political, and legal climate of early twentieth-century Canada. The gradual achievement of formal legal equality and new reproductive freedoms has not led to the disappearance of maternal neonaticide – only to a wholly different construction of "unwilling mothers" and "unwanted babies." Rather than locating the explanation for the killing of newly born babies by their biological mothers within a social welfare or mental health model, the authorities are attempting to amplify the available criminal justice punishment for crimes related to infanticide. While this book was being written, the federal government entertained the idea of removing "infanticide" from the *Criminal Code* and replacing it with "death by child abuse/neglect." It was suggested that this provision not require the specific intent to kill and that the minimum term of imprisonment without eligibility for parole be classed as second degree murder (life imprisonment). This suggestion came from the Office of the Chief Coroner for Ontario following several high-profile child abuse inquests.[24] The new offence, dubbed "child abuse homicide," amounted to a strict liability provision governing motherhood in criminal law. In a related move, the government is set to amend the current punishment framework for "abandonment," increasing it from two to five years imprisonment. The government is increasing the penalty, despite the fact that at least forty US states, France, Germany, and Italy have all decriminalized the crime of "abandonment" and established public spaces for women to leave their unwanted babies without fear of public censure or criminal prosecution in order to *prevent* infanticide. Today in Canada, the prosecutorial aim of punishing women who kill their infants is apparently no different than it was fifty years ago when Parliament passed the infanticide provision itself. But now, feminist discourses have been appropriated by law and order advocates to support the enhanced prosecution of women suspected of infant murder. In other words, the feminist discourse on women's reproductive responsibility, advanced in order to secure freedom of choice and to decriminalize abortion, has been appropriated by law and order advocates and incorporated into legal discourse in order to further retributive aims directed at the women on behalf of the baby. The baby, in turn, has acquired new quasi-legal status somewhat in line with the anti-abortion movement's attempt to assert foetal rights claims in law. In a climate where foetal rights are immanent, the newly born baby has become the wholly deserving victim around which calls for retribution are now organized; we see the emergence of the rights-bearing victim in the body of the baby, damaged or dead, while the mother, no longer a legitimate victim herself, continues to be the target of prosecution and, now, enhanced punishment.

These developments are connected to the rise in legal and *medical* status of the infant. Babies, newly born without medical assistance, used to be assumed to have been stillborn (and their mothers innocent). Now they are assumed to have been live-born (and their mothers guilty). Any humanitarian sympathy that existed for the women has been refocused on the baby. These developments are occurring within the context of a dramatic shift in the broader politics of criminal law, where the due-process rights of the accused are pitted against the rights of victims and potential victims to protection (Roach 1999). However, within the troubling emergence of the "due-process-versus-victim's-rights" model of criminal justice, only certain kinds of victims are truly deserving of state-sanctioned protection. The broader experiences of suffering by the women are always trumped by the obvious status of the (dead) baby as immediate victim. Proposals for the reform of the infanticide law must also be understood within the context of recent developments in the identification and management of child abuse, and its variant "shaken baby syndrome," where any kind of harm suffered by infants and children is construed as "child abuse" (witness the proposed "child abuse homicide" charge).[25] Here we see not just a conceptual affinity but also a practical cross-fertilization between feminist discourse (especially its positioning as part of a broader politics of victimhood) and the law and order discourse (with its emphasis on responsibility and the individual rights of the victim). Here, two seemingly disparate discourses merge/converge, bringing into being an impending system of regulation.

The socio-legal feminist critique of medicalization, with its emphasis on the women's rationality and agency, has been appropriated by "law and order" advocates to bolster their own arguments, although they have dropped the concern with the social contexts within which these women acted. And the development of the feminist critique of medicalization as a purely textual analysis of law, with largely symbolic force, seems to have been associated with a lack of direct feminist involvement both in cases where women kill their newly born babies and in current criminal law debates about the possible repeal of infanticide law. In part, this is because feminist activism was largely concerned with reforming law and procedure that reproduced the oppression of women as *victims* of violence.[26] Unlike feminist activism in other areas of criminal law reform (e.g., the amendment of traditional rape law and procedure, the decriminalization of birth control and abortion, the criminalization of woman abuse, and the nouveau-criminalization of obscenity) there have been no equivalent feminist discussions around the prosecution of women who kill their newly born babies. The purely textual forms of the feminist critique, and the obvious lack of organized response to the application of the infanticide law, have had the unintended effect of conceding conceptual territory to advocates of increased criminal sanction. Law and order advocates believe that the infanticide provision "devalues human life," and they have appropriated the language, rather than the intent, of the socio-legal feminist critique of medicalization in order to legitimize their claim that women be held wholly responsible for "infanticide" transmogrified as "child abuse." This development is especially significant in the present legal and political climate, when the "rights" of the foetus and baby threaten to acquire quasi-legal authority and to justify broader encroachments on and punishments of the pregnant, and recently pregnant, body.[27]

Attempts to locate infanticide within a framework of aggression in which infants are conceptually positioned as innocent victims of evil mothers, and whose right to life trumps all others, tend to dismiss both sociological and psychological explanatory frameworks as the product of ivory tower (and perhaps feminist) madness. Maternal neonaticide has become a problem of women's aggression, irresponsibility, selfishness, and "child homicide," demanding a different kind of criminal law response. The new explanatory framework is, of course, very much at home in the criminal justice arena as the criminal justice system is neither structured nor equipped to redress social injustices and inequalities, and, within the Canadian legal context, explanatory models of intentionalist maternal aggression tend to prevail over explanatory sociological models of social inequality. It also fits comfortably within the framework of contemporary political discourse, with its emphasis on individual responsibility, market economics, and minimal government.

During the twentieth century maternal neonaticide shifted from (1) an act understood in relation to socio-economic disadvantage to (2) an act understood as a psychiatric illness linked to childbirth and lactation to (3) an act for which no justification is legitimate because it is presumed that the infant-victim has a "right-to-life" that the courts must protect by punishing fully responsibilized mothers. My analysis demonstrates that, during a series of distinct phases in the treatment of defendants accused of maternal neonaticide, Crown prosecutors have persistently attempted to secure the most serious convictions and the most severe punishments available, despite the early legislators' attempts to deal with the problem in a manner that recognized working-class adolescent women's experiences of unwanted pregnancy. The pattern of prosecutorial effort, now reflected and potentially achieved in the new law and order discourses about "child abuse homicide" is, perhaps, the only completely consistent element of how the killing of newly born babies by their mothers has been viewed and responded to in Canada throughout the twentieth century. It indicates that any repeal of the infanticide provision is likely to result in adolescent women, whose offences have traditionally been (are still sometimes) regarded with considerable sympathy and responded to with appropriate leniency, becoming subject to aggressive prosecution and harsher punishment.

Chapter Breakdown

Chapter 1 sets out the prosecutorial conviction problem prior to the passage of the infanticide law in 1948. Concealment of birth and neglect to obtain assistance in childbirth were the charges most likely to secure a conviction for the killing of a newly born baby. Since only a live-born baby can be the victim of a homicide, the establishment of live-birth was crucial to the Crown's success. Yet forensic specialists were explicitly instructed to presume stillbirth rather than live-birth in these cases, thereby thwarting the Crown's efforts to obtain homicide convictions. Chapter 2 investigates the prosecution process prior to the law's passage. It does this by looking at the available indictment case files for the province of Ontario between 1853 and 1977 as well as at the capital case files in which women were sentenced to death for killing newly born babies. This chapter demonstrates that the authorities were prevented from obtaining indictments and convictions largely as a consequence of the inadequate evidence provided by coroners. The provincial cases reveal a strong inclination on the part of the authorities to secure indictments for murder; however, since grand jurors, who were convened under the antiquated system of indictment through a coroner's jury, were unlikely to issue these indictments and were disposed only to permit indictments for the lesser auxiliary charges, legislation in the form of the infanticide provision was adopted in the House of Commons in 1948.[28] The capital case files reveal that the women convicted usually made declarative statements to the authorities amounting to confessions that resulted in their conviction at trial. These convictions provoked considerable public protest. Eventually, the convicted women who were sentenced to death had their sentences commuted to life and were invariably released after serving a shorter period of time. This is the immediate background to the passage of the infanticide law in Canada in 1948.

Chapter 3 demonstrates that early twentieth-century medical knowledge, upon which rests English infanticide law (est. 1922, amended 1938), of which the Canadian law is a version, placed the killing of newly born babies by their biological mothers within its socio-economic context. The experts in mental medicine saw their "infanticidal" patients as overwhelmed by poverty. They believed that these adverse circumstances placed pressures on the recently pregnant and now lactating mind and body, causing women to kill their babies. This provides a counterpoint to the argument that the biomedical/psychological category "reproductive insanity" regulated single motherhood by individualizing and/or pathologizing deviance. In practical terms, it accomplished neither. This chapter also demonstrates, through a discussion of the House of Commons debates that occurred when the infanticide law was passed, that legislators intended to implement a more logical process for securing convictions for homicide when a woman was suspected of killing her newly born baby. Their aim was to assimilate the practices into one category – infanticide. The penalty could then be applied consistently in each case.

Chapter 4 provides a critical analysis of the available reported cases dealing with infanticide. Rather than diminish responsibility for manslaughter on the basis of pregnancy, childbirth, and lactation – as is the case with the English statute – Canadian infanticide law constitutes a separate charge. As a result, infanticide has not achieved the objectives as set out by reformers and has proven very difficult to administer. Once passed, the infanticide provision was very quickly amended to remove the Crown's dual burden of proving both intent and reproductive mental disturbance, which had turned out to constitute a new obstacle, rather than an aid, to conviction. The difficulties with using the infanticide law as laid out in *R. v. Marchello* (1951) led to its revision in 1955, when Parliament passed a law removing the Crown's burden to prove the reproductive mental element.[29] The amendment eliminated the need to prove mental disturbance, although the underlying psychological mitigation rationale was retained in the existing statute. Now we see the efforts on the part of the authorities to maximize convictions by tinkering, this time, with *procedural* elements of the criminal law. The identifiable legal barriers to conviction for infanticide, noted by those in law and order circles (particularly Crown prosecutors and judges), were well articulated and partially sorted out by the middle of the twentieth century. Following this, very few cases were reported. Existing case law deals with the perennial legal questions of live-birth and wilful intent. The development of jurisprudence on wilfulness reveals a trend toward enhanced responsibility for the women. Cases on sentencing reveal a growing dissatisfaction with the mitigation framework offered by the provision and a drift toward harsher punishment, especially when the baby is subject to maternal violence.

Chapters 5 and 6 describe the more recent development of new prosecutorial strategies for dealing with cases of maternal neonaticide, which locate it within a framework of child victimization, and attempt to cast it as a wholly willed and wicked act requiring intensive investigation and deserving of severe punishment. This framework is criticized on the ground that cases of maternal neonaticide are very frequently so unlike the abuse and victimization scenarios established in the "child abuse" framework (by its own moral and evidentiary logics) that to assimilate the one to the other is indefensible and can result in punishments that, from any standpoint, are inappropriately harsh. Chapter 5 discusses the rise of the child abuse detection movement and its links to the Office of the Chief Coroner for Ontario. It lays out a number of cases of child abuse homicide that occurred while the children were in the care of the Conservative government's child protection system. These deaths resulted in a very high-profile coroner's inquest in the mid-1990s. This inquest resulted in sweeping changes to the identification, detection, and management of the homicides of children, including abolishing the infanticide provision because it was seen as allowing women to get away with murder premeditated for nine months. Again, we see the authorities tinkering with both law and procedure in order to maximize the opportunity for a retributive response.

Today, the very idea of "infanticide" as a formal category of mitigation based on diminished capacity has become discredited as a means of partially excusing the killing of newly born babies. This "disappearance of infanticide" can be explained within the context of a consistent ethic of retribution, which is connected to the ongoing activities of the Office of the Chief Coroner for Ontario. Chapter 6 reviews the development of the newly minted category "child abuse homicide," which is deemed appropriate for responding to virtually all cases of infant death. An examination of the coroner's investigation case files and inquests (1980-98) suggests that the disappearance of the mitigating category of infanticide, like the disappearance of the death category "sudden infant death syndrome," occurred because it was seen as an obstacle to the discovery and prosecution of maternal child murder. This development occurs within the context of a much broader concern, beginning in the middle of the twentieth century, with the detection of child abuse and child abuse homicide and the concomitant amplification of criminal investigations.

By providing an interdisciplinary approach, bringing historical, sociological, and legal scholarship techniques to bear on the study of the application of laws governing the killing of newly born babies by their biological mothers, as well as the underlying medical discursive basis of infanticide and the introduction of the infanticide law, I am able to show that the critical textual analysis and account of the medicalization of women's deviance is ahistorical. I hope that, by revealing some of the political dangers inherent in hasty critiques of this law, and by demonstrating the value of a more complete and nuanced view to the development of legal and political interventions, I will be able to show the value of careful historical, sociological, and criminological analysis to critical legal scholarship.

1
Regulating Infanticide through Concealment of Birth

In this chapter I describe both the medical and legal procedural difficulties that substantially led to the passing of the infanticide provision in 1948. The primary impetus for the addition of infanticide to the *Criminal Code* lay in the difficulties experienced by the Crown in securing convictions for murder, which, until 1976, carried a mandatory penalty of death.[1] The second problem identified by legislators was the ad hoc manner in which the cases were being prosecuted in the various provincial jurisdictions, which often resulted in concealment of birth convictions. The statistical record for concealment of birth convictions prior to 1948 reveals its use as a substitute for murder in cases of maternal neonaticide. The extempore approach to the administration of criminal justice resulted in divergent punitive outcomes for the convicted women. This chapter provides essential background to my discussion of individual cases of infanticide processed at the provincial level in Ontario. When reading this material, I invite readers to think differently about the history of infanticide by opening their minds to a somewhat different, or at least more nuanced, interpretation of the events surrounding the prosecution of the cases. The history of the concepts operationalized throughout the criminal justice process in these cases has suggested that humanitarianism dominated the overall governing rationality brought to bear when women were accused of killing their newly born babies (Laqueur 1989). But compassionate lenience was not the only response to infanticide. Indeed, prosecuting authorities consistently sought to secure convictions for murder but were often thwarted in their prosecutorial ambitions by a variety of actors in the network of structures that make up the criminal justice system.

By paying special attention to the evidence presented and arguments developed, some of which challenge received wisdom, my aim is to provide a convincing critique of the idea that petit jurors (and later the Department of Justice authorities) acted with straightforward lenience toward women on trial for murder for killing their newly born babies. While mercy is part of the historical narrative discussed here, the lesser known history of the prosecution of these cases concerns frustrated attempts at indictments for murder at the provincial level. These attempts at indictment were largely frustrated where law and medicine intersect; that is, where the law requires medical evidence of live-birth to sustain an indictment/charge or conviction for murder. I argue that the ability of grand and petit juries to reject the Crown's murder indictments was connected to this medico-legal evidentiary obstacle, which barred indictments and convictions in these cases. Without the legal requirement to prove live-birth, no amount of compassion on the part of jurors could have prevented the women from being initially indicted (or later charged by police) for murder.[2] In other words, the jurors had to have something, other than their conscientious objection to the death penalty, to latch onto in order to acquit the women. The provincial indictment record highlights the importance of the forensic medical evidence required before a case can proceed to trial. Live-birth was the necessary threshold requirement to initiate a homicide charge in these cases since only a live-born human being can be the victim of homicide. Generally, absent medical proof for a murder charge, grand jurors substituted "lesser" indictments for concealment, as was allowed under the *Criminal Code* framework at that time.[3] At other times, "neglect to obtain assistance in childbirth" was used to prosecute cases, but even these charges were difficult to administer given that, in order for it to secure a life sentence, the Crown had to meet the formal requirement of proving that the woman *intended* for the baby to die. If the intent were only to hide the pregnancy, then the Crown was much more likely to be successful on a concealment rather than a neglect charge.[4]

In the first section of this chapter I outline the historical roots of concealment of birth law in order to historicize the Canadian provision. Concealment was, by the early twentieth century, the most popular of the auxiliary charges available within a broad legislative framework that provided authorities with a range of criminal responses. This was the case, in part, because an indictment or conviction for concealment could then be substituted for either on a charge of murder. The second section of this chapter discusses the effect of the formal requirements of the rules of evidence in criminal law administered during the period by the Office of the Coroner. The purpose of this section is to illustrate how a constellation of seemingly unrelated conditions – including home-based childbirth; paternalistic yet charitable sensibilities toward women (often working-class), their babies (often illegitimate), and the live-birth requirement; and the formal judicial independence of grand juries – could be combined with very substantial evidentiary and forensic pathological obstacles, resulting in any number of combinations and permutations of legal outcomes in these cases. Many of these outcomes were unsatisfactory from the point of view of Crown attorneys, and this led to the passage of the infanticide provision. The weakness of forensic scientific techniques for proving both live-birth and that the marks of violence observed by coroners on a baby's body were intentionally inflicted according to legal standards of intent are discussed in order to illustrate the medical evidentiary problems facing those attempting to secure convictions for murder and manslaughter, and even neglect in childbirth and concealment of birth.

In the third section of the chapter I provide information drawn from *Criminal Statistics* (Canada 1912-16; Canada 1917-48) on charge, acquittal, and conviction rates for "concealment of birth," along with certain demographic characteristics of the persons convicted. Concealment of birth is the only recorded charge from which it could be inferred that an infant had lost its life as the result of intentional or unintentional action on the part of the mother and had been secretly disposed of in some manner meant to hide the fact of pregnancy (often illegitimate) and birth. Since murder and manslaughter charges were not recorded by the age of the victim or relationship of the victim to the perpetrator, it would have been impossible for members of the Select Committee of Parliament reviewing the law to discover from *Criminal Statistics* alone how many convictions for murder or manslaughter were registered that applied specifically to infants. Concealment of birth was, therefore, the crime category most likely to represent what was popularly known as "infanticide," particularly since it was used as a substitute verdict when the Crown failed to meet its burden. By presenting the official criminal statistics collated on a yearly basis for concealment of birth, I demonstrate that the passing of the infanticide law in 1948 was connected to prosecutors' dissatisfaction with the existing framework of laws used to regulate maternal neonaticide. The classification of concealment of birth as the fifth most serious crime category, following murder, attempted murder, manslaughter, and murder, accessory after the fact, signifies its relative gravity in relation to other Class 1 offences.[5]

Collated statistics on this category of crime were maintained for nearly fifty years, until the latter was virtually replaced with "infanticide."[6] These records are included here to illustrate the available official record of conviction, acquittal, and sentencing patterns, as well as the demographic characteristics of those indicted and convicted of this offence. These records may have been used by state authorities to define, through quantification, the problem of maternal neonaticide. It should of course be remembered that both the Office of the Coroner (for those provinces in which the indictment system was operational) and the individual county assize clerks played a key role in the production of these criminal statistics on concealment of birth.

Historical Roots of Concealment Law

> From the Middle Ages until well into the nineteenth century,
> unmarried women bore the brunt of prosecutions for infanticide
> and concealment. The penalty of choice in eighteenth century
> France was "sacking." The infanticidal mother was forced to sew
> the sack she was later stuffed into, together with a dog, a cat and a
> rooster or viper, and drowned. Sacking, along with being buried
> alive or impaled was the punishment for all infanticides decreed
> by the Carolina, a code of criminal law published in 1532 by
> Emperor Charles V.
>
> – Maria Piers (1978, 69)

According to Hoffer and Hull (1981), maternal neonaticide as a social problem meriting a legal response appears around 1593 in European criminal justice systems. Anthony Fitzherbert's first authoritative manual for justices of the peace, *L'Office et Auctoritie de Justices de Peace* (1538), made no mention of bastard maternal neonaticide. But in 1593, during a period of increased interest in bastardy in England, Richard Crompton inserted a child murder case into a revision of Fitzherbert's legal manual. The case, as Hoffer and Hull (1981, 8) note, was hardly exceptional for the time and was told to Crompton "by word of mouth." The case added to the manual read: "A Harlot is delivered of an infant which she puts alive in an orchard, and covers with leaves; and a kite strikes at him with its talons, from which the infant shortly dies, and she is arraigned for murder, and is executed" (cited in Hoffer and Hull 1981, 8).

However, this reference did not introduce the term infanticide into the legal lexicon. This was only to follow much later in English law. In 1624 the *Act to Prevent the Murthering of Bastard Children* was passed in the English House of Commons after amendment by the Lords on 27 May 1624 to address the problem of women killing their newly born, illegitimate babies. The statute read as follows and is included here in its entirety to provide the reader with its full historical flavour:

> WHEREAS many lewd Women that have been delivered of Bastard children, to avoid their Shame, and to escape Punishment, do secretly bury or conceal the Death of their Children, and after, if the Child be found dead, the said Women do alledge, that the said Child was born dead; whereas it falleth out sometimes (although hardly it is to be proved) that the said Child or Children were murthered by the said Women, their lewd Mothers, or by their Assent or Procurement:

II For the Preventing therefore of this great Mischief, be it enacted by the Authority of this present Parliament, That if any Woman after one Month next ensuing the End of this Session of Parliament be delivered of any Issue of her Body, Male or Female, which being born alive, should by the Laws of this Realm be a Bastard, and that she endeavour privately, either by drowning or secret burying thereof, or in any other Way, either by herself, or the procuring of others, so to conceal the Death thereof, as that it may not come to Light whether it were born alive or not, but be concealed: In every such cases the said Mother so offending shall suffer Death as in the Case of Murther, except such Mother can make proof by one Witness at the least, that the Child (whose Death was by her so intended to be concealed), was born dead.[7]

Under this statute the courts presumed that single women who concealed their pregnancies and whose illegitimate infants were later found dead were guilty of murder. Punishment was execution, unless women could provide third-party corroboration that the baby had been stillborn – a provision that virtually guaranteed acquittal since midwives, sisters, and other female relatives could often be enlisted to attest to the baby's birth condition.

There have been a number of interpretations as to the significance of this act. According to O'Donovan (1984, 264), the law "sought to punish single women for becoming pregnant and for refusing to live with their sin. Thus the crime was created to affect moral and social behaviour." Jackson (1997a, 33) points out that many historians mistakenly argue that this was an unusual, or unusually harsh, law since it reversed the presumption of guilt. However, the universal presumption of innocence along with the legal burden of proof "beyond a reasonable doubt" did not become established legal maxims until the late eighteenth century (Beattie 1986). Hoffer and Hull (1981, 26) argue that the sex- and nuptial-specificity of the statute was not a significant departure from English precedent since concealment of the dead was proscribed by laws prior to the passage of the concealment act:

The statute's provisions were neither novel nor quite reversed the general presumption of the innocence of the accused. They entailed a return to earlier definitions of the crime of murder. Concealment of death was a crime in itself as early as Saxon times. It was proscribed in *morth*, the Saxon law of murder, and the proscription was repeated in the earliest forms of the Norman *lex murdrum*. To conceal or refuse to reveal the presence of a corpse was a capital offense. The relationship between concealment and secret murder was antiquated in common law by 1624, but not dead.

The regulation of concealment of death, then, was not limited solely to women prior to the *Jacobean Act*. The statute simply created a legal presumption whereby a woman who had concealed the death of an illegitimate child was presumed to have murdered it. No longer burdened by the problems of proving live-birth, the prosecution nevertheless had to establish that the child's death had been concealed. Jackson (1997a) offers the further qualification that the eventual enforcement of this law should not be read outside the context of English Poor Laws provisions aimed at preventing illegitimacy.

Illegitimacy and Concealment

Prior to the passage of the English concealment legislation in 1624, at common law a child born out of wedlock was, according to *Blackstone's Commentaries* (Blackstone 1966 [1769]), *filius nullius* (a child of nobody) or *filius populi* (a child of the parish [because responsibility for maintenance fell to the parish where the mother resided rather than to an unidentified father]) (Bailey 1991, 150; Jackson 1997a). *Blackstone's Commentaries* outlined the rights of the illegitimate baby as being "very few, being only such as he can acquire; for he can *inherit* nothing, being looked upon as the son of nobody" (Blackstone 1966 [1769], 447). An illegitimate child could neither inherit nor bequeath property, was restricted from holding any office in the church, and could only transcend its illegitimate status by "an act of parliament as was done in the case of John of Gant's bastard children, by a statute of Richard the second" (447). However, such dispensations were hardly the norm.

Early illegitimacy laws essentially delimited sexual deviancy and were calculated to prevent economic burdens being placed on parish rate-payers. The English concealment statute was designed, according to some, to prevent women from becoming pregnant with illegitimate babies by providing a harsh deterrent in the form of punishment for murder (Jackson 1997a; Hoffer and Hull 1981). Others argue that punishments for child destruction during this period were the result of religious condemnation of fornication and adultery, evidenced by the punishment of death. For example, Walker (1968, 126) argues:

Since fornication and adultery were strongly condemned by the Church, the criminal codes of medieval Europe treated this as a particularly heinous form of murder and prescribed hideous deaths for the mothers. Even the Code Napoléon retained this as one of its few capital crimes: if the child was murdered before it had been registered, the penalty was the guillotine. The justification was that until registration the child enjoyed less protection than the ordinary citizen from the normal deterrents of the law, since its existence was not known; consequently an exceptional deterrent was required. It was this philosophy of maximum deterrence which prompted Baron Bramwell to argue to the Capital Punishment Commission in 1865 that "the greater the temptation the greater the need for punishment in such cases."

Therefore, the materialist argument asserts that women who killed illegitimate infants were punished both for violating the rule prohibiting sex out of wedlock and for being financial burdens on the parish. Severe punishment, whether symbolic or real, was justified on the basis of its deterrent value in protecting infant life, but it was fundamentally linked to the regulation of single women's sexuality and, therefore, class and gender (Jackson 1997a; O'Donovan 1984).

Hoffer and Hull (1981, 22) describe the moral tones of the law as "accusatory and unrelenting" because of its use of the terms "lewd women" and "lewd mothers" and its concern with sexual promiscuity rather than murder. However, as Malcolmson (1977) and Beattie (1986) show, women brought to court on these charges were far from "lewd whores." In fact, according to Beattie (1986, 114), of the sixty-two indictments at the Surrey assizes (between 1660 and the end of the eighteenth century), three-quarters of those accused of infant homicide were unmarried women of solid reputation who went to the trouble of concealing their pregnancies and the births and deaths of their infants in order to *maintain* their reputations. Both Malcolmson (1977) and Beattie (1986) note that so-called whores would hardly ever kill their illegitimate babies in order to maintain their reputations since they had none to maintain. Fear of shame would therefore hardly be a motivation for prostitutes to kill an illegitimate child. In fact, their review of the historical record indicates that the overwhelming majority of those brought to trial were domestic servants whose employment depended heavily on their "good character."[8] Servants were particularly vulnerable to seduction and casual affairs because of their close contact with other male servants, masters, and the sons of masters, and they were at great risk when pregnancy occurred as this usually meant certain dismissal.

In addition, the relationship between age and occupational structure meant that a large number of unmarried women were employed in the domestic service sector throughout their childbearing years. As Malcolmson writes (1977, 203), "it may be that at any given time in the eighteenth century, as many as half of the unmarried women between the ages of about sixteen and twenty-five were living-in servants – chamber maids, scullery maids, cooks, dairy maids and the like." Given that such a significant number of women in their childbearing years were employed in the domestic service, many researchers have suggested a strong causal connection between employment in domestic service and maternal neonaticide. Since the loss of a servant girl's reputation had catastrophic economic and social consequences, it seems reasonable to infer that domestic servants were more likely than were single women employed in other occupations to conceal pregnancy and to commit maternal neonaticide in order to preserve the reputations upon which they were economically dependent.

The trope of the "fallen woman" was particularly conspicuous in relation to the class-based divisions within the middle- or upper-class households employing domestic servants. Sharp class divisions were strictly maintained, with severe proscriptions placed on moving beyond one's social standing. Maintenance of these class-based, upstairs-downstairs household divisions was accomplished partly through the tutelage of domestic servants. Domestic servants, more than any other employment group, were tutored by guidebooks on good behaviour and by popular literature. Assuming they could read, female servants were instructed to "beware" of menservants and the lascivious inclinations of masters and their sons. According to a typical guidebook on servant decorum: "If you are in the house of a person of condition where there are many men servants, it requires a great deal of circumspection how to behave. As these fellows live high, and have little to do, they are for the most part very pert and saucy where they dare, and apt to take liberties on the least encouragement" (cited in Malcolmson 1977, 202-3).

Although this example highlights the danger to a young girl's reputation when she encounters men of privilege, adolescent single women were seen as being in particular danger and usually fell under the careful scrutiny of the employer's female head of households. And what might have been overlooked in many empirical studies of court records is the extent to which the bodies of infants disposed of by domestic servants were readily detectable because of their geographic location in cities. It has been suggested that certain individual aggressive coroners were more concerned than were others with rooting out cases of maternal neonaticide and bringing women to court. They were, therefore, more likely to discover and promote prosecutions of women suspected of infanticide (Rose 1986).

Arguments about occupation notwithstanding, the concealment law itself functioned as a formal response to infant killing, later providing a reduced punishment framework within which to prosecute women who allegedly killed their newly born babies. It may also have functioned to regulate both class and gender, albeit not very effectively since its main purpose was to respond to the homicide of neonates. Within this broadly class- and gender-based context, working-class servant girls hid their unwanted pregnancies and disposed of the babies quickly after birth in order to preserve their reputations. In other words, their actions were in conformance with governing rules of propriety and were thus viewed by judges and juries as "rational." The perceived "rationality" of their actions was confirmed by their desire to maintain their respectability. Since women were viewed as motivated not by evil intent but, rather, by "decency" – which compelled them to maintain their honour and good character, not to mention employment – juries were reluctant to hold women entirely responsible and to convict them for murder. In other words, their acts were not rooted in sin, and they required no correction of character (Garland 1985, 111). Judged from the vantage point of contemporary standards, the failure to hang women for maternal neonaticide might be characterized as "lenient." However, as Hay (1975) has argued, respectability was one of the main grounds upon which judges commuted death sentences, so it is not surprising that otherwise respectable women who killed illegitimate infants tended to escape hanging.

Concealment of birth eventually came to be viewed as a direct substitute for a homicide conviction in cases of maternal neonaticide. This practice developed primarily because jurors were unwilling to convict for a capital crime in these cases. It is well established, particularly in the English context, that, with regard to the death penalty, eighteenth- and nineteenth-century laypersons and jurors were genuinely sympathetic to working-class women who were suspected of killing their unwanted babies (Laqueur 1989; Walker 1968; Ward 1999). Jackson (1996) has argued that the intense public scrutiny of single pregnant women, and their prosecution under the 1624 Jacobean statute of concealment (which, at the time carried the death penalty), was originally stimulated by English Poor Laws, which made it compulsory for the parish to support unaffiliated infants and their mothers. However, the focus of much of the historical scholarship has been on the issue of lenience. Backhouse (1984) has shown that compassionate responses were typical in Canada during the nineteenth century, and she describes the difficulty if securing convictions in cases that came to trial. However, the significance of the coroner's inquest and medico-legal obstacles to indictment and conviction have also played a part in the history of the infanticide law in Canada.

Canadian Concealment Law: Live-Birth, Stillbirth, Concealed-Birth
In British North America the concealment of birth statute reproduced the *Jacobean Act, 1624*, as amended in English law. By the time of its introduction concealment no longer held the reverse onus provision linking it to murder and was punishable by up to only two years imprisonment. The statute was adopted in Nova Scotia in 1758 and in Prince Edward Island in 1792. It was later extended to Quebec and Upper Canada by way of legislation that introduced English criminal law into the British colonies (Backhouse 1984, 449). By the early twentieth century Canadian cases of maternal neonaticide were governed neither by English Poor Laws (Guest 1980; Jackson 1997a) nor by the reverse onus presumptions of the 1624 Jacobean concealment statute. Today, section 243 of the *Criminal Code* maintains the offence of concealment of birth, which is also available as a substituted conviction

under section 662(4), where a count charges murder of a child or infanticide. Section 243 reads: "Every one who in any manner disposes of the dead body of a child, with intent to conceal the fact that its mother has been delivered of it, whether the child died before, during or after birth, is guilty of an indictable offence and liable to imprisonment for a term not exceeding two years." Section 662(4) allows for a substitution of the concealment of birth finding when the Crown fails to prove child murder or "infanticide": "Where a count charges the murder of a child or infanticide and the evidence proves the commission of an offence under section 243 but does not prove murder or infanticide, the jury may find the accused not guilty of murder or infanticide, as the case may be, but guilty of an offence under section 243."[9] It should also be kept in mind that both contraception and abortion were illegal in Canada at this time, with offences relating to abortion carrying especially severe penalties.[10]

According to *A Practical Treatise on the Office and Duties of Coroners* (Boys 1905), the Office of the Coroner was legally governed by the "born alive" rule, which, as outlined in the manual, stated that "no *murder* can be committed of an infant in its mother's womb. It is not until actual birth that the child becomes 'a human being,' so as to be embraced in the legal definition of murder" (Boys 1905, 129; emphasis in original). These included a range of circumstances that Boys calls "infanticide" (129). Although he defines infanticide in medical terms as "(1) The criminal destruction of the foetus *in utero;* (2) The murder of the child after birth," only the latter falls within the coroners' jurisdiction.[11] Coroners were governed by the legal definition of "human being" found in the *Criminal Code,* which then (1892) stated, as it does today (2005), that: "A child becomes a human being within the meaning of the Act, and so capable of being a subject of murder, when it has completely proceeded in a living state from the body of its mother, whether it has breathed or not, whether it has an independent circulation or not, and whether the navel string is severed or not. The killing of such a child is homicide when it dies in consequence of injuries received before, during or after birth" (130).

Therefore, the main legal concern in cases of maternal neonaticide was the question of live-birth. It was over this question that coroners and their juries exercised considerable discretion. Both the coroner's inquest juries and grand juries of the early part of the twentieth century acted with humanitarian sympathy toward the women accused, and I am able to show how, in order to prevent indictments, they were able to latch on to the technical difficulties in establishing both live-birth and intent. In effect, the less serious charges of concealment and neglect in childbirth were auxiliary laws employed to bridge a gap created by the law of homicide's definition of a human being. These laws facilitated a kind of conviction where doubt could be cast on live-birth and wilful intent. This same problem occurred in England before the passage of the *English Infanticide Act, 1922*. According to Davies (1968 [1937/38], 301), legal practitioners were vocal in their opposition to the auxiliary legal framework, which they viewed as problematic (as was the live-birth gap "through which many malefactors walked with impunity"). The legal requirement of determining when a foetus/newborn infant becomes a human being places biomedical science in a unique position vis-à-vis murder convictions for maternal neonaticide. The difficulties in establishing live-birth were more acute in the early twentieth century than they are at present, in part because the underdevelopment of medical techniques for determining live-birth and the home-based nature of childbirth created a situation in which conviction was practically unworkable within the criminal legal framework. The evidence from coroners themselves suggests that live-birth and/or intent were both exceedingly difficult to establish to the satisfaction of inquest and grand jurors who administered the law. The circumstances of childbirth produced an especially difficult relationship between law and forensic science – a relationship that remained unresolved until late in the twentieth century, when childbirth itself was medicalized and both infant and maternal mortality rates were reduced as a result of public health campaigns (see Commachio 1993). Once this change took place, the assumption that babies are still-born was reversed, along with consequent assumptions about maternal responsibility for infant survival.

The medico-legal difficulty of proving live-birth and/or intent to conceal or obtain assistance in childbirth was further compounded by the formal independence of both coroner's juries and, especially, grand jurors, who had the power to refuse or substitute indictments even in the face of overwhelming evidence against the accused. In addition to this, jurors were faced with a situation in which the very rules of evidence de facto prevented them from issuing indictments for murder and/or neglect to obtain assistance in childbirth and concealment. This conclusion qualifies the argument that jurors were wholly sympathetic to women's social circumstance and/or that illegitimacy played a determinative role in the so-called "lenient" disposition of these cases. At the time, there existed an authentic impetus toward retribution in these cases.

It should be noted that the suggestion that infanticidal women were treated with "lenience" is connected to the death penalty punishment for murder given to men and some women for other types of killings. Women were sentenced to a variety of disciplinary measures, which often included being supervised by various institutional authorities. Those found mentally unfit to stand trial were ordered into custody at the Toronto Psychiatric Hospital "until the pleasure of the Lieutenant Governor is known."[12] These measures were "punitive" to the extent that they often involved extensive moral regulation wherein the women were required to conform to established notions of femininity prior to their release. The dispositions for concealment and/or neglect in childbirth might be compared to dispositions for offences of similar severity to claim that women suspected of, or indicted for, maternal neonaticide were treated more or less punitively than were others indicted and tried for similar offences. These disciplinary, yet non-carceral, dispositions for concealment and neglect in childbirth might not have been particularly lenient in comparison to similar offences. For example, women were found not guilty for driving-related manslaughter, suggesting that concealment of birth may not have been the only instance of juror lenience. In the case files reviewed for this project a number of women indicted on manslaughter charges were found not guilty by petit juries for killing pedestrians or passengers through drunk and/or reckless driving.[13]

Coroner's Juries, Grand Juries, and the Prosecution of Infanticide

In early twentieth-century Ontario, women were brought to trial for killing babies by way of a coroner's inquisition and grand jury indictment. Before evidence was heard by a grand jury, a coroner's jury typically heard evidence of suspicious deaths at a coroner's inquest to determine whether or not there was sufficient evidence of culpable homicide to justify convening a grand jury to issue a formal indictment. If the coroner's jury found sufficient evidence it was to transmit that evidence to a magistrate or have a warrant issued to convey the accused person before a magistrate. Here the grand jury would convene, consider the evidence afresh, and vote on whether or not to issue a "true bill" of indictment. Once the members of the jury had heard the evidence, they were only required to issue a true bill of indictment if all twelve of them agreed to it. A true bill was required from a grand jury before an accused could be sent to the county jail (or released on her own recognizance) to await her trial. A true bill is a finding of the grand jury following a secret meeting at which the accused is neither present nor represented. Only the witnesses for the Crown are examined, and since there is no established standard to guide the grand jury in its decision on whether or not a true bill should be issued, it may act arbitrarily (Ontario 1968, 775).

Grand juries have been regarded both as a bulwark of freedom[14] and as an expensive, time-consuming, and secretive instrument of oppression in which no rules of evidence govern and upon which both friends and foes of a prisoner may serve.[15] According to the 1968 McRuer Report, "in Canada, grand juries were abolished in Manitoba in 1923, in British Columbia and Quebec in 1932, and in New Brunswick in 1959. Alberta, Saskatchewan, the Northwest Territories and the Yukon have never had a grand jury system. Thus, in Canada today, the grand jury system exists only in Ontario, Newfoundland, Nova Scotia and Prince Edward Island" (Ontario 1968, 774).

Grand juries were abolished in Ontario following the recommendation of the McRuer Report. Since both coroner's inquest juries and grand juries constituted the gate through which indictments had to pass before a case went to trial, they represented a unique feature of Canadian (and particularly Ontario) cases of infant homicide. Both juries were governed by a variety of formal legal and medico-legal requirements outlined both by the Office of the Coroner and the rules of evidence dictated by criminal law and procedure.

Establishing Live-Birth in Cases of Maternal Neonaticide

In Canadian law, the onus to prove live-birth was on the Crown, "as the law humanely presumes that every new-born infant is born dead; but if proved to have been wholly born alive, further proof shewing its capacity to live, be proved, its destruction would still be murder" (Boys 1905, 137). Furthermore, according to Boys's instructions, "in all cases where there is not the most clear and decisive proof that the child was born alive, it is the bounden duty of the coroner to tell the jury that they ought not to think of returning a verdict of wilful murder against the mother" (137).

A number of common law principles inherited from England guided what did or did not amount to wilful murder or manslaughter, all of which were governed by the born-alive rule. Once a child is born alive it acquires legal personality for the purposes of homicide law (Boyle, Grant, and Chunn 1994). Since only a legally defined "human being" can be the victim of a homicide, the determination of live-birth is the threshold test for criminal legal action. Legally defining maternal neonaticide as murder was exceedingly difficult and involved a variety of complex legal and biomedical tests. To further compound these complexities, infants often died simply because mothers allowed them to starve or freeze to death, which raised the question of liability for killing by omission.

The largely private nature of childbirth in the early part of the twentieth century made it difficult for coroners to prove the live-birth requirement for a murder charge. According to the manual for coroners, the best test of live-birth was respiration. If a child had breathed, then this could be considered proof of live-birth. According to Boys (1905, 132): "Respiration is the *best* test of a child having been born alive; and it has been decided that a child is born alive, in the legal sense, when breathing and living, by reason of breathing through its own lungs alone, it exists as a living child without deriving any of its living, or power of living, by or through any connection with its mother"[16] (emphasis in original).

According to Boys, the test was compromised (therefore allowing for reasonable doubt) by a few situations in which a child may breathe and subsequently die of natural causes. For example, Boys (1905, 131) states that "a child may breathe during birth, and before the whole body is brought into the world, which would not be sufficient life to constitute it a human being, and to make its destruction murder." However, in these cases Boys instructs that "there is a very strong presumption against the probability of the child dying unless through foul play, before being wholly born alive" (131n4). Or, "a child may breathe *in utero* after the membranes have been ruptured, but all such cases reported were in exceptionally difficult labours" (131). One of the most difficult murders to detect occurs when a child fails to breathe (but remains alive from the continuance of foetal circulation) and is then destroyed: "When a living child is destroyed while remaining in this state, there are no certain medical signs by which it can be proved to have been living when maltreated; although some indirect evidence of the existence of life previous to respiration may be obtained from wounds and ecchymoses found on the body of the child. The child being seen to move or breathe, would of course be evidence of life" (131).

One of the usual tests for the verification of live-birth was the floating lung, or "hydrostatic test." Discredited by the eighteenth century (Behlmer 1979; Jackson 1997a), but still used, the floating lung test "was based on the 17th century Dutch naturalist Jan Swammerdam's observations and entered the forensic literature in 1690 when Johann Schreyer used it in defense of a woman accused of infanticide" (Laqueur 1989, 186). The test involved placing the lungs in water to see if they floated as air in the lungs was taken as evidence that the foetus had taken a breath and was therefore legally considered to have been a human being who had been born alive. William Hunter warned of using this test in determining live-birth in a 1784 article entitled "On the Uncertainty of the Signs of Death" published in *Medical Observations and Inquiries*. Here he cautioned against conviction based on this test, his point being that "lungs may float because of putrefication or because a mother breathed into her stillborn infant's mouth" (Hunter, cited in Laqueur 1989, 186-87). According to Behlmer (1979, 410), "by the mid-nineteenth century even English physicians were conceding that a conviction for murder should not hinge upon whether lung tissue sank or 'swam.' Victorian medical men had grown increasingly reluctant to draw hasty conclusions in cases of suspected infanticide."

Thus, even though the lung test was routinely performed during autopsies on babies in Ontario throughout the early twentieth century, it had long been discredited among forensic experts since it was possible for air to enter the lungs of a stillborn child by means other than respiration. In addition, since proof of independent existence was a general requirement in addition to the proof of live-birth, indictments for murder were inevitably extremely difficult to sustain.

Although Boys recognized that the hydrostatic test had been discredited by his time, he nevertheless recommended its use in conjunction with a consideration of other circumstances. Indeed, he provided detailed instructions for its use. He argued that "employing this test as conclusive evidence of the child having breathed or not, is now exploded, yet when used by an intelligent physician, thoroughly acquainted with its real value, and who considers its result with other circumstances, it is a proper and important test to employ in many cases of infanticide" (Boys 1905, 135).

Boys (1905, 133; emphasis in original) implored practitioners to be cognizant of the weaknesses of the test for proving live-birth: "A person using the hydrostatic test in cases of alleged infanticide should remember that the lungs floating is not *a proof* that the child has been *born alive,* nor their sinking *a proof* that it was *born dead.* At most it can only prove the child has *breathed* or not. The fact of living or dead birth has, strictly speaking, no relation to the employment of this test." In addition, a number of events were likely to produce air in the lungs and therefore produce a false positive (or negative) lung test. If the baby fell on the floor during delivery or if the mother had attempted to resuscitate it, then air would surely be present in the lungs. Like Hunter, Boys too recognized that air could enter the lungs by other means of expansion. For example, the lungs would float in water if they were putrefied. He also believed that absence of air in the lungs "is no proof of natural dead birth; as the mother may cause herself to be delivered in a water-bath, or the mouth and nostrils of the child may be covered in the act of birth" (133). Because, according to the legal requirements, medical forensic science could not prove live-birth beyond a reasonable doubt, intentional homicide was often practically impossible to prove in a court of law. These were the technical impediments to homicide prosecutions which, in conjunction with the paternalistic sympathy of coroner's jurors, often restricted indictments to concealment and/or neglect.

Intent to Conceal: *R. v. Pichè*

If homicide was difficult to prove on the basis of live-birth, then concealment, as a substitute, presented its own evidentiary difficulties. Concealment was not, according to Boys (1905, 139), properly within the province of the coroner's jury and thus did not fit easily into the scheme whereby coroner's juries issued true bills: "In a case of infanticide, the coroner's jury should not find as to the concealment of birth, if any there be; for, the concealment, under the present law, is no presumptive evidence of infanticide, and has no connection with the cause of death, to inquire of which is the purpose of the coroner's inquest."

Boys's manual points out that concealment should not operate as a presumption of guilt (as it may have operated in previous centuries in England and Europe). In any case, *intent* to conceal birth was a requirement for conviction and was by no means always easy to prove. According to *R. v. Pichè* (1879),[17] the only reported case of concealment of birth in Canada, evidence of intentionality of concealment as set out in English common law was required for a conviction.

R. v. Pichè (1879) outlined a wide array of circumstances in which it is evident that concealment of murder was the underlying intent and yet proof of actual *mens rea* remained difficult, if not impossible, to establish. One typical defence was the "benefit of linen defence," where women would provide the courts with clothing they had made for the baby, thus proving that they had planned for and expected the live-birth of their infant, thereby corroborating intent to keep the baby rather than to kill it. In *Pichè* the appeal court considered the relevant case law from England in order to determine whether or not there was sufficient evidence of intent to conceal or secretly dispose of a body for a proper conviction. The Court of Appeal outlined a number of circumstances dealing with this question of intent to guide the handling of these cases. The legally relevant facts in *Pichè* were that the accused woman was living in a house alone at the time of the delivery of her child. The house was some sixty yards from that of a neighbour, John Orange, who went to the house to see what was wrong at the request of his wife. The following passage, as described by the Court of Appeal, reveals a typical case of maternal neonaticide and eventual conviction for concealment:

> She said she was sick, and thought she should die. She said she wanted to see her mother. The witness went for his wife's mother, Mrs. Coghlan, and they both went to the prisoners house. He lighted a lamp. The prisoner was then sitting down-stairs. She said she was bad with cramps. She did not want a doctor till her mother should come next morning. Mrs. Donnell was sent for and came, and Mrs. Kenna came. On the suggestion of the women present the witness was sent for a doctor, and he brought Dr. Wright. The doctor got there about 11 p.m.
>
> Mrs. Donnell said she went to the prisoners about 10 p.m. The prisoner complained of being cramped. They helped the prisoner up-stairs, and she went to bed. The doctor asked prisoner what was the matter with her. She said was cramped and sick. He asked her where was her child. She said she had not had any. The witness asked the prisoner where was her child. The prisoner said it was behind the chest. The witness pointed to the place. Mrs. Coghlan went and found the dead body of a child. It was lying between the trunk and the wall on the top of some clothes. It was wrapped in a small shirt. It was not dressed in anyway. The witness did not observe anything about the room before the body was discovered.
>
> Dr. Wright said: "I asked her what was the matter. She said she was cramped. I told her she had been delivered of a child. From examining her I was satisfied she had been delivered of a child. The delivery had been quite recent. The after-birth was still retained. I asked her before I made the examination if she had been delivered of a child, she said no. I then exam-

her. I asked her again, and she denied. I told her I knew she had been delivered of a child. After I told her so I removed the after-birth. I found it had been severed by a sharp instrument. The child was discovered from half a minute to a minute after I removed the after-birth. One could not see the body of the child from being in the room till it was moved from behind the chest. This was the same room the prisoner occupied. The appearance of the child's body corresponded with the appearance of the after-birth. The child had been born alive as shewn by the hydrostatic test. Mrs. Donnell told the prisoner that child was there, and must be found.

The prisoner's counsel contended no offence was proved.

The learned Judge convicted the prisoner, and he reserved the case as before stated. (*R. v. Pichè* [1879], 409-11)

In discussing the facts of the case, Wilson C.J. relied on established jurisprudence to determine whether or not there was sufficient evidence of intent to conceal in *Pichè*. Concealment, or "secret disposition," depended on the circumstances of each particular case, and in *Pichè* the woman's initial denial of pregnancy counted toward her conviction.[18] Like the presumption of guilt that operated under the earlier Jacobean concealment statute, pregnancy denial here apparently amounted to evidence of wilful intent to conceal the body of the child. Further adding to the presumption of guilt was the medical evidence provided connecting the deceased body of the baby to the existence of an "after-birth" found with the woman.

Common law principals reviewed in *Pichè* illustrate that women might be convicted of concealment even though the body of the baby was not concealed particularly well. Discussing an earlier case of poor concealment, Wilson C.J. noted that the intention to conceal was nevertheless evident:

It must have been thrown there from a public house yard, to which yard the prisoner had no right of access. The body could be seen by one looking over the wall of the yard into the field, but not by any one using the yard in the ordinary way. There was no gate into the field but from a butcher's yard, the butcher using the field as a grass field for grazing. There was no path in the field that would take any one within sight of the body, and no one going into the field in their ordinary occupation would go near the body or see it, nor would they see it unless they went to the part of the wall where the body lay. The body was discovered by chance by a child. There was nothing to conceal the body but this situation. (*R. v. Pichè* [1879], 411)

Thus, even though the body was completely exposed in this situation, it was clear that the intent was secret disposition in a place where, even though completely exposed, the body would likely not be seen. Other cases cited by the *Pichè* court (1879)[19] were disposed of according to similar principles.

The jury in *R. v. Sleep* (1864), 9 Cox C.C. 559, found the accused not guilty of concealment when she admitted to having given birth to a child and to having put it in a box in her bedroom. The judge in *R. v. Sleep* disagreed with the jury, arguing that placing a body in an open box was secret disposition. Similarly, in *R. v. Clarke* (1866), 4 F. & F. 1040, a jury acquitted a woman servant who placed the dead body of her child "in a dust bin a day or two after its birth, having been accidentally strangled by the umbilical cord." The judge in this case "was of the opinion the dust bin was a place in which the body might be disposed of so as to conceal it" (*R. v. Pichè* [1879], 411-12). The accused was acquitted since it could not be established that she herself disposed of the body with the intent to conceal its death. In *R. v. George* (1868), 11 Cox C.C. 41, a woman claimed to have miscarried a six-month-old foetus and thrown it in a slop pail along with the afterbirth. Upon inspection, however, no foetus or afterbirth was found. Shortly after the delivery the accused was asked to leave her house of employment. Shortly thereafter, "a servant girl, on going into a bedroom near the one which had been occupied by the prisoner, saw an old dress hanging partly out of a large box in which old clothes were kept, a hat and bonnet had also been taken out of the box and thrown on the floor. The lid of the box was not quite closed, but kept up a little by a smaller box, which was placed inside of it on the top of some old clothes. The smaller box, which belonged to the prisoner, was found to contain the dead body of a full-grown child. Neither of the boxes was locked or fastened in any way" (*R. v. Pichè* [1879], 413).

The judge in this case determined that the child was put in the box in order to be discovered rather than to be secretly disposed. Since the accused admitted to having miscarried (although the discovered body was determined to be a full-term infant), and since the boxes themselves were not locked or fastened, the jury determined that the body was placed in the boxes with the intention that someone discover it and thus acquitted the accused. This case illustrates that common law required high standards of intent to conceal a body.

Similar cases required similar standards of intent for convictions of concealment. Dead infants discovered in boxes, garbage cans, open fields, outhouses, and the like had not been considered by judges or juries to have been secretly disposed of with *intent* to conceal the birth. What is remarkable is that the decision made as to the women's intentionality is left entirely with the judge or jury, as the case may be. And evidence of the woman's moral character appears irrelevant, having little effect on the final decision. In *Pichè* it appears that an especially significant piece of evidence that counted toward conviction was the fact that the accused lived alone – or that she was single. Like the open field into which no person treads, the house of a lone woman is deemed to be a space in which concealment is intentional. According to Wilson C.J.,

The circumstances which bear against the prisoner are, that she lived in the house where she was delivered "alone, about sixty yards from the house occupied by John Orange," the person who went to her house to find out what the matter with the woman was, and, as I understand the evidence, that was the nearest house to the house of the prisoner: that she placed the body where it was found: that the body: "could not be seen by one in the room till it was moved from behind the chest," and that she denied having had a child until Mrs. Donnell said to the prisoner "the child was there, and must be found;" and then she said the child was "behind the chest."(*R. v. Pichè* [1879], 414)

In the opinion of Wilson C.J., if the house had been occupied by others, then the accused would not have been considered guilty of concealment. "The most open place, as it is said, might be the most secret place of deposit if removed from the ordinary haunts or visitation of others. So the most public place of deposit might also be the most secret place, if it were not likely to be resorted to, or were not likely to be suspected as a place of concealment for such a purpose" (*R. v. Pichè* [1879], 415). The judge conceded that this case might just as easily have been decided in favour of the accused had it been addressed by a jury stressing different evidence:

It is possible a jury, or even another Judge, may have formed a different opinion upon the same facts ... It might, for instance, have been presented to the jury that although the prisoner had the house wholly to herself and was delivered of her child while alone, and placed the body between the chest and the wall in the manner represented, she did not intend to exclude others from the house at the time she so put away the body of the child; and the fact, although she called for no help, that when seen by Mr. Orange, her neighbour, she said she wanted to see her mother, was some evidence that she did not intend at or from the first to conceal the birth of the child, or the place where she put the body. And it might also have been urged on her behalf that she did not object to those persons who did come to her house when summoned by Mr. Orange being admitted and going up with her, and to her, to the room where the body was, when there would be a great change that they might discover the child. (*R. v. Pichè* [1879], 416)

The irony here is that, if the accused in *Pichè* had simply claimed that the child had been stillborn and left the body in plain view, then no jury or judge could have convicted her of concealment since there would have been no proof of intent to conceal. Of course the question of whether the accused would have been convicted on a murder charge is a relevant consideration, but in that instance intent to kill (or malice aforethought) would have to have been proven along with actual live-birth.

English common law principles used to guide Canadian cases of concealment provided judges and jurors with few guidelines for finding a woman
guilty of this charge. A finding of guilt for concealment turned on the question of intent to conceal, which, historically, had been interpreted on the
side of innocence. Despite the obvious vagaries in these cases, concealment
was, along with neglect in childbirth, a vital charge substituted for murder
or manslaughter in cases where the Crown, at least, suspected maternal
neonaticide. It was also, perhaps surprisingly, an indictment that was collated as a separate category in Canadian criminal statistics and, therefore,
was an important source of information available to those responsible for
criminal law policy concerning the broader "problem" of maternal
neonaticide.

Canadian Concealment of Birth Statistics, 1912-48

One of the ways in which objects of criminological concern are both manu-
factured and understood is through the use of statistical data. Hacking (1983)
has argued that the printed number provided more than just "information," that it was itself a technology of power belonging to modern states.
Statistics helped to determine the form of laws and the character of social
facts, engendering concepts and classifications in the social sciences while
creating a vast bureaucratic machinery devoted to the collection and collation of such "facts." Haggerty (2001) has shown, in the Canadian context,
that official aggregate crime data are an important tool of governance because they transform phenomena into something counted and real – something to be acted upon by government officials.[20]

With the importance of official statistics to the state and with the state's
governance of populations in mind, this section reviews Canadian concealment of birth conviction, acquittal, and sentencing statistics. These provided legislators with knowledge about the nature and extent of the crime
of concealment, which had become a virtual substitute for infant murder.
Between 1876 and 1911 these statistics were collected, collated, and published by the Minister of Agriculture. This task was accomplished by the
Ministry of Trade and Commerce between 1912 and 1916, and by the Dominion Bureau of Statistics when the *Statistics Act, 1918*, established it as a
separate government body responsible for overseeing the collection of data
on crime. This act replaced the *Criminal Statistics Act, 1876*, which had ini-
tiated the criminal statistics series (Coats 1946).[21] Both acts required that
the individual county trial courts submit information on "criminal business" and that the wardens of penal institutions provide similar demographic
knowledge of their inmates. The Dominion Bureau of Statistics reports list
"the number of charges, acquittals and convictions, by judicial district, by
class of offences, and by disposition, together with other information on
each convicted person and on cases in which the prerogative of mercy of

the Crown had been exercised" (Zay 1965, 634). Popularly known as "court" statistics, since they were kept by each judicial county's court workers, these data are the earliest Canadian source for statistical knowledge of crime.

These data quantified and described a broad range of social demographic and criminal justice variables. The statistics were submitted by each individual judicial district (county) for each province[22] in Canada for all *Criminal Code* offences, including Class 1, "Offences against the Person,"[23] which reported, in order of their severity: "Murder," "Murder attempt to commit," "Manslaughter," "Abortion and concealing birth of infants,"[24] "Rape and other crimes against decency," "Procuration,"[25] "Bigamy,"[26] and so on. For each "Offence against the Person," the following criminal justice and demographic information was obtained for most years, with slight variation over the period under review for each judicial district (county) of all Canadian provinces: "Number of Charges"; "Acquitted (Male/Female)"; "Detained for Lunacy"; "Convictions"; "Ages and Sexes of Convicted (Male/Female)"; "Occupations"; "Religions"; "Use of Liquors"; "Educational Status"; "Civil Condition" [indicates married, single, widowed]; "Birth Places"; "Residence"; "Total Pardons" [includes Male, Female, Total]; "Places of Imprisonment Whence Liberated."

The Dominion Bureau of Statistics aggregated data for murder, manslaughter, and a range of other offences, though not for concealment of birth. The purpose was to track crime trends. However, this was accomplished in different ways in different years (e.g., comparison to previous year; comparison of five-, eight-, or ten-year periods). These comparisons were discussed in the "Introduction" to the yearly volumes. These discussions included, among other criminal justice variables, observations on increases and/or decreases in the overall crime rate, the numbers of females committing particular offences, and sentencing trends. For example, murder and manslaughter increases and/or decreases were noted, as were the increases or decreases in the number of offences committed by women.[27] The tables reproduced below differ from the tables maintained by the Dominion Bureau of Statistics only in that I have aggregated the data by decade between 1912 and 1948. These data were not published in this aggregate format by the bureau. I have aggregated the data in this way for the purposes of manageability. Otherwise, the tables presented below precisely reflect the original categories and layout.

Despite the fact that a fairly complete statistical record exists for the years 1912 to 1948, there were (and are) many factors that diminished the comparability of data between the individual years and the decades (Zay 1965, 634). The enforcement of law with respect to maternal neonaticide during the early part of the twentieth century was particularly vulnerable to individual or community responses to the baby's death. After the discovery of a baby's body, made all the more difficult because of the relative ease of body disposal (particularly in rural jurisdictions), someone in the community had to have been motivated to report the incident to the coroner or the police. If the incident did come to the attention of the authorities, then a true bill, or indictment, had to have been issued by a grand jury before the case would be recorded in the court statistics as a "charge." Thus, once the matter had been sent to a grand jury for consideration, that institution played a significant role in the production of these statistics since it was ultimately responsible for issuing an indictment. And, as I have indicated previously, there were a variety of auxiliary charges laid in these cases in an endeavour to get some kind of conviction.

In addition, changes and/or improvements in collecting and delivering court data affect the comparability of these data over time. At certain times, registrars, clerks, and the officials of magistrate's and family courts were paid by the case reported, but this system of remuneration was eventually abolished as a cost-saving measure. Moreover, identical standards in recording across individual county courts cannot be assumed. Certain courts may have had more or less personnel responsible for the tabulation and reporting of their business. As a result, it is possible that county courts located in cities may have had a more sophisticated system of reporting than did those located in the rural districts, given that the former would have employed more clerks. On the other hand, rural county courts may have had relatively fewer cases and therefore more time in which to keep accurate records of charges and convictions. In short, and this only reflects what is now one of the most established criminological maxims, neither urban nor rural statistics should be regarded as valid indicators of levels of particular crimes (Zay 1965, 634).

In addition to the problem of comparability between years, it is difficult to compare charges, convictions, and acquittals between provinces as not all provinces relied on the grand jury system of indictment (Zay 1965, 635). Given the significant role of grand juries (in the provinces that required them) in the preferment of indictments in possible maternal neonaticide cases, this procedural difference in the indictment process may have had a significant impact on the numbers of cases brought to trial in the different provinces. And finally, population increases do not appear to have been accounted for when aggregating these data in order to discuss increases or decreases over time. However, the purpose here is not to compare these potential differences or to analyze comparability over time but, rather, to examine how the infanticide law came into existence. Concealment of birth statistics were the only official source of statistical knowledge defining the boundaries of this problem, and, therefore, it is worth understanding how the perpetrators were constituted in and by the official record as legislators (and/or their researchers) should have relied on this data as a source of knowledge about the nature and extent of maternal neonaticide or infanticide, and its prosecution, in Canada. Although it is not known whether these demographic indicators were consulted by the legislators responsible for the enactment of the infanticide provision in 1948, their impression of the characteristics of "infanticidal mothers" is remarkably similar to the picture that emerges from the official demographic record.[28]

In Ontario it was grand juries, made up of laypersons from the community, who consistently refused to issue true bills on indictments for murder and who consistently substituted charges for either concealment or neglect in childbirth, as allowed by law or dictated by circumstance. In the other provinces discretion would have been in the hands of an individual Crown attorney (or police officer acting on his/her behalf) for the judicial district in which the crime occurred. Given that Crown attorneys may have been likely to have had professional allegiance with the criminal justice system and therefore to be inclined to lay a charge, it could easily be argued that relatively more charges were laid for murder, manslaughter, concealment, and neglect in childbirth in the absence of the grand jury.

In part, precisely because concealment of birth was the watered down version of the suspected crime of murder that state authorities were attempting to prosecute, these statistical figures point to a potential criminal justice problem. It may have been that many people thought that, because of the convictions for concealment of birth, women were getting away with murder. Conviction rates (expressed as a percentage relative to charges) for concealment of birth rose slightly from 70 percent in the 1910s and 1920s to almost 90 percent during the 1930s and 1940s.[29] This high rate of conviction for concealment of birth was not likely seen as a criminal justice success but, rather, as a failure to properly address an emerging socio-legal problem – namely, "infant murder." As we shall see in Chapter 3, legislators equated the crime category of "concealment of birth" as processed by the courts to "infant murder" and sought to rationalize the homicide framework and to remove the discretionary power of juries in a manner that would satisfy both those who pressed for conviction and those who viewed the mandatory punishment framework for murder as too harsh.

Aggregate Concealment Charges:
A Socio-Legal Phenomenon Quantified

Unlike today's published crime statistics, early twentieth-century court statistics provide the researcher with demographic knowledge on a case-by-case basis concerning those brought before the county court in every judicial district across Canada. Along with the numbers of charges, convictions, and acquittals, statistical information is readily available on the sex; age; marital status; religion; employment; place of birth; use of alcohol; detention for lunacy; lengths of actual stay in a jail, penitentiary, or reformatory, along with sentences that included the option of fines. Life sentences were recorded along with death sentences and commutations. Lengths of stays in individual jails were recorded since the information on prisoners was provided by the warden of each jail and prison in Canada. It is also possible to know how many prisoners, male or female, and for whom and for how many, the prerogative of mercy was granted. These data were tallied for each judicial district in Canada. In Ontario alone there were forty-seven judicial districts for which returns were tallied, aggregated both by province and for the country as a whole.

Of the returning counties throughout Canada, a range of observable demographic and legal response characteristics for the crime of concealment of birth are evident. Table 1.1 reveals that between 1912 and 1919 (i.e., during the first decade for which statistics were produced), the typical woman convicted of concealment of birth was likely to be employed as a domestic servant (47 percent), to be single (62 percent), and to be born in Canada (38 percent). Between 1920 and 1929 there was little overall change. Of those women convicted of concealment of birth between 1920 and 1929, 48 percent were employed as domestic servants, 58 percent were single, and 61 percent were born in Canada. From 1930 to 1936 the demographic data on "occupation" and "civil condition" were not reported, but between 1937 and 1948, 55 percent were employed in the domestic service, 64 percent were single, and 69 percent were born in Canada.[30]

In terms of potential jeopardy vis-à-vis prosecution, women working in domestic and personal service were often living on their own without a male member of their family to act as a go between with the authorities on their daughter's behalf. Without fathers to shield them from prosecution – either by way of securing a perhaps costly defence attorney or by way of diverting the matter entirely from the criminal system – domestic servants were likely to be in a more vulnerable position than other women.

Additional data on maternal neonaticide for the period 1913-15 are recorded in separate statistics for infanticide, although this is before the introduction of the separate *Criminal Code* offence of "infanticide." The collation of these data ceased after 1916, when the publication of the records was taken over by the Dominion Bureau of Statistics. Charge and conviction rates are documented for each of these years in the bureau's statistical tables (see Table 1.2).[31]

Table 1.2 demonstrates that, of these seven defendants, six were acquitted. Of these acquittals, it is worth noting that one person was a male. Here we see two instances in which a man and a woman (likely a couple) were charged with infanticide for a single incident. In the sole conviction registered, the accused was living in a city at the time of the crime, was between sixteen and twenty-one years of age, single, employed as a domestic with elementary school education, Roman Catholic, and born in an "other foreign country." This was her first conviction and she was sentenced to serve

Table 1.1

Characteristics of women convicted of concealment of birth, 1912-19

Totals for Canada, 1912-19*		1912	1913	1914	1915	1916	1917	1918	1919	Total	% of (60) convictions
Occupation	Agriculture	–	–	–	–	–	–	2	–	2	3
	Commercial	1	–	–	–	–	–	–	–	1	2
	Domestic	3	6	–	8	3	1	4	3	28	47
	Industrial	–	–	1	2	2	–	1	–	6	10
	Professional	–	1	–	–	–	–	–	–	1	2
	Labourer	2	1	–	–	–	–	–	–	3	3
Civil condition	Married	2	3	–	4	2	–	2	3	16	27
	Widowed	1	1	–	–	–	–	2	–	4	7
	Single	3	7	6	7	5	2	6	1	37	62
Religion	Baptists	1	–	–	–	1	–	–	–	2	3
	Roman Catholics	–	5	1	4	1	1	4	–	16	27
	Church of England	–	1	1	–	–	–	1	–	3	5
	Methodists	–	3	1	1	1	–	1	–	7	12
	Presbyterians	–	1	–	3	2	–	1	–	7	12
	Protestants	–	–	–	1	–	–	2	–	3	5
	Other denominations	4	1	1	1	1	–	–	–	8	13
Birthplace	British Isles	–	1	2	1	–	–	2	–	6	10
	Canada	1	9	–	7	–	–	6	2	23	38
	United States	–	–	–	–	–	1	1	1	3	5
	Other foreign countries	4	1	2	3	–	–	1	1	12	20
	Other British possessions	–	–	–	–	–	–	–	–	–	–

* Numbers do not equal total charges (86) or convictions (60) for this period. There is apparently no reason for this other than lack of information from individual reporting county clerks.

Source: Aggregated from Canada (1912-16), *Criminal Statistics*, and Canada (1917-48), *Statistics of Criminal and Other Offences*, for the years 1912-19.

Table 1.2

Charges, acquittals, convictions and sentences for infanticide, 1913-15

		1913	1914	1915
Charges		2	2	3
Acquitted*	Male	–	1	–
	Female	2	1	2
Convicted (male and female)		–	–	1
Commited to jail	< 1 year	–	–	–
	1 year and over	–	–	1
Reformatory		–	–	–
Other		–	–	–

* For this and all other similar tables, the sex of acquitted defendants, but not the sex of the convicted defendants, was recorded.
Source: Aggregated from Canada (1912-16), *Criminal Statistics*, for the years 1913-15.

"one year and over" in jail. Finally, her "use of liquors" was described as "moderate" versus "immoderate."

In addition to the statistical data for infanticide, eight years of data from the first decade of the twentieth century are available on concealment of birth. Table 1.3 reveals the total number of charges laid, along with acquittals, convictions, and sentences. In these years a total of eighty-six charges for concealment of birth were issued, with a total of sixty convictions. The conviction rate of 70 percent did not necessarily represent a success rate, at least in the eyes of Crown attorneys, since the usual sentence was in the "other" category, which likely represented probation dispositions. Out of total of sixty convictions, thirty-three were disposed by the "other" sentence, representing 55 percent of the total convictions. Nevertheless, a significant number of those convicted were sentenced to short jail terms. Thirty-five percent of all convictions were disposed of as jail terms of one year or less. Yet, some of those incarcerated were granted mercy and were liberated from jail. For example, in 1917, of the three convictions for concealment, one woman was granted the prerogative of mercy and liberated from jail after serving between one-quarter and less than one-half of her sentence of less than one year (Canada 1917, 252). Thus, while charges frequently led to convictions, sentences were likely to be non-carceral, with those who served jail sentences being released after serving only a portion of their entire sentences. Sentences for concealment of birth remained relatively "lenient," with the non-carceral "other" category representing 46 percent of all convictions between 1920 and 1929, falling to 43 percent in 1930-39, and falling to 34 percent between 1940 and 1949 (see Tables 1.4, 1.5, 1.6).

Table 1.3

Charges, acquittals, convictions, and sentences for concealment of birth, 1912-19

		1912	1913	1914	1915	1916	1917	1918	1919	Total	% of (60) convictions
Charges		9	16	8	14	11	6	17	5	86	n/a*
Acquitted	Male	–	2	–	–	–	–	3	–	5	n/a
	Female	2	3	2	2	4	3	4	1	20	n/a
Convicted (male and female)		7	11	6	12	7	3	10	4	60	100.0
Committed to jail	With fine	–	–	–	–	–	–	–	–	–	–
	≤ 1 year	2	5	–	5	3	1	3	2	21	35.0
	≥ 1 year	–	–	1	–	–	1	–	–	1	1.7
	2-5 years	–	1	1	–	–	–	–	–	2	3.3
Reformatory		–	–	–	1	1	–	1	–	3	5.0
Other		5	5	5	6	3	1	6	2	33	55.0

* Figure excluded in all the comparable tables. The percentage of charges that resulted in convictions for each decade is shown in Table 1.7 below.
Source: Aggregated from Canada (1912-16), *Criminal Statistics*, and Canada (1917-48), *Statistics of Criminal and Other Offences*, for the years 1912-19.

Table 1.4

Charges, acquittals, convictions, and sentences for concealment of birth, 1920-29

		1920	1921	1922	1923	1924	1925	1926	1927	1928	1929	Total	% of (78) convictions
Charges		3	12	11	2	17	9	12	16	9	7	98	n/a
Acquitted	Male	–	1	–	–	2	–	1	–	–	–	4	n/a
	Female	–	3	1	–	2	1	2	3	1	2	15	n/a
Convicted (male and female)		3	8	10	2	12	8	9	13	8	5	78	100.0
Committed to jail	With fine	–	1	–	–	–	–	–	2	–	–	2	2.6
	≤ 1 year	1	1	3	2	5	5	–	1	1	2	21	27.0
	≥ 1 year	–	–	–	–	–	–	1	3	2	–	6	7.7
	2-5 years	–	3	1	–	–	–	–	1	–	–	5	6.4
Reformatory		–	1	–	–	2	–	1	3	–	1	8	10.3
Other		2	3	6	–	5	3	7	3	5	2	36	46.2

Source: Aggregated from Canada (1917-48), *Statistics of Criminal and Other Offences*, for the years 1920-29.

Table 1.5

Charges, acquittals, convictions, and sentences for concealment of birth, 1930-39

		1930	1931	1932	1933	1934	1935	1936	1937	1938	1939	Total	% of (122) convictions
Charges		9	16	8	22	15	13	8	16	20	14	141	n/a
Acquitted	Male	–	–	1	–	1	1	–	–	3	1	7	5.7
	Female	2	1	1	1	2	1	2	1	–	1	12	9.8
Convicted (male and female)		7	15	6	21	12	11	6	15	17	12	122	n/a
Committed to jail	With fine option	–	1	–	1	–	–	1	1	1	–	5	4.1
	≤ 1 year	2	6	–	3	–	2	1	3	5	6	28	23.0
	≥ 1 year	1	–	–	1	2	1	2	–	–	–	7	5.7
	2-5 years	1	1	–	5	–	1	–	–	–	1	9	7.4
Reformatory		1	1	2	3	3	4	2	2	2	1	21	17.2
Other		2	6	4	8	7	3	–	9	9	4	52	43.0

Source: Aggregated from Canada (1917-48), *Statistics of Criminal and Other Offences*, for the years 1930-39.

Table 1.6

Charges, acquittals, convictions, and sentences for concealment of birth, 1940-48

		1940	1941	1942	1943	1944	1945	1946	1947*	1948	Total	% of (104) convictions
Charges		17	19	19	8	17	17	9	–	12	118	n/a
Acquitted	Male	–	1	–	–	–	2	–	–	–	3	3.0
	Female	3	2	3	1	1	–	–	–	1	11	10.5
Convicted (male and female)		14	16	16	7	16	15	9	–	11	104	n/a
Committed to jail	With fine option	–	–	–	–	2	3	–	–	–	5	4.8
	≤ 1 year	4	6	4	4	4	6	3	–	1	32	31.0
	≥ 1 year	–	3	1	1	1	1	1	–	3	11	11.0
	2-5 years	–	–	–	–	–	–	1	–	1	2	2.0
Reformatory		–	5	5	–	4	4	–	–	1	15	14.0
Other		10	2	6	2	7	1	4	–	3	35	34.0

* Data omitted for this year due to inconsistent reporting of categories by the Dominion Bureau of Statistics.
Source: Aggregated from Canada (1917-48), *Statistics of Criminal and Other Offences*, for the years 1940-48.

The statistical data reveal that, when incarcerated, these single women were sentenced, for short periods, to reformatories rather than to provincial jails. Between the years 1920 and 1948 the rate at which women convicted of concealment of birth were sent to reformatories varied from 10.3 percent (1920-29) to 17.2 percent (1930-39) and 14 percent (1940-48) of the total convicted. Sentences of jail terms less than one year ranged from 27 percent between 1920 and 1929, to 23 percent between 1930 and 1939, and 31 percent between 1940 and 1948. Sentences of more than one year in jail ranged from a low of 6.4 per cent (1920-29) and a high of 11 percent (1940-48). Second offences accounted for harsher sentences of between two and five years. Very often the convicted were released after only a few months of incarceration. The data presented in Tables 1.4, 1.5, and 1.6 also support most legislators' impressions that sentences tended to be lenient. Table 1.7 illustrates that overall conviction rates for concealment of birth increased from 80 percent between 1920 to 1929, to 87 percent between 1930 and 1939, to 88 percent between 1940 and 1948. The high overall conviction rate for concealment during this period, not to mention the slight upward trend in the charge and conviction rates, conforms with the impression of legislators at the time of the adoption of the infanticide provision that infant homicide was a unique and unaddressed socio-legal problem (although the actual offence or conviction rates were probably not rising in relation to the overall population).

Finally, during the period under review, few defendants were listed as detained for "lunacy."[32] This finding is really not surprising, even though maternal neonaticide was eventually to be governed under a medico-legal framework that mitigated culpable homicide through the use of the concept of "mental disturbance." A few indictment case files for the province of Ontario (discussed in Chapter 2) reveal that indictments for murder were dismissed because the defendant was deemed "unfit to stand trial." The question of mental illness in these cases was, however, never really very strong since infanticide was understood as resulting from a fleeting mental

Table 1.7

Concealment of birth charges, acquittals, and convictions, 1920-48

	1920-29	1930-39	1940-48	% increase (1920-29 to 1940-48)
Charges	98	141	118	20%
Acquittals	19	19	14	–37%
Convictions	78	122	104	33%
Conviction Rate*	80%	87%	88%	10%

* Expressed as a percentage of total charges

condition precipitated by childbirth and/or lactation, somewhat akin to a state of inebriety (Sullivan 1911; Morton 1934). The weaker psychiatric concept of "disturbance of mind" did meet the conventional standard of "disease of the mind" causing a "defect of reason" sufficient for a successful claim of legal "insanity" (Roach 1996).

Although I have no direct evidence that the legislators or their assistants consulted the available statistics on concealment of birth, the *Hansard* record does indicate that, when the infanticide provision was amended, five to six years after the provision was enacted, as part of a broader revision of the *Criminal Code* that considered questions relating to the homicide framework (and capital punishment in particular), they did consult *Statistics of Criminal and Other Offences*.[33] It is not, therefore, unlikely that the government would have relied upon *Statistics of Criminal and Other Offences* when considering enacting an infanticide provision. If this was the case, then the data I have presented would have formed the criminal statistical basis of the authorities' constitution of "infant murder" as a significant legal problem requiring an innovative legislative response, which would have complemented the legislators' impression of the inadequacies of the existing *Criminal Code* framework for addressing maternal neonaticide derived from other sources.

2
Unwanted Babies:
Humanitarianism and the Infant

Infanticide is not a random, unpredictable crime. Instead, a
quick survey of history reveals that it is deeply embedded in
and responsive to the societies in which it occurs. The crime of
infanticide, or child murder in the first year of life, is committed
by mothers who cannot parent their child under the circumstances dictated by their unique position in place and time. The
factors in such circumstances vary from poverty to stigma to
dowry, but the extent to which infanticide is a reflection of the
norms governing motherhood is a constant that links these
seemingly disparate acts.
– Michelle Oberman (2003, 4)

For comparative purposes, this chapter examines material from the criminal assize clerk county indictment case file records for the Province of Ontario
as well as the federal records of women convicted of murder for killing newly
born babies. The part of the provincial records examined contains information on findings issued by coroner's juries in cases of suspected maternal
neonaticide. The usual process by which a case of suspected maternal
neonaticide was pursued involved the notification of the police and the
Office of the Coroner. The matter was subsequently investigated by a
coroner's jury, which, if it saw fit, would, upon finding evidence of a suspicious homicide, send the matter to a magistrate and grand jury to issue an
indictment. As I indicated earlier, juries might reject all, or the most serious, charges considered. Following indictment, the accused would be sched-
uled for trial. Here, again, petit jurors' reluctance to convict, especially on
the most serious charges, would often come into play. At least one coroner,
the author of a manual for coroners, was particularly concerned about the
evidentiary problems confronting indictment and later, in the case of petit
juries, conviction.

These case file narratives illustrate how, through a complex filtering process structured by the involvement of the witnesses, suspects, police, Crown attorneys, and coroners and their inquest juries, legal responsibility was established within the narrow framework governing the work of the laypersons of the grand jury. The provincial grand jury exercised a considerable degree of discretionary power, albeit constrained by the rule of law. Although the contents of jury deliberations are obviously not accessible, some cases conform to the established nineteenth-century story of juror and judge sympathy (Backhouse 1984) – cases where there is a marked reluctance to indict or, in the case of petit juries, to convict. This reluctance to convict for murder may have been affected by high-profile murder cases such as that of Maria McCabe,[1] who confessed and pled guilty to the murder of her illegitimate child at the Wentworth Fall Assize in 1883. She was sentenced to death, but the sentence was later commuted to fourteen years to be served at the Kingston Penitentiary, where she served approximately seven years of her term before being released. A petition for her release was eventually granted on the grounds that she committed her crime while in a state of "wild distress," having been the victim of seduction and dismissed from her employment at the age of sixteen. Her release was supported both by members of the Hamilton women's community and state authorities, including the Crown attorney who prosecuted the case. The evidence suggests that the general public did not countenance a death penalty for the killing of a baby, particularly an illegitimate one, since women in these circumstances were both the victims of their seducers and of society's moral disapprobation of sexual relations and childbirth outside marriage. According to the jurors in this case, Maria McCabe was justly convicted for "infanticide." However, they expressed their desire for clemency to the assize court judge on the grounds that the "distressing circumstances" of the crime mitigated her offence – that "justice" could only be served if her sentence was commuted.

Over the course of the twentieth century, however, coroner's jury findings of wilful murder for the Province of Ontario and later convictions (either by judge or petit jury) could be obtained, especially for the lesser charges. Thus, there was not an especially lenient approach to these circumstances as criminal responses were countenanced as "just." This can be seen in the official criminal statistics for the whole of Canada, which indicate increasing numbers of charges and convictions, and an increasing conviction rate, for "concealment" between 1912 and 1948.[2] I also describe one case of maternal neonaticide where there appears to have been considerable pressure from relatives and witnesses to prosecute and convict for murder, and I discuss capital cases in which murder convictions were easily obtained. The Crown attorneys' complaints about juror sympathy and reluctance to convict may well have been overstated, given that there is evidence that there were numerous convictions for concealment and neglect, and even some for murder. There is little doubt that culpability was mitigated in reference to the socially ascribed life chances and living conditions of mainly single working-class women, the unwanted ex-nuptial infant, and their combined social destiny. However, this explanation overlooks the medico-legal framework within which decisions about guilt and innocence were made. As Boys's manual for coroners made explicit, convictions for any of the charges had as much to do with the available forensic medical evidence as they did with a generalized juror compassion for the women.

Finally, this chapter qualifies the argument, best advanced by Laqueur (1989), that the humanitarian sentiment developed in and through both popular infanticide stories and forensic autopsy narratives of cases of infanticide. In slight contrast to Laqueur, I argue that humanitarianism was fixed on the baby around whom both humanitarian sentiment and legislative action were eventually focused.

Ontario Criminal Assize Clerk Indictment Case Files, 1853-77

Insight into the law, medicine, and lay knowledge, as these came together in the criminal justice process, can be gained by examining criminal assize clerk indictment records for cases of maternal neonaticide. The cases discussed in this section are drawn from Criminal Assize Clerk Indictment Case Files that cover the whole of Ontario for the period 1853 to 1977, now maintained at the Archives of Ontario. The series contains records that show which indictments were preferred, with information on the initial charges laid and final indictments issued, with the latter frequently being for lesser offences than had initially been charged. The record was not, apparently, supposed to contain case records where a coroner's jury refused to issue any indictment ("no bill"),[3] although a few of these files in which no bill was issued are contained in the series. These particular files contain only the information, complaint, and the "no bill" finding. In addition, the eventual trial outcome from these indictments is only occasionally indicated through correspondence retained in the file.

These files were created by a Crown attorney in a judicial district, and the files for all Ontario were submitted to York County Judicial District Court by the assize clerks of each county. Once the files began to be maintained by each judicial district, the historical record virtually vanishes. Many files sat in basements of county courthouses and were damaged by flood, fire, and/or pests. Case files were often poorly stored in the basements of the individual courthouses, where they were subject to invasion by rodents and insects.[4] For this reason, for the period covering 1930 to 1977 only those indictment records from York County (now Toronto) have survived.

All cases where it could be ascertained from the index that the victim was an infant were selected for review. These cases include: all cases of "concealment," "neglect," "abandonment," "failure to provide necessaries of life," "killing unborn child," as well as a range of apparently ad hoc designations that include "killing illegitimate child," "child murder," and even "murder (infanticide)." This last designation was occasionally in use decades prior to the passage of Canada's infanticide law.[5] In cases where the generic indictments of murder or manslaughter were brought, the existence of an infant-victim is only evident where additional charges of concealment and/or neglect were also brought. I was not necessarily able to identify all murder and manslaughter cases where the victim was an infant. As we might expect, indictments for the more serious generic charges tended to be refused, and indictments for the less serious infant-victim specific charges were preferred. The record available to me is therefore incomplete. First and foremost, in most cases the final outcome at trial is not recorded.[6] In this important sense, each case file is incomplete. Finally, most of the records for cases in which no indictments were issued were not retained and are, sadly, lost to history.

Juror Reluctance to Indict and Convict:
Lawyer and Juror Inventiveness and the Difficulty of Proof
In this section I discuss individual cases in which attempts were made by the district Crown attorneys to indict women for killing their unwanted babies. I have endeavoured to discuss a range of cases that represent the differing circumstances in which the deaths occurred, the legal responses to the suspect, and, when possible, the outcome of the case. Different charges, such as murder or attempted murder, were often unsustainable, were refused, and/or were substituted with concealment of birth or neglect to obtain assistance in childbirth. Sometimes, of course, women pled guilty to the lesser charges of concealment or neglect and were sentenced accordingly, although the broader sample from which the cases I discuss in detail are drawn indicate that, sometimes, these sentences were merely perfunctory.

Often, as many as three or four charges would be laid in order to gain a conviction for at least one of the offences charged. These charging practices illustrate the measures taken by Crown attorneys in their attempts to gain convictions, especially for the more serious charges, in cases of suspected child murder. In fact, it appears from these records that the practice of charging women solely with murder was abandoned by about 1892, when Crown attorneys began to seek three and sometimes four different indictments. For example, Josephine Flaro was charged in Stormont County in 1892 with "murder," "concealing birth of child," and "manslaughter." In 1897 Charlotte Saunders was charged in Northumberland County with "Infanticide," "Concealing Child Birth" and "Neglecting to Obtain Assistance in Child Birth." Between 1897 and 1900, "Neglecting to Obtain Assistance in Child Birth" charges were laid against Annie Humeston of Kent County (1897), Mary

McGraw of Middlesex County (1897), Helen Darrah of Hastings County (1898), Edith O'Donoghue of Leeds and Grenville County (1898), and Annie Flavelle of York County (1900). After about 1900, multiple combinations of charges continued to be brought before the grand jury for consideration, with neglect and concealment being the most popular (and almost always in conjunction with a murder or manslaughter charge). Eventually, the practice of indicting on charges of murder or manslaughter was abandoned in favour of the multiple indictment practice because grand juries simply would not issue a true bill of indictment on a charge of murder; instead, they would substitute concealment or neglect for murder charges, even when the indictment had not been sought by the Crown.[7]

Lucy Nadgwan:[8] Indictment for Murder Refused

In 1901 the Crown attempted to indict Lucy Nadgwan of the Indian Reserve of Cape Croker, Bruce County, on the little-used charge of "Killing Unborn Child." In this particular case, the infant was killed *during* the act of birth, so it could not be said to have been wholly born-alive and to have had independent circulation. The affidavit of the Crown attorney stated that "Lucy Nadgwan ... did unlawfully cause the death of a certain male child whose name to the jurors is unknown which child had not become a human being in such manner that she the said Lucy Nadgwan would have been guilty of murder if such child had been born."[9]

Upon hearing the evidence, however, the coroner's jurors replaced the indictment for murder with indictments for "killing unborn child," "concealment," and "neglect." Although the handwritten record is not entirely clear, it seems that Lucy Nadgwan pled guilty to "killing unborn child" at her trial held 18 September 1901. There is no record of what happened at the trial itself or of what her punishment was. In this case, we see the classic pattern, much complained of by Crown attorneys, in which lesser charges are substituted by the jury for the more serious charges sought by the Crown.

Rachel Boakes and Louisa Kalkhorst (Parry Sound):[10] "Neglect to Obtain Assistance in Childbirth"

In 1904, in the district of Parry Sound, two women, Rachel Boakes and Louisa Kalkhorst, were separately indicted on the offence of neglect to obtain necessary assistance in childbirth. In Rachel Boakes's case it seems likely, from the indictment record, that she worked as a servant for the Hicks family in the township of Chapman in Parry Sound. Martha Hicks suspected that Rachel had hidden her dead baby somewhere in the bushes, and she told her two children to go out and look for it. The children, Hugh and Alice Hicks, provided affidavits that they found the baby alive, wrapped in a wet coat and lying behind a log. The baby lived for four days. Rachel Boakes's indictment sheet read:

Rachel Boakes is convicted before the undersigned a justice of the peace for the said district for that she the said Rachel Boakes at the township of Chapman in said district on the 16th day of May 1904 being then and there with child and about to be delivered of such child did, there and then, with intent that her said child should not live neglect to provide reasonable assistance in her delivery whereby and in consequence of such neglect her said child died shortly after birth. And I adjudge the said Rachel Boakes for her said offence to be imprisoned in the common Gaol of the said district of Parry Sound in the said district of Parry Sound to await trial at the first court of competent jurisdiction.

Even though Rachel Boakes was imprisoned to await her trial, she was found "not guilty" by a petit jury at trial.

Like Rachel Boakes, Louisa Kalkhorst had a baby who died. Kalkhorst was also suspected of wilful murder and was indicted by a grand jury on a charge of neglect to provide assistance at childbirth. In this instance the accused provided a deposition in her own defence, admitting to having given birth alone but not to having intentionally killed her baby. Evidence provided to the coroner's jury, dated 26 September 1904 at the township of McMurrich, Parry Sound, included affidavits from her brother, father, and a male friend. Each provided confirmation that Louisa was pregnant. In her own defence Louisa provided a statement recorded by the police as follows:

That I was about to give birth to a child but did not wilfully neglect to provide assistance so that the child might die. There was no one present whom I could send for assistance my father and brother knew that I was unwell but don't know whether were aware that I was about to give birth to a child. I told Mr. McRae that I had not given birth to a child, I now acknowledge to I told him an untruth. The child was born between nine and ten in the forenoon and I asked my brother about six in the evening to bury it. My father came into my room shortly after the child was born but only remained a few minutes. I don't know whether or not he was aware that I had given birth to a child. I told him of the birth of the child about 10 days after the child was born. The reason I did not tell my father sooner was because I did not wish to put any more trouble on him than I could help. I took up the child a few moments after it was born and found it was dead.[11]

Dr. Louis Ferguson's post-mortem examination found that the child was born alive but did not discover any evidence of foul play. He stated: "I think the child would have lived had it had proper assistance at birth." Since Louisa Kalkhorst admitted to giving birth unattended, and the doctor's medical evidence indicated that the child was born alive but did not live as a consequence of unattended birth, she was found guilty of neglect.

The "confession" in Kalkhorst's statement seems hardly more compelling evidence in relation to the charge of neglect than that available from the record in the Boakes case. Boakes could conceivably have been convicted of a very serious charge, manslaughter or even murder, but the jury at her trial was unable to convict her even of neglect. This reluctance was entirely typical.

Eliza Logan:[12] "Concealment" Conviction despite Evidence of Foul Play

In 1902, in the Simcoe County district, Eliza Logan was indicted on three charges: "murder," "neglect to obtain assistance at childbirth," and "concealment of birth." A warrant was issued for her arrest on 25 March 1902 in Collingwood, Ontario. The affidavit of the police magistrate Fred Maidens stated: "I went to the home of the prisoner with [name of a physician] who made an examination, she told me she had given birth to a child, that the child was born dead she wrapped it in an apron and left it down the railroad. She also said she kept it for some time. The child was a girl. The magistrate committed the prisoner to Barrie, Ontario for further investigation and time."

Eliza Logan confessed to police magistrate Maidens that she had a child on 23 February 1902 and took it down to a ditch, where it was found two weeks later. She claimed the child she had was a female and that she neither told anyone she was having a child nor visited a doctor. Grand jurors in this case issued indictments for the murder of an infant, for neglect to obtain assistance in childbirth, and for concealment of birth. The coroner who inspected Logan for signs of delivery and who autopsied the infant's body issued a report in which he observed that the umbilical cord revealed signs of manual separation from the mother's body and that the hydrostatic "floating lung" test indicated live-birth. According to the coroner's autopsy report, the child was born alive and had died from violent means: "The cause of death in my opinion: The injury to the head was received while the child was alive and was sufficient to cause death and death occurred very soon after birth."

Despite this overwhelming evidence of foul play in the death of the baby, Eliza Logan was found not guilty of murder and neglect but guilty of concealment of birth. It appeared as though this was the only indictment that would sustain a conviction, likely because she confessed to the police magistrate to having secretly disposed of the dead body of the infant. This case illustrates the classic "concealment" scenario, which frustrated Crown attorneys and which was discussed by the legislators who debated and passed the infanticide provision.

Grace Hamilton,[13] Jean Fraser,[14] Vera Fish:[15] Successful Convictions for "Concealment"

Numerous attempts were made by police magistrates and Crown attorneys to obtain indictments for concealment of birth. The series index indicates that there were sixteen attempted prosecutions for concealment between 1877 and 1930. These attempted prosecutions do not include all those cases where grand jurors substituted concealment indictments for murder, resulting in many more convictions for concealment than are listed by the series index. Nor, crucially, do they contain all the cases where concealment indictments were sought and a no bill finding was issued.[16] However, the record does contain two files where a plea of guilty was entered, following which an indictment for concealment was issued, and one case where the investigation revealed that the body of the infant suffered considerable violence and a conviction for concealment was registered. Grace Hamilton gave birth to an infant in Toronto and was indicted on a charge of concealment, to which she pled guilty. An infant was discovered in a box inside a clothes wardrobe in her room. Hamilton was sentenced to one year's imprisonment in a county jail on the charge of concealment.

Jean Fraser also pled guilty to a charge of concealment at her trial in York County, held between 26 March and 30 April 1926. In this case, the judge directed the (petit) jury to find Fraser not guilty of murder in exchange for her plea of guilt. The coroner's autopsy found no external signs of violence on the infant's body and concluded that the cause of death was neglect and exposure subsequent to its birth. Fraser was released on her own recognizance to return to the court in one year for sentencing. In her case, it appeared a murder charge would have been unsuccessful since there had been no sign of violence on the infant's body. Without any sign of violence, the Crown would have a difficult time proving intentional killing, so perhaps the murder charge was dropped in exchange for her plea of guilt to concealment.

Vera Fish, aged twenty-two years, was indicted on two counts of concealment of birth in Halton County in the Province of Ontario on 14 September 1926, following the discovery of an infant in a river. Fish confessed to having given birth but not to having anything to do with the child discovered in the river. The burnt body of her child was discovered in the oven at her home. The coroner's autopsy indicated that the body of the infant was "burnt and roasted" but that one lung floated, suggesting live-birth. Fish was found not guilty of the concealment of the birth of the infant found in the river, since it was not her child, but she was found guilty of the concealment of the infant discovered in her oven. The accidental nature of the discovery of Vera Fish's dead baby tends to suggest that, in certain contexts, it was easier then than it is now for women to conceal their dead babies.

Pearl Anderson:[17] Conviction for Manslaughter despite Infanticide Scenario

At a Coroner's Inquest in the town of Collingwood, Simcoe County, Ontario, jurors determined that an infant died at the hands of Pearl Smith (alias Anderson) as a result of exposure due to being placed in the cedars near the railway track. The evidence provided to the coroner's jury indicated that the accused had sought the help of Jessie Bessou, matron of the Woman's Hospital and Rescue Home of the Salvation Army in Toronto. According to Bessou's witness narrative, Pearl Anderson had come to her for help with her pregnancy. Anderson told Bessou that she was in trouble, was married, and lived in Collingwood but that her husband abused her and failed to provide for her. Her lack of a wedding ring signalled to Bessou that she was perhaps lying about the marriage, but Anderson explained that she had sold her wedding ring to pay her expenses in Toronto. She claimed that she and her wretched husband lived in a shack in Webbwood, Ontario. According to Bessou's depositions, Pearl Anderson was "poorly clad and not very clean and was suffering from disease of a syphilitic nature." For this she was treated in the Woman's Hospital; however, when she gave birth to the child on 22 December 1911 it had symptoms of secondary syphilitic disease on its face. After remaining in the hospital for two weeks, Pearl and the baby were discharged and sent to live with her sister in Collingwood in January 1912. When Anderson arrived home in Collingwood, her parents would not take her and the baby in. And so, after wandering around in "the willows," Anderson left the baby to die of exposure. The baby was found at the side of the road, not far from her sister's house. Her sister provided evidence to the grand jury that Pearl had told her the baby had died within two hours of its birth. The coroner's autopsy determined that the infant had died from exposure. At eighteen years of age, Pearl Smith was indicted on two separate charges: abandonment and murder. She pled guilty to manslaughter and was sent to live at the Salvation Army, in Toronto, for five years.

In this case, we see a guilty plea entered to a very serious charge and resulting in a significant sentence. Life under the watchful eye of Jessie Bessou at the Woman's Hospital and Rescue Home of the Salvation Army may not have been all that comfortable, and the sentence should probably be regarded as a genuine punishment. In comparison to the sentence of one year's imprisonment Grace Hamilton received for concealment, Anderson's sentence was certainly not lenient, particularly since women generally did not serve their full carceral sentences.[18]

Annie Flavelle:[19] Damning Evidence Leading to Trial for Murder in Possible Private Prosecution

The criminal procedure for indicting a woman on any one of the charges used to govern child killing began with the discovery of a dead baby and an opinion of a coroner's jury. Once the body was discovered and taken to a coroner, he would swear out a coroner's affidavit before a justice of the peace of the county district. In this case, the coroner's affidavit, sworn before the justice of the peace in Toronto on 19 February 1900 read: "I, M.J. Greig, Coroner of the City of Toronto, do swear that from the information received, I am of the opinion that there is reason for believing that a infant [sic] child did not come to her death from natural causes, or from mere accident or mischance, but come to her death from violence or unfair means, or culpable or negligent conduct of others under circumstances requiring an investigation by a Coroner's inquest."

Next, the coroner would issue a "Warrant to Constable to Summon Jury." The record indicates that Sergeant E. Hales received the warrant at the police station at 2:55 p.m. on that same day. The next day, fourteen (rather than the twenty-four dictated by the warrant) coroner's jurors were assembled by P.C. James Roe of no. 4 Division to commence the inquisition. The records indicate that jurors met at the morgue to view the corpse, inquire into the cause of death, and to issue a finding that read, in part: "That this child met its death at 322 Wilton Ave. in the City of Toronto about 11am Monday February 19th 1900, by direct violence at the hands of some person or persons." The document is signed and sealed by each of the jurors and the coroner.

Both James and Sarah Hayes, Annie Flavelle's aunt and uncle, provided sworn evidence to the coroner's jury, but this did little to help her case. Annie Flavelle had been living with them at the time of the infant's birth and death. James Hayes, a grocery store owner, testified that he "saw her and the child yesterday about noon and at the time the child was dead and she was in bed. I asked her who was the father of the child and she told me that it was Mr. Miller, a bar-tender at Stoufville. I saw a long tear on the side of the face [of the baby] which was pointed out to me by Dr. Ball." Sarah Hayes also provided evidence to the effect that Annie was responsible for the infant's death. She testified that:

Mip [sic] Flavelle came in at the store door at about 10 a.m. Feb. 19th. 1900. She told me that she was not well. (I had not seen her before for two weeks.) She told me that she *had cramps*. I got hot water and put her feet in it. After a time she went up stairs and went to bed. She told me that she had no sleep the night before so I pulled down the blind and left her. Fifteen minutes later she had gone to the bathroom. She stayed in the bathroom a while and then went back to bed. At this time she told me that she *had diarrhoea* very badly and that was why she had gone to the bathroom. I offered her some diarrhoea mixture, but she thought that she would not need it. I went down stairs and got her some tea and toast. But when I took it up *she was in the bathroom again*. The bathroom door was locked. I then went down stairs and was called to the store. Shortly after the children told me that Annie must have fallen out of bed, *as they hear a thud*. I went up stairs again and *found Annie on the floor beside the bed in a sitting posture. She had a wrapper on and I think that she had removed her under-clothes*. She complained again of pain and said that *she wanted to go to the bathroom* again.

But we got her to bed again. She then told me that she had left a dirty napkin under the bed. I looked there and found a baby. When I found her on the floor she told me that her changes had come on. *When I found the child so far as I knew it was dead.*

She told me that she had *made a mess in the bathroom*. I found some blood on the floor, but not a great deal. (emphasis in original)

In addition to Sarah Hayes's testimony, Martha Campbell, a friend of Sarah Hayes, was present when the baby was found. Martha Campbell testified to the coroner's jury as follows: "She told Mrs. Hayes to look under the bed and there we found the baby which was dead. I noticed the cut on its face. Afterwards I saw the paper in its mouth. The only thing that Annie Flavelle would say was that she was cramped and cold. I heard her tell who the father of the child was."

Along with the Hayeses and Martha Campbell, the two doctors who performed postmortem examinations on the infant provided testimony before the coroner's jury. Drs. Jerold Ball and Gideon Silverthorn testified that they believed the child had been born alive. Events were swift after the infant was discovered. Dr. Ball testified that he was called by Mr. Hayes and attended at the residence on Wilton Ave at 12:30 p.m., when he was shown the baby by Mr. Campbell. According to Dr. Ball:

It was dead and the body was cold. I saw that the child had been badly used. There was a tear on the face, extending from the corner of the mouth toward the ear, about two inches in length. There were several bruises – one on the nose especially noticeable. I saw a little wad of paper on the back of the tongue. I asked the mother several questions which she did not answer. I heard her tell Mr. Heys [sic] who the father of the child was. The condition of the girl showed that she had been recently delivered.

I assisted to make the p.m. and agree with the report.

I saw the tests which were applied to prove live-birth and agree that the child was living when born, had breathed fully and had made efforts to swallow.

I think it possible that the injuries to the child's face may have been produced by the mother unintentionally in the frenzy of labor pains.

I saw the wads of paper removed from the throat and do not think it possible that the child could have breathed with this paper in its mouth. I believe that suffocation with the other condition found caused death.

Similarly, Dr. Silverthorn indicated to the jury members that he had read the postmortem report and that he too believed that the child had been born alive and that it had been suffocated. "The plugs in the mouth, in connection with the other conditions found were sufficient to cause death. I do not think that a mother trying to deliver herself would be likely to produce the injuries described. I tested the lungs fully as described and they bear out the fact that the child was born alive." The detailed postmortem report of Drs. Ball and Silverthorn was also provided to the jury members as evidence. Based on their personal observation of the wads of paper in the infant's mouth and the lung test, both doctors concluded that the infant had been born alive and that the cause of its death was suffocation along with the injuries to the face and head described in their reports.

Based on the evidence provided by the Hayeses, Mrs. Campbell, and the doctors, the coroner's jury determined that the infant met its death by means of violence. At this stage a true bill is typically issued by a grand jury and a copy is attached to the indictment file. However, on 20 February 1900 an "Information and Complaint" brought by William E. Stuart, Deputy County Coroner of the City of Toronto, is sworn before George Taylor Denison, Esquire, Police Magistrate, to the effect that Annie Flavelle "did murder an infant child." It appears as though Annie Flavelle was "remanded" until 27 February and that she appeared in police court on 12 March 1900.

Annie Flavelle pled not guilty to murder at her trial. However, given that the doctor testified that the baby was born alive and that the physical evidence of the wad of paper in the mouth of the infant, along with the testimony provided by Mrs. Sarah Hayes, indicated her guilt, it is quite possible, in light of the overwhelming evidence of foul play and the willingness of relatives to testify against her, that her trial might have resulted in her conviction for murder. This is, however, unclear from the indictment record.

Capital Cases: "Sob Sister Stuff" v. "Irresponsible Men"

In Canada, prior to the passage of the infanticide provision, when women were charged with murder (in provinces lacking grand juries these charges occurred without having to be vetted) confessions of guilt left juries little option but to convict and sentence the women to death, but with a strong recommendation for mercy. On occasion, the women were convicted by a jury despite overwhelming mitigation.

For example, in 1919 Viola Thompson[20] suffocated her two-week-old daughter by stuffing her mouth with a cotton handkerchief and wrapping her nose and mouth with a wide bandage. The baby girl was later found by a fireman beside a railway track, where Thompson boarded a train to take her home. The baby, dressed in a flannelette nightdress, was frozen and dead. The jury found the defendant guilty of murder, with a strong recommendation of mercy. The defence tried to show that the defendant was not mentally responsible for her acts, but the evidence of diminished capacity was rejected by the trial judge, who sentenced Thompson to death on 27

September 1919. Dozens of letters sent to the Department of Justice to request clemency explained Thompson's actions. Viola Thompson was repeatedly brutally assaulted by her husband Jim Thompson, whom she
married when she was seventeen and he was forty-eight. Mr. Thompson
had seven children at the time of their marriage, and they then had four
more together. Jim Thompson was described as a madman who viciously
beat Viola. The letters written on her behalf described a man who was drunk
most of the time and who beat her so badly she would often turn up at
neighbours' homes bleeding and severely bruised. Given these circumstances,
it was argued that Jim Thompson provoked her to kill her baby and that the
baby's death was his responsibility to bear.[21] Viola Thompson begged the
minister of justice for her release so that she could to return to her four
children, who had been left in the care of her husband. Thompson tried to
put the baby in a home because her husband did not want it. The infant's
home required her to pay $125 and to stay with the child for six months.
She claimed to have been driven to commit the crime only as a "last resort."
On 15 February 1926, Viola Thompson was granted a ticket of leave from
Kingston Penitentiary, where she had been imprisoned for six and a half years.

Even though the life circumstances of nineteen-year-old Annie Rubletz,[22]
who was initially charged with concealment of birth but who later confessed to intentionally smothering her second illegitimate baby, are described
in the most sympathetic of terms, given the mandatory death sentence for
murder the petit jury had no option but to sentence her to hang. Tried in
the Court of King's Bench in Yorkton, Saskatchewan, in June 1940, Rubletz
had been seduced first by her brother, with whom she had a baby that was
later put up for adoption, and later by her sister's husband, for whom she
worked as a farm labourer. In part, the jury's conviction was an inevitable
outcome of the judge's charge to them since he refused to allow them to
substitute a conviction for concealment. The judge noted that he was aware
of this practice among other judges but that this was not how he interpreted the law. In fact, he states his position explicitly in a letter to the
secretary of state in Ottawa: "From the discussion with the jury ... you will
notice that apparently the jury were very loath to find the accused guilty
and I am satisfied that if I had instructed them that in the circumstances
mentioned in 952 [then the section covering concealment of birth] they
might find her guilty of concealment of birth, they would have acquitted
her of the charge of murder and salved their conscience by finding her
guilty of concealment. Apparently, however, they did not appreciate what
would be the effect of making the findings of fact."[23]

Apparently, a complete rejection of the law was unsatisfactory to the trial
judge, who nevertheless joined the jury in recommending mercy, "in view
of the youthfulness of the accused and the sordid circumstances surround-

ing her life and the unmoral atmosphere in which she evidently was brought up, I wish strongly to join the jury in recommending her to clemency."[24] Annie Rubletz was later detained at the women's jail in Prince Albert, Saskatchewan, after being sentenced to hang on 7 January 1941.

Naturally there was an enormous campaign for a reversal of her sentence. There were numerous letters sent to the minister of justice on her behalf, and numerous letters to the editor published in the *Regina Leader Post* called for mercy in the Yorkton child murder case. Most were opposed to the death penalty in principle, but there was also a strongly expressed sentiment that blamed the father of the illegitimate baby. According to one letter to the editor, signed "yours in fair play. A Business Girl," "I'm not condoning child murder, but I don't think that a girl who finds herself in that plight is responsible for her actions. Anyway, why should the girl always have to bear the brunt of it while the man's name is never mentioned. Oh no! He crawls off into some corner like the coward that he is, until the shouting is all over, and then he ventures out again large as life, – 'A heck of a fellow with the women.' Why isn't he hounded down and his name dragged through the mire also?"[25]

Another writer suggests a similar approach to men: "It is high time the men in these cases were punished too. They go on leaving girls to bear the shame of it all, probably ruining many more, unknown to anybody."[26] However, there was also a strong sentiment of the reverse nature. Another writer argued: "We must all admit there is something very brutal in a girl's nature who will deliberately murder her own baby. This sob sister stuff and coddling of criminals should have no room in Canada, as I believe justice should take its course."[27] Here we see the usual pitting of opposing opinions in the letters to the editor section of a newspaper. Nevertheless, these were, and are today, competing sentiments addressing the question of responsibility.

A broad range of people wrote letters to the minister of justice pleading for Annie Rubletz's clemency, including a soldier, a vicar, and the Saskatoon Council of Women. Rubletz was granted clemency and her sentence reduced to one year in the Battleford women's jail. According to the *Montreal Standard*, 22 February 1941, "the fight to save 19-year-old Annie Rubletz, Ukrainian girl from the gallows has ended successfully and the big sympathetic heart of Saskatchewan beats easier now."[28]

Despite the fact that it seems obvious from these cases that many of these women deliberately killed their babies, the fact that, often, only convictions for crimes with lesser penalties (such as concealment or neglect) were obtained may reflect more than juror sympathy. While other writers impute sympathetic motives to juror members dealing with these cases, one should not discount the medico-legal framework within which these jurors rendered their judgments, as the contemporary coroner's manual by Boys

(1905) indicates. Cases conforming, more or less, to the nineteenth-century pattern of juror sympathy and consequent Crown frustration (Hoffer and Hull 1981; Rose 1986; Malcolmson 1977; Walker 1968) were evident in the early twentieth-century Ontario indictment record (e.g., Lucy Nadgwan, Rachel Boakes, and Eliza Logan). However, in some cases where indictment or conviction on serious charges were refused, the medical evidence as to live-birth available to the jurors was, in light of the instructions laid out in Boys's manual for coroners, inadequate, given the formal medico-legal requirements. The ambiguity of the medical evidence may well have been sufficient, in and of itself, to thwart prosecutorial ambitions.

Indeed, as these cases have demonstrated, there was a certain "public" will to prosecute these women, otherwise the discovery of the dead baby would not have been brought to the attention of the authorities whose professional allegiance to the criminal justice system called for nothing less than attempted indictments and convictions. In Ontario grand jurors appeared to do their best to issue indictments sustainable by the evidence they were provided. In addition, as we have seen in the case of Annie Flavelle, family members and others connected to the case could sometimes be responsible for pressing the justice system for a punitive response. I described cases in which convictions were obtained for a range of offences, sometimes following guilty pleas, and where substantial punishments were handed down (e.g., Louisa Kalhorst, Pearl Anderson, and Maria McCabe).

Finally, there are instances of convictions for infanticide, but, as the case of Annie Rubletz reveals, these convictions were constrained by the rule of law, as enforced by the judge. Clemency was a nearly inevitable outcome in this case, and cases like it, in which the men responsible for the women's dire circumstances were held accountable, and the punishment of death for murder was perceived as an outrageously harsh treatment of women. Library and Archives Canada series RG 13 (1867-1976, the years for which records were kept until the abolition of the death penalty) reveals no case in which women were hanged for killing their newborn babies.

Thomas Laqueur and the Rhetoric of Humanitarianism

In "Bodies, Details, and the Humanitarian Narrative," noted historian Thomas Laqueur (1989, 197) argues that narrative forms (such as the novel), the inquiry, and especially the autopsies performed in cases of infanticide as reflected in coroner's inquest reports and indictment files, had "a specific rhetorical purpose more or less related to the production of humanitarian sentiment and reform." The humanitarian narrative, of which these stories are a part, have three main characteristic features. First is their "reliance on detail as a sign of truth" (177); second is their reliance "on the personal body, not only as a locus of pain but also as the common bond between those who suffer and those who would help and as the object of the scientific discourse through which the causal links between evil, a victim, and a benefactor are forged" (ibid.); and third, "humanitarian narrative exposes the lineaments of causality and of human agency: ameliorative action is represented as possible, effective, and therefore morally imperative" (178). Laqueur further argues that these documents, along with other kinds of inquests (such as those conducted into industrial disasters), shaped "the human comprehension of death" and "have the capacity to engender the kind of moral concern that arose in the late eighteenth century" (197). As I have indicated, Laqueur argues that humanitarian sentiment comes into being at the site of the "body," as it is rendered in the medico-legal discourse of the inquest/autopsy: "Case histories and autopsies thus constitute humanitarian narratives not only because of their policy implications or because doctors were leading figures in a wide range of reform movements both in Great Britain and on the Continent, but also because they make bodies the common ground of humanitarian sensibility and explicate the history of suffering. Humanitarianism, while devoted to saving human lives, focuses its attention most powerfully on the dead and becomes a guide to the mastery of death" (182).

More important, it is the unique details of the dead and damaged body that gave rise to a humanitarian discourse in which suffering is central; it was the "corpse ... [that] enabled the imagination to penetrate the life of another" (Laqueur 1989, 177). He argues that "great causes seem to spring from the power of a lacerated back, a diseased countenance, a premature death, to goad the moral imagination" (178). Laqueur claims that humanitarian sentiment and concern for *women* is produced in and by those autopsy reports on infants who were victims of infanticide. These detailed reports of the infant's bodies created "sympathetic passions" and "bridged the gulf between facts, compassion, and action" for women (179). Discussing a late eighteenth-century case in which a leading British surgeon, William Hunter, "published an extraordinarily compassionate defense of women accused of murdering their infant children" (185), compassion toward women is inspired through the retelling of a particular narrative trope:

> The social narratives that Hunter interweaves with forensic medicine are absolutely standard eighteenth century fare. Indeed, they gain power precisely because they are repeated in so many different contexts and become, through repetition and through association with the authority of medicine and law, the means for comprehending the actions of others. A coroner's inquest tells of a maid to Lady Tyrconnell who had kept her pregnancy secret from her fellow servants and who then delivered a premature but, according to the surgeon's evidence, live baby girl. In this version, the maid

was saved by the detailed evidence of a housekeeper who testified that the accused had prepared baby clothes and had thus probably not intended, by murder, to hide her pregnancy forever. In printed reports of Old Bailey trials, in execution broadsheets of cases in which the defense failed, in ballads, and in forensic medicine texts, the tale is retold with slight modifications. The narrative form for "humanitarian" sympathy and action is thus widely disseminated. (Laqueur 1989, 187)

Laqueur's description of the formation of a humanitarian sentiment focused on the mother through the processes of investigation of the death of the infant and the autopsy of its body is not entirely satisfactory. Laqueur contrasts "tragedy" to the "humanitarian narrative." Tragedy is a narrative in which "someone or something did something that caused pain, suffering, or death and that could, under certain circumstances, have been avoided or mitigated" (Laqueur 1989, 178). The development of a humanitarian sentiment is a departure from the earlier narrative form of tragedy. But Laqueur's description of the discourse that grew up around the infanticidal mother fits with a tragedy narrative rather than with a humanitarian narrative as the reader is meant to identify with the protagonist – who is not the baby but, rather, the maid to Lady Tyrconnell. In this narrative it is not the body of the baby with which we identify but the experience of the maid-mother. According to his own definition, the story of the seduced maid is retold as "tragedy" in trial reports, execution broadsheets, ballads, and in forensic medicine texts in which the reader feels sympathy for the maid-protagonist. This sympathetic identification with the predicament of the mother is broadly correct as a description of nineteenth- and early twentieth-century juror sentiment, including, as we have seen, juror sentiment in Canada. Crown attorneys were, throughout the nineteenth and early twentieth centuries, frustrated by jurors' appreciation of the tragic circumstances in which the minor and coerced sexual wrongdoing of adolescent women with very little social power was amplified by circumstances beyond their control into the dire problems they faced as unwed mothers – circumstances that led directly to infanticide. But Laqueur's thesis is, perhaps, slightly overstated with respect to the claimed transition from tragedy to humanitarianism. From the evidence I have presented in this chapter, drawn from the Ontario indictment case files and the federal capital case files, this juror sentiment seems to have existed in Ontario during the first half of the twentieth century (although I have also shown that the "uncomplicated story" of juror sympathy is overstated when one considers the difficulties of medical proof and the willingness of jurors to indict and convict in some cases).[29] Of course, it may be that nineteenth- and early twentieth-century jurors' sympathies for infanticidal mothers – sympathies that thwarted the basic objectives of the medico-legal process in which they were engaged – were somehow the product of earlier medico-legal processes of the same kind. There is no indication that juror sympathy was in any way the product of the careful exposure of the suffering of the baby-victims of the infanticides they were investigating.

Despite this, it is certainly possible that the processes Laqueur describes played some part in the gradual development of a socio-legal discourse relating to maternal neonaticide, albeit one which would serve infanticidal mothers very poorly: the discourse of the innocent baby-victim of infanticide, dead and marked by violence, whose suffering must be avenged, and whose memory can best be served by the protection of future innocents. This discourse emerges only in its full ferocity at the end of the twentieth century, and it is the subject of later chapters of this book. More immediately, as we shall see in the next chapter, the twentieth-century Canadian "infanticide" provision, an apparent example of "humanitarian ameliorative action," was, in fact, implemented to rationalize an uneven system of criminal law and, according to the dominant discourse at the time, was meant to appropriately punish women for a crime against both their children and society. Infanticide narratives in the form of the indictment case file and the coroner's autopsy, "which eventually make babies in dungheaps a thing to inspire compassion" (Laqueur 1989, 200), do, as Laqueur argues, trigger ameliorative reform. But in the instance of maternal neonaticide, at least during the twentieth century, the passions inspired and the reforms implemented are directed at infants rather than, as Laqueur suggests, at the women. The reform solution subsequently offered in 1948 to the prosecutorial problem of securing convictions in the infanticide provision was, in part, justified as an ameliorative measure on behalf of the infant-victims. This legal reform is undoubtedly linked to what Duden (1993, 3) refers to as a changing "social perception of the unborn." If humanitarian sentiment and subsequent ameliorative action developed in relation to sympathy for women, as Laqueur describes it, then this impulse would have logically resulted in leaving well enough alone. There would have been no "humanitarian amelioration" required since women were hardly ever indicted or convicted for murder in cases of maternal neonaticide. When they were convicted they were likely to have confessed, and in all cases they were granted clemency. Women were *already,* as common practice, being charged with and convicted of concealment of birth, which carried a culturally acceptable, but legally problematic, punishment framework.

Laqueur (1989) argues that autopsies and coroner's inquests, including cases of maternal neonaticide, formed a crucial site in which eighteenth- and nineteenth-century humanitarianism developed through the linking of an investigated damaged body (which stimulates sympathy for the victims) with a commitment to, and confidence in, the amelioration of the circumstances deemed to have led to injury. Laqueur contrasts this with a sense of the tragic that turns upon an identification with the flawed nature of the protagonist, and which the new humanitarian sentiment is claimed to have replaced. In cases of maternal neonaticide, Laqueur suggests a significant (although rather obscure) link between the details of the babies' damaged bodies revealed by medical examination and calls for sympathetic criminal justice responses toward the mothers. My research does not cover this time period and is not set up to support or refute Laqueur's ambitious and provocative thesis. However, in the early part of the twentieth century in Canada it is quite clear that sympathy for the mother was a sentiment jurors brought with them to the inquest or trial and that it was informed by a sense of the tragic, as Laqueur conceives it. How consistent this is with Laqueur's thesis is, at least, debatable. In his discussions of other kinds of "humanitarian narrative," Laqueur is at pains to insist that humanitarianism is stimulated by a new narrative strategy, but his discussion of the material concerning maternal neonaticide is ambiguous, and the material itself, at least as it relates to sympathy for the mothers, does not necessarily reflect this part of his thesis. In addition, in the second half of the twentieth century, law and order advocates, linking their arguments to a wider child protection discourse, have assiduously invoked sympathy for the damaged newly born baby in order to generate antipathy toward defendant-mothers and, thereby, to bolster their calls for severe punishment. Whether or not Laqueur's identification of a particular set of narrative mechanisms stimulating a new humanitarian sentiment in the eighteenth and nineteenth centuries, and his assimilation of narratives concerning maternal neonaticide to this model, hold good, by the end of the twentieth century something quite different and, for the defendant-mothers, much more dangerous, is occurring.

By the end of the twentieth century the prosecutorial sentiment is always expressed in terms of the protection of, and justice for, the *infant*. Here, the humanitarian and punitive sentiments form a Janus-faced unitary dynamic. While Laqueur's distinction between tragic and humanitarian narratives is important, the paternalistic sympathy of early twentieth-century jurors, informed by a sense of the tragic as it may be, represents the final flowering of humanitarian concern for the infanticidal mother. With the passage and application of the infanticide provision, along with broader changes in official attitudes to infant suffering and death during the second half of the twentieth century, humanitarianism comes to be focused only on one subject – the infant-victim of the wicked infanticidal mother.

As I have argued, there was ample opportunity for humanitarianism to be exercised in the cases discussed. Series RG 22-517, Supreme Court of Ontario (York County), Indictment Cases Files 1930-77, further reveal that successful murder and manslaughter indictments for maternal neonaticide were dealt with by way of alternate substitutions for concealment of birth (Agnes

Fox, 1934) or were found "unfit to stand trial," sent to hospital, and typically released within a few days to a few months (Jean Gruintel, 1935; Edna Damonde, 1935). Thus, sympathy was already operative and no "humanitarian amelioration" was required. The cases I have described illustrate the complexity of the investigation, indictment, and trial processes, and of juror responses. The complexity revealed in these cases undermines the idea that judges' and jurors' paternalistic charity was the sole cause of Crown attorneys' failures to indict and convict women. This idea was, however, communicated by Crown attorneys and judges to the legislature and was, as I show in the next chapter, the basis upon which the infanticide provision, with its new psychiatric rationale and diminished punishment framework, was enacted.

3

The Insanities of Reproduction: Medico-Legal Knowledge Informing Infanticide Law

The current Canadian legal category "infanticide" is, unlike murder or manslaughter, a sex-specific category of culpable homicide that requires a biological relationship between the perpetrator and the victim. Infanticide requires three co-existing circumstances: (1) the child must be the child of the perpetrator mother; (2) the child must be newly born (less that twelve months of age); and (3) at the time of the act or omission the mother must not have fully recovered from the "effects of childbirth or lactation" and "by reason thereof, the balance of her mind [must be] disturbed."[1] This chapter describes the development of English psychiatric theories of the "insanities of reproduction" discussed by experts in mental medicine in the late nineteenth and early twentieth centuries, paying special attention to the knowledge base for the *English Infanticide Law, 1922*, the text of which is reproduced in Canadian law. Here I document the rise of early criminological, specifically medico-legal, knowledge that was later altered in and by Canadian law to produce the modern legal category of infanticide.

Evidence from scientific journals devoted to mental science qualifies three central critiques advanced in the literature concerning the effects of infanticide law. The first critique is directed at the text of the infanticide law itself. This is part of the contemporary critique of the "medicalization" of women's deviance, and of legal approaches to women, advanced from a modern feminist perspective. This perspective objects to infanticide law on the ground that it links women's deviance to reproductive difference, thereby perpetuating a sexist bio-psychiatric understanding of the underlying cause of infanticide (Edwards 1984; Scutt 1981; Showalter 1985; Smart 1989, 1992). This claim has some historical as well as conceptual merit in that certain medical knowledge, which theorized the signs and symptoms of pregnancy psychoses as having at least partly organic origins, was drawn upon in the development of the infanticide law. However, this chapter shows that the psychiatric knowledge base equally emphasized the socio-economic and cultural precipitators of maternal neonaticide and the mental disturbance supposedly associated with it. In addition, in the Canadian context, the legal relevance of the psychiatric mitigation of infanticide law has, in any case, been significantly diminished.

In the second critique of infanticide law discussed here, Ward (1999) advances an engaging critique of the medicalization thesis to argue that autopoiesis theory provides an unsatisfactory but somewhat better framework for understanding the gap between medical and legal knowledge contained in the *English Infanticide Act, 1922*. Drawing on Teubner's (1989, 1993; and see 1988, 1990), and hence Luhmann's (1988; and see 1985, 281-88), theories of law as an autopoietic system of communication, Ward (1999) challenges the medicalization interpretation. Modelling discourses as systems of communication operating independently from the intentions, strategies, and even consciousness of participating individuals, Luhmann posits an increasing fragmentation of discourses characteristic of modernity (Luhmann 1982), with each discourse constructing its own categories, that is, its own realities, which are radically incompatible with those of alternate discourses. Law is viewed as an especially basic discourse fundamental to the possibility of society (Luhmann 1985, 105). From this perspective, medicine cannot colonize law (any more than law can colonize medicine), but can only place external pressures on law to which law responds by developing, through legal procedures, new *legal* categories which, despite appearances, are never medico-legal in a genuine sense.

The contention that psychiatric concepts are reconstituted within legal discourse is qualified in the Canadian context, where law is shown to have less systematicity than autopoiesis theory suggests. The developments in Canada show law subverting psychiatric medicine in a far less subtle way than Ward describes for the English case. Evidence presented here shows that, in the Canadian context, legislators largely *ignored* the scientific knowledge bases upon which experts in mental medicine established their causational theoretical framework and merely adopted the text of the *English Infanticide Act, 1922*, in 1948. However, they did this in a way that was to have significant repercussions, which further qualified the degree to which Ward's analysis of infanticide law applies in the Canadian context. Rather than the infanticide construct functioning to mitigate the punishment attached to a manslaughter charge by evidence of mental disturbance consequent upon childbirth and lactation, as is the case in the United Kingdom, the Canadian statute allows a separate, lesser charge of infanticide to be brought in cases where a biological mother kills her newly born child.

Initially, this was interpreted as placing a requirement on the Crown to prove the element of mental disturbance beyond a reasonable doubt. Failure to meet the burden of proof in the Canadian case essentially meant that a woman's homicidal act was "wilful," and yet, as a result of the double jeopardy provision, which holds that a person may not be tried for the same crime twice, she would be acquitted of infanticide and not retried. In an amendment to the *Criminal Code of Canada* adopted in 1955, expert psychiatric testimony to establish infanticide on the basis of the effects of childbirth or lactation was no longer a formal requirement. All that the Crown had to do was to establish wilfulness. Thus, while Ward is certainly correct in insisting that the psychiatric basis of mitigation in infanticide cases was transformed into a distinctly legal formulation when it was adopted into law, Canadian legal developments are even less "biomedical" than Ward's autopoiesis thesis suggests. The Canadian law retains the biomedical language but as a mere discursive shell, with no necessary legal consequence.

The final critique qualified here is one that analyzes late nineteenth-century ethnographic accounts of the practice of neonaticide (especially among Australian Aboriginals), which were drawn upon to explain white Western maternal neonaticide when infanticide law was developing in England. Despite the availability of the anthropological discourse as an explanatory model for mitigation, it is largely absent from the theories put forward by English mental science experts as the root causes of infanticide among their patient-inmates. The critique of colonial anthropology, best represented by Reekie (1998), locates the ethnographers' explanations of the underlying causes of neonaticide practised by Aboriginals as examples of racializing discourses. These ethnographic accounts were then applied to maternal neonaticide more generally to describe the practice in purely biological or atavistic terms (Reekie 1998). This chapter describes a significant original ethnographic account, showing that, despite some statements that are certainly racist, the authors' explanations of various types of neonaticide are primarily socio-economic and/or cultural. Notwithstanding the practice of describing criminality in atavistic terms during the early part of the twentieth century, neither the anthropological experts nor the experts in mental science deployed the racist Lombrosian discourse to account for infanticide. That both the experts in mental science and ethnographers relied on culturally organized socio-economic conditions to account for the practice has been largely unnoticed in the critical literature on infanticide law.

This chapter shows that the psychiatric theory underlying infanticide law, and its various source theories, was less reductively biomedical than a medicalization thesis suggests. Here I endorse the value of a social history approach to legal analysis. In Canada, infanticide law was contingent upon solving the social and political problems of failing to obtain convictions for homicide proper, without sentencing women to death, which laypersons empanelled on juries would not countenance. The wording of infanticide law, including the text of the Canadian statute, can certainly be read as reductively biomedical, and within the context of the United Kingdom a legitimate debate arises as to whether this subversion of the original psychiatric basis of the law amounts to the biomedicalization of a legal doctrine or the transformation of a body of psychiatric theory into a pseudo-medical construct tailored to the requirements of law. However, the adoption of the *English Infanticide Act, 1922,* in Canadian law occurred in such a way as to virtually shelve the psychiatric questions, with the law effectively functioning without the prop of biomedical theory, transformed or otherwise.

Early- to Mid-Twentieth Century Infanticide Discourses

This section provides an overview of English mental medicine and, more broadly, medico-legal knowledge (developing from the nineteenth century through to the mid-twentieth century) to illustrate the kinds of discussions that took place among mental scientists who were trying to explain the underlying causes of neonaticide. In addition, I examine contemporary anthropological understandings of neonaticide because they informed some of the published medical discussions. Anthropological ideas that circulated during this period attributed the practice of infanticide among aboriginal tribes to cultural practices occurring within the context of patriarchal socio-economic arrangements. By the late nineteenth century, anthropologists such as Fison and Howitt (1967 [1880]), who studied Australian Aboriginal tribes, had a fairly well developed discourse on infanticide that was not unlike the discourse being developed by English medical specialists in insanity. Both viewed the motivation for infanticide as a product of human agency exacerbated by extenuating socio-economic arrangements.

I look to the medical experts because it was partly their expertise upon which lawmakers relied to form the basis of the *English Infanticide Act, 1922.* Neonaticide was discussed in very different terms by medical practitioners and lawyers, respectively, and, of course, with very different goals in mind. More often than not during this period, medical specialists in insanity were interested not in colonizing law but, rather, in discovering the origins of, and cure for, a variety of mental diseases. Their aim was a pragmatic one to the extent that they were concerned with identification, classification, and, ultimately, finding a treatment for a "mental disturbance."

Asylum doctors, experts in mental medicine, offered a range of theories about the underlying causes of the "insanity of reproduction."[2] This was the formal scientific knowledge base available to early twentieth-century Canadian medical practitioners confronted with instances in which women killed their unwanted babies.[3] These early discourses, produced mainly by asylum medical officers, offered diagnoses of infanticidal mothers that blended socio-economic data and developing ideas about the frameworks of the mind. Nevertheless, it was the distinctly individually oriented interpretation of mental pathology that was operationalized in both the logic and wording of the *English Infanticide Act, 1922,* the text of which was adopted in Canadian law in June 1948.

Nature, Biology, and Atavism

Havelock Ellis provided a précis of an article titled "Considerations on Infanticide [Quelques considérations sur l'infanticide]" in the regular "Sociology" section of the *Journal of Mental Science* (*JMS*) in 1902. (The *Journal of Mental Science* later became the *British Journal of Psychiatry* and was one of the main professional journals partly devoted to medico-legal issues.) In this article, the author attempts to link maternal neonaticide among women to what is occurring in nature: "There are biological reasons why a woman in whom, for whatever cause, abnormal mental conditions are set up, should be impelled to destroy her child. This impulse is not confined to the human female, but is found throughout nature, and leads, for instance, a bird whose young have been confined in a cage to enter the cage and kill them, while many animals, if interfered with after parturition, will kill or eat their young" (Ellis 1902, 366).

In this paper reviewed by Ellis, the biological impulse is advanced as the motivation behind maternal neonaticide, and it urges a consideration of the biological impulse accompanying childbirth when a "mother is not in full possession of her faculties" (Ellis 1902, 366). The notion that women have sovereign rights over the fate of their children is not explicitly rejected as "uncivilized." According to Ellis (ibid.): "The author considers that this tendency is recognised outside civilisation, and that it lies at the basis of the wide-spread belief that the mother is the mistress of the child she carried in her womb, that it belongs to her like any other object that she produces, and that no one has any right to contest her rights over her infant's life."

Here the practice of infanticide is not linked specifically to customary neonaticide to distinguish between the "civilised" and "uncivilised" society but, rather, to the biologically programmed behaviour of animals who kill as a result of the belief (mistaken or not) that danger will come to their offspring.

During this period, criminals were sometimes compared to "savages" – a term used to racially classify those deemed lower on the evolutionary scale of advancement than others. Criminality was compared to savagery and was deemed a result of degeneration that occurred within the borders of civilized societies. These theories explained deviance in terms of biological and/or physiological defect or pathology, the most influential among them being Lombroso's theory of atavism, which explained criminal behaviour in evolutionary terms and deemed it curable through scientific advancements (Pfohl 1994, 104-7). In both the paper reviewed by Ellis and the Lombrosian framework, human deviance (of which maternal neonaticide is an example) is evidence of retreat from civility and is seen, in quasi-Darwinian evolutionary terms, as a biological degeneration.

In 1911 W.C. Sullivan[4] commented on an article referenced as "A Case of Infanticide with Mutilation [Un caso di infanticido con depezzamento criminale]" in the "Sociology" section of the *Journal of Mental Science*. Here Sullivan (1911) provides a précis of an article he claims would be of interest from the point of view of both mental medicine and criminal science. The question of the underlying pathologies of those who engage in mutilation is discussed in the article under review within the context of a case of maternal neonaticide and is distinguished from criminal mutilation, where "the murderer is always insane, epileptic, or very degenerate" (Sullivan 1911, 402). First, the article divides mutilation into three categories: the religious or sacrificial, the judicial, and the criminal. The criminal variety is then divided into two main forms, the offensive and the defensive, "the former being a mere mutilation for the satisfaction of feelings of hate or in obedience to morbid sexual impulses, while the defensive form is an attempt on the part of the criminal to avoid detection" (402). This typical case of maternal neonaticide is provided as an example of relatively *normal* behaviour rather than as belonging to the "congenital criminal class, because in this form of crime *the social* are much more important than the anthropological factors" (1911, 402; emphasis added).[5] Sullivan's description of the case is worth reviewing at length, given the effort used to distinguish the practice of infanticide from criminal degeneracy:

A servant girl, having strangled her newly born child, dismembered the body and put the pieces down a latrine. The way in which the body was cut up, as shown by a photography of the pieces, resembled in several respects the method followed by cooks in preparing fowls and other animals for the table. This mode of dismemberment, which has been noted in several cases of criminal mutilation, has been termed by Lacassagne "*le procédé de la cuisinière*"; it is usually indicative of the defensive form. In this particular case, the point of interest, because it had been suggested in defence of the accused girl that the mutilation of the body was evidence of a delirious condition with homicidal and destructive impulses at the confinement, it is being further asserted that the girl was predisposed to such impulses by the fact of being weak-minded. The author maintains in opposition to this view that the culprit did not present any somatic, functional, or psychic anomalies which, according to the Italian school, are distinctive of the criminal degenerate, and he finds this negative evidence in harmony with the defensive character of the mutilation. (Sullivan 1911, 402)

Maternal neonaticide and the secret disposal of the infant's body are not explained as the actions of a criminal degenerate: the actions are normalized here and are contrasted to the abnormal criminal type viewed in Lombrosian terms as inherently criminal. Here the girl is characterized as weak-minded but not of the criminal degenerate type described by Lombroso.

We see here two quite different accounts of maternal neonaticide, neither of which is strictly biomedical in the sense understood within formal psychiatric theory. In the first account Lombrosian atavism is deployed to explain an instance of maternal neonaticide. This kind of explanation was sometimes drawn upon by the medical specialists of the mind when describing their cases. In the second account, this idea is explicitly rejected, with the method of killing cited as an example of the rationality of the perpetrator.

Anthropological Discourse and Infanticide

It has been argued that colonialist anthropological discourses "represented infanticide as the ultimate expression of the ignorance, primitiveness and savagery of indigenous peoples" (Reekie 1998, 115). Citing Fison and Howitt (1967), Reekie (1998, 116) argues that anthropologists characterized the Aboriginals who practised "infanticide" as "primitive," "lacking in moral sensibility," and "incapable of understanding the wrong they were committing." However, a careful reading of Fison and Howitt (1967) suggests a different interpretation, one that shows the ethnographers were sensitive to the effects of lifestyle as well as to patriarchal socio-economic arrangements. These anthropological works may have been bound up with the constitution of an "Other" through the production of racialized knowledge, as Said (1978) has argued, but their accounts of infanticide were not tightly linked to notions of biological or racial difference.

In their description of the practice of customary neonaticide among Australian Aboriginals, Fison and Howitt (1967, 190) argue that the practice was the result of exigencies of circumstance rather than atavism, mental illness, or aggression toward infants. The nomadic lifestyle of the Australian Kurnai made it difficult for them to tend to large numbers of children. According to Fison and Howitt (ibid.): "On speaking to a number of the Kurnai upon this subject, they gave me the following explanation. It was often difficult to carry about young children, particularly where there were several. Their wandering life rendered this very difficult. It sometimes happened that when a child was about to be born, its father would say to his wife, 'We have too many children to carry about – best leave this one, when it is born, behind the camp.' On this, the new-born child was left lying in the camp, and the family moved elsewhere."

Fison and Howitt are careful to note that the practice was not one born out of aggression or lack of feeling for children as the infants were left to die rather than killed directly by one of the tribe members: "The infant, of course, soon perished. The Kurnai drew this singular distinction, that 'they never knew of an instance of parents killing their children, but only of *leaving behind* new-born infants.' The aboriginal mind does not seem to perceive the horrible idea of leaving an unfortunate baby to die miserably in a deserted camp, crawled over by ants and flies, and probably devoured by wild dogs" (Fison and Howitt 1967, 190; emphasis added).

Reekie (1998) cites this last sentence as evidence of the ethnographers' racism rather than as providing a fuller context for their discussion, which seems aimed at explaining to the naïve or judgmental English reader that the Kurnai do not develop the same immediate attachment to infants as do English parents: "It may be that the feelings of affection arising from association and dependence have not in such a case been aroused, and the natural parental feelings seem to be overborne by what they conceive to be the exigencies of their circumstances" (Fison and Howitt 1967, 190). Here the ethnographers can be seen to be educating their readers with respect to cultural differences in parental attitudes and attachments to children.

Furthermore, the practice of female customary neonaticide is accounted for in relation to patriarchal social arrangements that result in girls and women becoming encumbrances when parents are required to provide dowries to potential husbands. Fison and Howitt saw female customary neonaticide as being precipitated by this requirement. They rely on this social arrangement to provide motivation for customary neonaticide rather than on any kind of racist notions about atavistic degeneration. Fison, writing alone, describes the practice as a logical one:

> Savages are perfectly logical people in their own way, and do not act without a motive, which, to their minds at least, is a sufficient one. So thoroughly have I been convinced of this by my sixteen years' residence among them and observation of their ways, that I do not hesitate to assert that, whenever their acts appear capricious to us, we may be quite sure there is something hidden from us in which lies what to them is sufficient motive. Now, the savage has no hesitation in killing his infant children, whether male or female, if they be in his way, but he does not kill any one of them for the mere sake of killing; and he certainly would not kill his daughters rather than his sons without a sufficient motive. (Fison and Howitt 1967, 135)

According to Fison, the killing of female babies is motivated principally by socio-economic arrangements among the *more advanced* tribes: "It is among the more advanced tribes that the motives for female infanticide are found, and, I believe, the practice also to a greater extent than among the lower savages. Thus, where a costly dower has to be given with a girl in marriage, female infanticide is known to be very common. A daughter [sic] there is a special cause of impoverishment to her parents, whereas a son is a cause of enrichment" (Fison and Howitt 1967, 137).

Other similar kinds of patriarchal social arrangements among Aboriginal tribes account for the practice of customary neonaticide. Fison and Howitt identify patrilineage and patrilineal ancestral worship as principal causes of female customary neonaticide:

> Another motive for killing female children rather than male is found, among agricultural tribes who have descent through the father, in the fact that a woman can transmit neither the family name nor the family estate. She passes out of the line by marriage [sic]. And, with tribes who have that line of descent, and now accept its consequences as regards ancestral worship – *i.e.*, who offer house sacrifice to male alone and by males alone – this is a very grave, the very gravest consideration. The dead are dependent upon their male descendants for those offerings without which their shadowy existence would be to the last degree wretched; and therefore every man is anxious to have sons, not daughters to succeed him. If, therefore, he practice infanticide at all, he will surely kill his daughters, not his sons. (Fison and Howitt 1967, 138)

In tribes that are matrilineal, the impulse is toward male customary neonaticide. Thus, the motivation for customary neonaticide, female or male, is connected to the effects of patriarchal and, to a lesser extent, matriarchal social arrangements on peoples' perceptions of difficulty. It is mendacious to portray Fison and Howitt's account of the motivations behind customary neonaticide as advancing especially racist ideas about Aboriginals, particularly when their apparent aim was mainly to provide an account of a social practice that was very clearly, in their view, motivated by complex social arrangements having to do with survival and economic necessity.[6] Similar ideas about economic hardship were deployed by experts in mental medicine to account for the motivation behind maternal neonaticide among working-class patient-inmates of the asylum.

Developing Psychiatric Discourses:
Puerperal, Lactational, and Exhaustion Psychoses

Marcé's influential research on puerperal psychosis, published as *Traité de la Folie des Femmes Enceintes* (1858), anticipated a link between the hormones of pregnancy and mood. Written prior to the discovery of the endocrine system, the research attributed the cause of puerperal psychosis to an interplay between reproductive process (the uterus) and disorders of the mind. As a result, the traits associated with pregnancy psychosis were understood as both physical (organic) illness and functional (mood) illness. The relation between the two was understood in terms of a chronic dysfunction of the complex mind-body interaction, which produced changes in mood and behaviour (Hamilton and Harberger 1992, 10). In many cases, exhaustion from lactation was observed and recorded as a major physical complaint among women. Marcé was likely the first to publish findings that he thought suggested an interaction between physical illness (organic disorder) and functional illness (mood disorder) in these cases – an idea that was later partially taken up as a mitigating rationale in law. According to Marcé: "That which gives puerperal psychosis its special quality is the coexistence with it of a functional and organic modification of the uterus and related organs ... The coexistence of this organic state raises an interesting question of pathologic physiology: one immediately asks if there exist connections between the uterine conditions and the disorders of the mind, and if these disorders do not develop in consequence of modifications of the genital apparatus; in a word, if the psychosis is sympathetic" (quoted in Hamilton and Harberger 1992, 10). Following Marcé's work, experts in mental medicine began to develop the idea that lactation mixed with exhaustion might cause different forms of mental disorder.

By the late 1920s a broad range of medical accounts of mental pathology had become fashionable in the literature. Throughout the early twentieth century, prior to the passage of the infanticide amendment in Canada, a number of articles on the insanities of pregnancy and childbirth ("puerperal," "lactational," and "exhaustion" psychoses) appeared in various English medical journals. The professional views varied only slightly during the early part of the twentieth century, the variations often reflecting differences in the demographic characteristics of women confined to numerous asylums (these women being the basis for the new expertise). Both lactational insanity and exhaustion psychosis dominated the literature as the sort of mental derangement likely to account for maternal neonaticide.

The journal literature on mental medicine contained case study reports on infanticidal patients. These were important sources of knowledge because they dealt with the relationship between mental science and questions of legal responsibility. The classification of mental diseases was the focus of many medical experts during this period, and the classification of mental diseases due to reproductive function and dysfunction made up a portion of the overall discourse of mental science. As the major source of expert knowledge on medico-legal issues, the theoretical and clinical information published in the *Journal of Mental Science* was a widely read source of professional expert knowledge. These discourses would have been more or less "available knowledge" for Canadian physicians and coroners as well as for lawyers, judges, and legislators.

In 1927 J. Stanley Hopwood, junior deputy medical superintendent of the State Criminal Lunatic Asylum at Broadmoor, wrote about the characteristics of women inmates who, between 1 January 1900 and 31 December 1923, had either killed their own children (not over one year of age, except when lactation was extended beyond that period) or had killed older children (sometimes more than one child) following childbirth and while still breastfeeding. During this period, of the 388 women admitted to Broadmoor,

166, or 42.8 percent, had been charged with child murder (Hopwood 1927, 94-96). On the question of insanity, Hopwood (96) determined that child murder by nursing mothers accounted for more than 25 percent of the total number of murders committed by persons who were not considered responsible for their actions. He divided the insanities connected with childbirth into three categories – (1) insanity in pregnancy, (2) puerperal insanity, and (3) lactational insanity – but he deals only with puerperal and lactational insanity. Hopwood argues that neonaticide in puerperal insanity was uncommon because mania is associated with puerperal fever, during which time homicidal acts are not possible. It is only when insanity develops later in the puerperal period, "[taking] the form of melancholia with delusions of unworthiness ... [that] ideas of suicide and homicide are more common" (96). According to Hopwood, it is under lactational insanity that child murder is likely to occur:

> Many mothers, who for various reasons are totally unfitted to do so, undertake the nursing of their children, and their systems are unable to withstand the severe strain which lactation entails, with the result that an attack of insanity develops. As this condition is in the nature of an exhaustion psychosis the insanity usually develops during the later months of lactation, or even after the weaning of the child has taken place. It is in cases of lactational insanity that child murder occurs most frequently. In this condition the onset is more insidious than in puerperal insanity, and the symptoms are usually less pronounced, and although the relatives recognize a change in the patient, they often fail to realize that it is the start of a serious mental condition until a tragedy takes place which could have been avoided had medical advice been sought earlier. (96-97)

Lactational insanity, in the form of exhaustion psychosis, accounted for 75.5 percent of his cases and was the most typical type of insanity linked to "child murder," particularly when the mother had more than one child: "As the commonest insanity connected with childbirth is an exhaustion psychosis, it is to be expected that patients of an unstable temperament would feel the strain of the puerperium and lactation more acutely in a later than in their first confinement, and thus the marked exhaustion, with attendant mental breakdown, is more likely to occur in multiparæ than in primiparæ" (Hopwood 1927, 101-2).

The majority of the infanticidal patients under Hopwood's care were somewhat older women ("the greatest number of cases occurred between the ages of 26-30, but a large number also occurred between and ages of 31-35 and 36-40" (Hopwood 1927, 100), and married ("By far the greater number of receptions were married women – married, 128; single, 33; widowed, 5" [101]). His conclusion – that "child murder" is provoked by exhaustion psychosis, suffered by lactating women with more than one child and who are constitutionally weak – differs from the then conventional understanding of emotional breakdown caused by the birth of an illegitimate child. Hopwood notes that "illegitimate [unwed] mothers" are unlikely to be insane and therefore committed to the asylum as "murders committed by unmarried mothers often take place at the time of confinement, or very shortly after, and that at the trial the charge is frequently reduced to one of concealment of birth, and the question of the sanity or otherwise of the prisoner is not raised by the defence" (101). Note that this article was published some years after the passage of the *English Infanticide Act, 1922*. Hopwood seems either to be referring to an earlier time or suggesting that the infanticide charge is *not* being levelled against "traditional" infanticidal mothers who kill their newborn children but, rather, that the old practice of charging with "concealment" is continuing. Hopwood certainly draws a sharp distinction between these cases and those that he considers to be genuine cases of "exhaustion psychosis," which are clearly covered by infanticide law.

The key predictor of "exhaustion psychosis" was class affiliation. Hopwood's (1927, 101) diagnosis of exhaustion psychosis agrees most easily with his observations about working-class motherhood:

> It is a noticeable fact that practically all the cases belong to the working or lower middle classes. This is not surprising, as in these classes the strain of bringing up a family is far greater than in those of higher social standing. They are often faced with financial difficulties, and are therefore unable to obtain domestic help; this means that they have to resume the duties of looking after their children and the house before they are in a fit state to do so. They are apt to neglect themselves, and are often unable to obtain sufficient nourishment, and as their work must necessarily take up the greater part of the day they have little time for exercise in the fresh air and other relaxations. In this class it is the rule, rather than the exception, to nurse the baby, and lactation is often unduly prolonged with the idea of preventing conception.

Hopwood provided an overview of other factors, such as heredity, method of killing, suicidal ideas, alcohol, epilepsy, amenorrhæa, and amnesia, but his main approach was "sociological." Showalter's (1985, 59) criticism that the "definition of puerperal violence ... ignored the social problems of unmarried, abused, and destitute mothers and the shocks, adjustments, and psychological traumas of the maternal role" is clearly not applicable. Hopwood clearly articulates and incorporates into his framework an understanding of the unique reproductive difficulties faced by poor women, particularly those with many children.

Some contributors were concerned with the proper functioning of the *English Infanticide Act* itself. Physicians like J.H. Morton (1934), governor and medical officer of H.M. Prison, Holloway, were concerned that the courts were interpreting the term "newly born" too narrowly and that they were failing to consult medical experts on the meaning of the expression "the balance of her mind being disturbed." Morton endeavoured to educate the English courts on the meaning and appropriate application of the medical terms they were using. As a medical expert, Morton's position was unique vis-à-vis women who had committed neonaticide and the courts who were sentencing them to prisons like Holloway.

In a paper delivered to the Annual Meeting of Prison Medical Officers in 1933, and published as "Female Homicides" in the *Journal of Mental Science* in 1934, Morton reviews 126 cases of women who killed children and adults during the years 1923 to 1932. Out of these, 64 women came within the *Infanticide Act, 1922*. Their ages ranged from 17 to 40 years, with the majority of them being in their twenties and 80 percent (51) being single (Morton 1934, 68). Out of the 51 single women, 80 percent had not arranged for delivery, and of the 11 married women, none had arranged for delivery.

Morton (1934, 64) was of the opinion that a woman who killed her newly born child was not insane: "Just as certain people believe that anybody who commits suicide is insane, so others regard the killing of a child by its mother as an indication of insanity. With neither of these theories can I agree." Morton draws on the natural scientific model of neonaticide described above, comparing the killing of a newborn infant (i.e., a child not more than twenty-four hours old) to the instinctual killing of offspring by certain animals in order to protect their young from perceived harm:

> I understand that certain animals are liable to destroy their offspring, but this usually occurs within a few hours of the birth of their young. I do not know if there is any scientific explanation for this, but I have always understood that it occurred either when the mother saw or thought she saw the possibilities of danger, or destruction of her offspring, or in those cases where the young animal was born abnormal or deformed. May not, then, a woman, as a result of the strain of her pregnancy, culminating in the severe trial of her confinement, lose her reason for a short period immediately following her confinement and also destroy her offspring? (68)

According to Morton's (1934, 69) literature review, certain articles identify four varieties of mental disorder associated with childbirth: pregnancy, parturition, puerperal, and lactational insanity, while later authors "describe the insanity of pregnancy, puerperal insanity and lactational insanity" in terms of "either a depressive or confusional psychosis." Despite the use of the terms "insanity" and "psychosis," women who killed their newborns were diagnosed as only temporarily mentally impaired, and this was sometimes seen as the consequence of a biological mechanism that compelled women to kill their offspring when they perceived them to be in danger. Thus, childbirth was viewed as producing a kind of irresistible impulse in animals as well as women of a certain socio-economic stratum. This description viewed maternal neonaticide not as evidence of insanity but, rather, as a biological response resulting in temporary loss of reason. Morton's reliance on this kind of biological determinism was not unique and existed along with the cultural and socio-economic mitigation frameworks. In 1941 the *Journal of Criminal Psychopathology* published "Medico-Legal Aspects of Infanticide" by G.M. Davidson, MD, who argued for an infanticide provision to be added to the New York Penal Law, which would leave the determination of the precise level of criminal responsibility of infanticidal mothers to mental science expertise. Davidson claimed that infanticidal mothers frequently had some degree of diminished responsibility and that, in some cases, they suffered from mental illnesses that wholly negated their responsibility (in line with insanity law). By way of explaining the diminished responsibility of infanticidal mothers, Davidson (1941, 509) provides a psychological version of Lombrosian atavism: "Infanticide, i.e. by the mother of her offspring, of the quoted variety, may be psychiatrically interpreted as a regression of the individual to a primitive form of activity akin to other biological weapons of defence, such as sham-death. The latter applies to the person; the former is to save the offspring. While the act is animal, the human psyche usually provides the wish fulfillment in seeing the offspring in heaven (in dreams)." As noted in my discussion of Ellis's review of the French article on infanticide, biological explanations of "irresistible impulse" certainly exculpated, and even operated to normalize, maternal neonaticide.

Despite his reliance on biological ideas, Morton (1934, 70), like many of his contemporaries, explained the cause of neonaticide primarily in class-based socio-economic terms – as an attempt to control fertility:

The majority of the patients whom I have seen and examined have been drawn from the poorer classes, who have had to get about their household duties at the earliest possible moment after confinement, and, in some cases, before they were fit to do so. Many of them have had financial worries, and perhaps insufficient or poor and unsuitable food. The majority of the cases were in poor physical health, anaemic and badly nourished ... I therefore maintain that the predisposing cause of their mental breakdown has been their insane heredity, coupled with overwork and fatigue, and that all these cases should come under the heading of "exhaustion psychosis." I am well aware that the law is very conservative, and that there are many judges and barristers who are familiar with the terms "puerperal" and "lactational insanity," and I think when we give evidence in courts we are justified in using these terms.

In fact, there was controversy over the causes of neonaticide and its underlying pathological mechanisms. Some viewed puerperal insanity, with its origins in puerperal fever and resultant septicaemia, as the underlying aetiology, while others favoured lactational insanity. The two differed in that puerperal insanity had a biomedical cause (i.e., puerperal fever), while lactational insanity was rooted in the effects of childbirth. It was thought that puerperal fever could bring about a delusional state in women, but this explanation eventually fell out of favour because, as such women were usually too weak with fever to leave their beds, it was not likely to be associated with maternal neonaticide. The two strands of reasoning bring to mind Marcé's discussion of the aetiology of puerperal psychoses, where an "organic," or physical, disorder is linked to a "functional," or mood, disorder, especially in cases where the lactating body experienced stress or exhaustion due to socio-economic circumstance. In their descriptions of the root causes of infanticide in women, experts in mental science seemed well aware of the interplay between mind and body, and they rarely attributed mental disturbance in recently delivered and lactating women to one cause or the other. In most cases, the mental disturbance was seen as inextricably linked to the class-based experiences of the women and the demands made on their bodies by the baby (and, in many cases, other small children).

By 1942 the concept of puerperal psychosis was completely out of vogue. According to Ian Skottowe, MD, DPM, medical superintendent, Buckinghamshire County Mental Hospital, and physician for nervous and mental disorders, Royal Buckinghamshire Hospital, there was "no specific psychiatric syndrome which occurs exclusively in the child-bearing epoch" (Skottowe 1942, 158). He noted that other experts shared this view: "This is accepted by modern writers, including Kilpatrick and Tiebout (1926), Strecker and Ebaugh (1926), James (1935), Harris (1936), Smalldon (1940) and Cruikshank (1940). The old conception of 'puerperal psychosis' (McDonald, 1847) as a special entity is no longer tenable, although it is a convenient term in everyday use, so long as it is understood to refer to the setting in which the psychosis occurs and is not in itself a diagnosis" (Skottowe 1942, 158).

While puerperal psychosis may have been out of vogue, the idea of diminished responsibility based on either pregnancy or lactational insanity was not. Puerperal psychosis simply fell out of favour because puerperal fever had been rejected as the underlying aetiology of the psychosis itself, which was manifested in an infanticidal act. Both pregnancy and lactation were strongly situated as underlying special "problems" or "experiences," which, when coupled with social stressors, precipitated "wrong" thoughts and led women to kill their babies.

There were, then, diverse interpretations of the causes of the mental disturbance in neonaticide cases, each connected in some way to the physical processes and social stressors associated with pregnancy, childbirth, and lactation. In one strand there was a continuance of the old "atavism" discourse, which had transmuted an anthropological understanding of customary neonaticide into a mitigation of the "infanticidal act" as the result of "irresistible impulse" observed in the natural realm. There is also a strand that depicted the "infanticidal disturbance" as the product of the combination of socio-economic stressors and the constitutional demands of pregnancy, childbirth, and lactation, particularly among working-class women. The underlying rationales of their diagnoses contain the notion that female fertility control is a universal feature of the natural world and the dominion of women.

Ironically, the bio-psychiatric terms[7] that, from the point of view of a feminist critique of infanticide law, supposedly represent the abandonment of sociological accounts of the women's actions in favour of individualistic medico-legal knowledge that decontextualizes and depoliticizes women's experiences (Comack 1987, 1993; Edwards 1984; Johnson and Kandrack 1995; Showalter 1985; Smart 1989), in this case turn out to have been theorized by many medical specialists in insanity as substantially socio-economic in character. These asylum experts viewed the problem of maternal neonaticide from the point of view of working-class women's experiences of pregnancy and childbirth, thus paring a particular kind of paternalistic awareness of the severe stresses of poverty and uncontrolled fertility with the unique kind of "exhaustion" this brought about for women. This awareness operated to mitigate murder charges brought against working-class women, who were viewed substantially differently than were women of the physicians' class.

The Canadian Infanticide Amendment, 1948

When Mackenzie King's Liberal government introduced amendments to the *Criminal Code of Canada,* which included "infanticide" as a form of "culpable homicide" (Bill no. 377), in June 1948, Canadian lawmakers had the well established *English Infanticide Act, 1922,* upon which to draw. Passed during the height of psychological ambition in law, the *English Infanticide Act, 1922,* intended to create an offence that fell somewhere between "murder and concealment" (Davies 1968 [1937-38]) and would be mitigated by a degree of mental derangement somewhere between sanity and insanity. The new clause required the courts to interpret the relationship between *actus reus* and a disease of the mind *de novo* (Walker 1968) without having to satisfy the requirements of the M'Naghten rules. The practice of "illegitimate mothers" killing newly born infants for socio-economic reasons was reframed in legal discourse as rooted in mental derangement brought on by the effects of pregnancy, childbirth, and lactation. By the 1930s aseptic practices in obstetrics[8] had reduced the frequency and mortality rate of puerperal fever. The causes of neonaticide were then attributed to "lactational insanity" and/or "exhaustion psychosis."

The law's appeal to the bio-psychological "effects of childbirth and lactation," rather than to the socio-economic factors that underpinned the mental scientists' diagnoses of exhaustion psychoses, effectively met the criminal law's requirement that the individual, rather than society, be held accountable, even for an event widely thought of as only quasi-criminal.[9] As Ward (1999) argues in the British context with respect to the passage of the *Infanticide Act, 1922*, and its amendment in 1938: "Rather than a simple replacement of a legal by a medical model of crime, the infanticide acts involved a *reconstruction* of medical concepts to fit the needs of law ... Medical discourse, with its distinction between normal (rational) and pathological (somatically determined) mental processes, afforded a way of drawing this line without overtly recognizing social pressures as a defence in a way that would threaten basic legal tenets of responsibility. But this medical distinction was reconstructed within legal discourse in a way quite at variance with medical knowledge" (174; emphasis in original).[10]

Early twentieth-century English criminal law had constructed the issue of responsibility for neonaticide in *individualistic* terms, even though, in mental science discourses, neonaticide was viewed as bio-socially determined. This legal interpretation of responsibility is at variance with medical knowledge, which mainly explains the provocation to commit neonaticide by referring to socio-economic factors external to the individual perpetrator-mother. Women were very rarely held entirely responsible for the death of their babies. The English infanticide statute, in accordance with the legal convention that held the individual responsible for a crime, evidently operationalized only biomedical knowledge of the mind. However, in the case of maternal neonaticide psychiatric knowledges (and earlier legal practices) were more inclined to extend responsibility to "society" or unjust social arrangements and the experience of "working-class motherhood."

The *English Infanticide Act, 1922*, allowed reduced punishment for a woman who killed her newly born infant when it could be established that she had not fully recovered from the effects of giving birth to the child and, by reason thereof, had the balance of her mind disturbed (Walker 1968, 131).[11] Canadian legislators were able to adopt this idea with the confidence that it had been applied in England since 1922. According to the Canadian minister of justice (Ilsley): "Many years ago in England, the crime of infanticide was created by statute. It applies to cases where there is not the degree of mental derangement amounting to insanity ... We have taken the wording of the English statute. Those words are found in section 7, and there are English cases on this section. Therefore we are not without precedent to guide judges and juries in determining the circumstances in which a charge of infanticide is proper" (*Hansard Parliamentary Debates*, 14 June 1948, 5185).

Like the rationale underpinning the *English Infanticide Act, 1922*, the Canadian statute was intended for those circumstances that could be mitigated by a special defence category that did not require a full-blown defence of insanity. In contrast to the English act, which kept infanticide on the same footing as manslaughter (with a maximum punishment of life imprisonment), the Canadian act outlined a three-year maximum penalty. This three-year maximum punishment was later raised to a five-year maximum in 1954, when Parliament standardized within the Canadian *Criminal Code* punishment framework. At the time, Stanley Knowles (CCF, Winnipeg North Centre) was the only member of Parliament to question whether five years was not too harsh a penalty, asking if it were

> not a rather severe sentence in view of the definition of infanticide that we have already been given ... As I understand the definition, there is imported into it exceptional or unusual circumstances. It seems to me that causing the death of a child, in the sense of it being outright murder, is covered in other sections. Causing the death of an unborn child is covered in clause 209. But I come back to the questions, namely, in view of the fact that infanticide is defined as something that happens under exceptional and understandable circumstances, is it not rather severe to increase the penalty from three to five years? (*Hansard Parliamentary Debates*, 25 February 1954, vol. 3, 2446)[12]

When the original omnibus bill containing the infanticide amendment was debated during its second reading, legislators who contributed to the debate (all of whom were lawyers) were concerned with a range of issues, some of which had to do with the practice of maternal neonaticide and some of which did not.[13] The discussion of the proposed infanticide amendment covered the potential legal controversies raised by the introduction of what amounted to a defence of diminished responsibility in order to circumvent the death penalty. There was no debate about the scientific validity of the medical concepts of mind incorporated into law, either in the House or in the newspaper reports that followed. The relevant headline in the *Globe and Mail* (15 June 1948, 3) the following day did not even refer to infanticide: "Death Penalty to Stay in Canadian Statutes, Ilsley Tells Commons." Key issues raised by John G. Diefenbaker (PC, Lake Centre) and Stanley H. Knowles (CCF, Winnipeg North Centre) concerned the possible abolition of the death penalty, including the law's deterrent value, the kinds of circumstances to which it would apply, and public opinion on the matter. These concerns eclipsed any kind of in-depth discussion of the infanticide amendment. Other issues were also much more significant at the time. For instance, Ilsley had redrafted a section of the *Criminal Code* dealing with "criminal sexual psychopaths," which would allow courts to issue indeterminate sentences following a conviction for a sex crime, to "remove sex offenders from circulation for an indefinite period and give them treatment which might lead to their release without menace to society" (*Globe and Mail*, 15 June 1948, 3). In the shadow of these discussions, infanticide law was merely the vehicle for raising broader issues associated with the practice of capital punishment; the debate over the infanticide amendment provided legislators with the opportunity to raise broader questions about provocation, diminished responsibility, and punishment relating to a range of apparently more pressing social issues.

It is important to be aware of the context within which these discussions took place because, when the infanticide amendment was introduced in Canada, the mandatory penalty for murder was death, and for manslaughter it was life imprisonment. Within this context the passage of the infanticide amendment would have been considered a means of providing judges with the flexibility to issue appropriate punishment based on the circumstances surrounding individual cases.[14] It provided an avenue for dealing with a social problem through the criminal justice system in a way that gave judges the authority to punish women fairly. For a variety of socially located reasons, both the death penalty and life imprisonment were popularly and judicially viewed as inappropriate sanctions for many cases of maternal neonaticide.

The debate described below is reproduced here in order to show how these kinds of quasi-social and legal questions were, in fact, much more in the minds of legislators than were the medical concepts upon which the amendment was conceived. There seemed little or no question that pregnancy, childbirth, and lactation produced, or could produce, a state of diminished capacity in women and function to partially exculpate them for culpable homicide. The content of the debate illustrates that infanticide law arrived in Canada not as new biomedical or psychiatric knowledge but, rather, as a mechanism for dealing with the legal problem of too few and inappropriate convictions. What is evident from the discussions is the fact that infanticide law, as outlined in the *English Infanticide Act, 1922*, provided a practical solution to a legal problem. While this amendment perhaps had the long-term effect of medicalizing the popular understanding of neonaticide, at the point at which the law was passed, medical specialists in insanity had little, if anything, to do with altering the law. Both the established English statute and its appeal to childbirth and lactation as provocation/diminished responsibility constituted a convenient and entirely sensible way to deal with a pressing legal problem. Thus, though it may appear that the Canadian *Infanticide Act, 1948*, represented an instance of the outright medicalization of women's deviance, it was a legal solution to a conviction and punishment problem as well as a response to a legal procedure problem. It was not until later that scholars began to see that the juridical-medical version of infanticide law had the overall effect of pathologizing the practice of maternal neonaticide.

The infanticide amendment was suggested, according to the news reports, by the Ontario provincial attorney general (*Ottawa Evening Citizen*, 15 June 1948, 8), was supported by Diefenbaker,[15] and easily passed in Parliament. The contemporary legal practice of charging women with concealment of birth was thought to discredit the application and practice of law (*Globe and Mail*, 15 June 1948, 3). As a substantive charge allowing for partial exculpation, infanticide law rationalized existing legal practices and addressed the punishment problem during a time in Canadian legal history when legislators were concerned with the potential negative effects of discretion both on the part of both juries and prosecutors. Minister of Justice Ilsley described the situation in the House of Commons as follows:

My information is that there are cases where the mother kills her newborn child, and that in the normal case of that kind it is useless to lay a charge of murder against the woman, because invariably juries will not bring in a verdict of guilty. They have sympathy with the mother because of the situation in which she has found herself. Therefore, crown prosecutors, and those who lay charges, if they are to obtain convictions lay charges of concealment of birth; or a charge that is equal to concealment of birth. Anyone who looks at the section will see that it is really not concealment of birth, but rather concealment of the body. However, this charge is known as concealment of birth. Sentences of a few months, or even shorter are imposed. To a minor extent that brings the law into disrepute, because the offence is murder; that is, unless the woman is insane ... We have placed the penalty at three years. It is purely a matter of judgement; the time may be too short, or it may be too long. I am told, however, that even in cases where manslaughter has been charged and convictions obtained – and I should think quite improperly, because I cannot think how a charge of that kind would have any of the elements of manslaughter – sentences have been rarely more than two years. (*Hansard Parliamentary Debates*, 1948, 5185)

The record clearly suggests that lawmakers were attempting to deal with the negative discretionary effects of popular sympathy toward mostly single and white working-class women who killed their unwanted, mostly illegitimate, babies in order to conceal their shame. Much of this sympathy expressed itself through mandatory minimum penalties for murder and manslaughter. Diefenbaker further made it clear that the infanticide provision was necessary in order to circumvent sympathetic jurors and to gain convictions for a unique kind of homicide: "For in a great number of cases in which a woman finds herself in the position of having on her hands a newborn child, loses her power of control and the child dies in consequence of some act on her part, over and over again juries have refused to convict, regardless of the evidence. I presume that the reason for the amendment is to make it easier to get a conviction for the offence of homicide short of murder or manslaughter" (*Hansard Parliamentary Debates,* 1948, 5184).

This led to some discussion about the dangers of implementing new categories of culpable homicide in order to dodge the death penalty rather than abolishing it altogether.[16] Diefenbaker asked whether a complete revision might be effective:

> In view of the fact that something is being done to amend the criminal code by sections, I ask the minister if any consideration has been given to this matter [the death penalty]. I have the feeling that taking the code in this manner, and having a kind of selective amendment of it, may cause some difficulties in the future which I think are fairly obvious. But if the decision has been made to follow this course in order to meet certain *ad hoc* matters that have arisen in the last year, and if it is thought that this is the best way of doing so short of a complete revision, naturally I support it. (*Hansard Parliamentary Debates,* 1948, 5184)

It is clear from the *Hansard* record that the infanticide law was not a straightforward case of psychiatric theory being imported into law; rather, it was a case of trying to provide a widely accepted solution to a range of historically specific legal problems. The first problem was juror and judicial discretion operating in the face of a mandatory penalty of death for murder, and the second was the laying of concealment of birth charges, which were sometimes thought to be too lenient and were always thought to be inappropriate. The infanticide amendment provided a suitable middle ground. Indeed, given that they had a number of years in which they could view the results of the English infanticide provision, the legislators seemed more or less content to have been presented with a ready-made solution to a small but troublesome criminal justice problem. They seemed to have been barely concerned with the character and merits of the underlying psychiatric rationale for the measure they were adopting.

Far from codifying the established practice of jurors' lenience toward mainly young, white, single, working-class women, the Canadian infanticide amendment had the unintended consequence of individualizing, and thus rendering more serious, a type of killing previously exculpated by jurors (and sometimes judges) on socio-economic grounds. In this respect, Canadian infanticide law operated as a further sanction rather than as a mitigating partial defence to murder (the latter being the likely intention of legislators relying on the expertise of mental scientists). The juridical-medical rendition of neonaticide, the product of the appropriation of certain aspects of medical knowledge, rendered moot the more "sociological" account described in the English mental science literature and formerly relied upon by Canadian jurists. These accounts mitigate women's responsibility based on their working-class affiliation, lack of reproductive freedom, and aversion to illegitimate babies.

Initially, the new infanticide law proved difficult to use. The law was soon revised because it was read as requiring the Crown to prove the element of psychiatric disturbance. In *R. v. Marchello* (1951) the Ontario High Court laid out the required elements to be proven for an infanticide conviction. In his decision McRuer J. noted that the Canadian law was burdensome to the Crown because psychiatric evidence of mental disturbance on the basis of pregnancy or lactation did not function to reduce the penalty for manslaughter, as did the amended *English Infanticide Act, 1938;* instead, the mental element had to be proven beyond a reasonable doubt in order to sustain a conviction for the separate charge of infanticide. McRuer J. laid out the elements to be established by the Crown under the new law as follows: "(a) the accused must be a woman; (b) she must have caused the death of the child; (c) the child must have been newly born; (d) the child must have been a child of the accused; (e) the death must have been caused by a willful act or omission of the accused; (f) at the time of the willful act or omission the accused must not have *fully* recovered from the effect of giving birth to the child; and (g) by reason of giving birth to the child the balance of her mind must have been then disturbed" (*R. v. Marchello* [1951], 141; emphasis in original).

In 1955 the Canadian Parliament responded to the concerns raised in *Marchello* and passed a new provision, entitled "No acquittal unless act or omission not wilful." This amendment eased the burden on the Crown to establish the reproductive-psychiatric element but still required proof of intent for a conviction of infanticide. The removal of the requirement of the Crown to prove the psychiatric component resulted in the elimination of discussions at bar of the mental science expertise that had located maternal neonaticide within a socio-economic framework (Kramar 2000). Now a strictly individualized biomedical account of infanticide was left "standing alone" in a statute that was never subject to close medico-legal examination in Canadian courtrooms. What is perhaps of particular interest to medico-legal scholars is that there is no evidence that any systematic attempts were made by medical specialists in insanity to bind medicine to law either by lobbying for an infanticide provision or, later, by providing testimony in individual cases before the courts following the passage of the law in 1948.[17]

Nevertheless, a strictly individualized or medical account of the basis of maternal neonaticide in legal discourse is what one might expect given the criminal law's orientation toward individual responsibility and accountability. In its contemporary legal guise, infanticide law undeniably allows for a humanitarian response while codifying biological difference and abandoning the class-based accounts that mitigated maternal neonaticide. The infanticide provision, adopted in Canada as an independent charge, shifted the broad conceptual understanding of maternal neonaticide while altering the available legal framework to facilitate homicide convictions. The newly established grounds for infanticide held that childbirth and lactation partially, but not entirely, mitigated responsibility for murder. Only the very individualized aspects of the psychiatric theories of causation, which discussed "infanticidal mothers" in strictly biomedical and/or psychiatric terms of reproductive processes, were readily imported into Canadian law (albeit eventually only as a nominal mitigation framework).

Discussions of infanticide law raise questions about the relationships between diminished mental capacity, culpability, sympathy, and punishment. Academics usually ask whether these women were viewed as "mad," "bad," or "sad" (Edwards 1984; Wilczynski 1991, 1997b; Ward 1999). This chapter examined the development of two distinct bodies of knowledge, law and medicine, during the period leading up to and including the passing of the Canadian infanticide law. It provided a critical examination of the range of issues important to each body of knowledge and assessed whether mental medicine colonized the practice (established by juries) of accepting a socio-economic model of provocation in order to fully or partially exculpate women for neonaticide. As a mechanism for thinking about and responding to maternal neonaticide, the new Canadian law was unable to integrate the emergent socio-economic explanatory mitigation framework developed by ethnographers and mental science experts. My examination of discourses on the "insanities of pregnancy and childbirth" suggests that experts in mental science were as likely as were jurors to account for diseases of the mind – such as "lactational insanity" or "exhaustion psychosis" – in socio-economic terms (although, as we have seen, the population they had in mind probably differed somewhat from the one that proved to be so hard to convict). In fact, stress or exhaustion (accounted for in bio-socio-economic terms) during pregnancy, following childbirth, and throughout the lactation period explained the mental disturbance that resulted in the reactionary practice of maternal neonaticide.[18]

On the other hand, the Canadian members of Parliament viewed the *English Infanticide Act* as a practical solution to a legal dilemma. As O'Donovan

(1984, 261) argues, regarding the passage of the English legislation in 1922, infanticide law "was the product not of 19th century medical theory about the effects of childbirth, but of judicial effort to avoid death sentences which were not going to be executed. But medical theory provided a convenient reason for changing the law." However, even a claim that the psychiatric rationale of infanticide law acted as a "convenient reason" is probably over-stated in the Canadian context. As part of a concerted effort on the part of the judiciary, certain medical theories about pregnancy and lactation were, at most, a helpful rationalization for instituting a smoother legal process from the laying of a charge of infanticide to conviction and punishment. Canadian legislators seemed not at all interested in the available theories of pregnancy and childbirth insanity but, rather, were content merely to adopt a provision that would enhance the prospects for indictment and convic-tion. The debate in the House of Commons makes it clear that the infanti-cide amendment was a solution to a straightforward legal problem rather than a well thought out appropriation of sexist psychiatric knowledge. In-deed, the juridical-medical version of maternal neonaticide was *at odds* with the primarily socio-economic antecedents of exhaustion psychosis and lac-tational insanity offered by the experts in mental medicine. Ironically, it is this difference that gives some credence to the medicalization thesis in that the limited wording of the statute does produce, at least textually, a dis-tinctly biomedical element.

What has been described as the central paradox (Ward 1999) of infanti-cide law – that it operationalized a psychiatric explanation for the killing of newly born (and sometimes illegitimate) children when, in almost every discourse outside of law, the practice was much more likely to have been accounted for in socio-economic terms – is perhaps not as paradoxical as it appears. The criminal law tends to individualize responsibility for culpable homicide and, therefore, only incorporates exculpatory explanations that mitigate individual responsibility. Socio-economic mitigating factors are thus excluded from the domain of criminal law, allowing only for those kinds of explanations that address individual responsibility. The infanticide amend-ment incorporates only those aspects of the twentieth-century medico-legal discourse that account for maternal neonaticide in terms of individual mental derangement.

Given that social explanations are exterior to questions of criminal respon-sibility, and that the socio-economic basis of the mitigation framework was obscured in the infanticide provision, Canadian legislators unwittingly operationalized a crude rendition of psychiatric theories of the insanities of reproduction – one that viewed maternal neonaticide in wholly bio-psychiatric terms as the product of a diseased mind. This distortion and simplification of psychiatric discourse was, on the face of it, even more marked in the Canadian than in the English case because the juridical-medical understanding of maternal neonaticide codified within the Canadian Infanticide provision (1948) differs from the English provision in that it created a new and separate category of culpability – a category in which the key requirement was to show the mere existence of the mental disorder and its connection to childbirth, lactation, and homicide. In the English scheme the evidence of mental disturbance was introduced to mitigate responsibility for manslaughter, so that a broader range of psychiatric evidence, including socio-economic precipitators, could easily be introduced as part of the mitigation. Ward (1999) has shown that the infanticide law's appropriation of bio-psychological knowledge was quite at odds with the socio-economic understanding of the root causes of infanticide. Ward's (2002, 250) analysis further highlights the fundamental contradiction between sociological/humanitarian mitigation frameworks and the abstract individualism inherent within criminal law.

This kind of reformulation of psychiatric discourse has been used to support the autopoietic theory of law, which, according to Ward (1999, 174), "views law as an autonomous and self-reproducing system of communications which constructs its own knowledge of the world. Concepts from other systems of knowledge, such as medical science, can never simply be incorporated into law, but are 'reconstructed' within legal discourse ... Law 'enslaves' psychiatric concepts, putting them to work to answer its own questions about responsibility, etc."

This chapter provides evidence for a slightly more contingent and less subtle process. In Canada, at any rate, the reconstruction, or "enslavement," of mental medicine's theory about maternal neonaticide within legal discourse (case law) was not quite as immediate as Ward's thesis might suggest. At least initially, the infanticide provision was taken to require convincing mental science evidence about the existence and causes of mental disturbance leading to maternal neonaticide – something that proved difficult to obtain. Thus, although the Canadian provision required psychiatric evidence only for its own strictly legal purpose of determining the level of responsibility for culpable homicide, this proved to be too much psychiatry for the law. This problem was only resolved later by the passing of a 1955 amendment that, rather than reconstructing, or enslaving, mental science theory, simply removed the need for psychiatric evidence, leaving the underlying quasi-psychiatric rationale of infanticide law as a discursive shell that served no other purpose than to provide for a generalized mitigation in cases of maternal neonaticide.

4
Unwilling Mothers: The Disappearance of the "Unwanted" Baby

This chapter provides an analysis of the reported legal cases dealing with the killing of newly born babies by their biological mothers with homicide and childbirth related offences following the enactment of the infanticide provision in 1948. The social, medico-legal, and bio-political context within which the cases of mothers suspected of killing newborn babies were adjudicated changed dramatically in the half century following the enactment of the infanticide law. By 1948 a series of dramatic changes related to rapid industrialization led to a significant rise in the population, urbanization, and immigration. Labour unions were formed by the working classes, a number of national women's groups were born, and the role of the Church was redefined. In this context, the *Criminal Code* became an important tool for governing and responding to economic, political, cultural, and religious changes that brought with them a range of social anxieties related to "foreigners" and "dangerousness," particularly as they affected the newly working independent single woman (Cellard and Pelletier 1988; Strange 1995). By the time the infanticide provision was adopted in Canadian law, the shift of childbirth from home to hospital and the lowering of both maternal and infant mortality had begun to revolutionize the management of the newborn infant population. By the late 1930s childbirth occurred mainly in hospitals, and birth registrations were legally mandated under provincial law. This institutionalization of childbirth altered the infant and maternal mortality rates and made it more difficult for women to assert their innocence when a baby died at home following a concealed pregnancy.[1] Well before this professionalization of childbirth, Mitchinson (1991, 142) has shown that the *Upper Canada Journal of Medical, Surgical and Physical Science* (1852) urged "registration of births and deaths [to] prevent concealed births known only to the mother and midwife." The inference was that midwives and the home birth were complicit in the practice of infanticide. According to Mitchinson, home births would have implicate[d] midwives with infanticide, suggesting they were perhaps not "wholly trustworthy" in reporting births and might "tacitly condone" infanticide. Such a view recognized the attempt of practitioners to distance themselves from minority practitioners and to develop a cohesive and unified code of ethics for the practice of medicine. In this case doctors' loyalty belonged to the state, through the registration of births, and to the fetus. The midwife's loyalty, it seemed to be suggested, was to the birthing mother. But although physicians disapproved of infanticide, they were not up in arms about it; neither were Canadians in general. (144)

More broadly, public health interventions aimed at reducing infant mortality placed the infant in a special relationship vis-à-vis state protection and public assistance, and measures such as adoption, homes for unwed mothers, mothers allowances, the eventual decriminalization of birth control – coupled with (limited) availability of hospital abortion – helped to eliminate the concept of the excusably "unwanted baby."

More recently, the increasing legitimacy and legalization of abortion has had the unintended effect of decreasing sympathy for women unwilling to mother and who kill their babies at birth rather than have an abortion. While certain anti-choice discourse portrays abortion as an especially culpable and heinous form of infanticide, feminist pro-choice discourse, which emphasizes rational choice in sexually active and pregnant women, also tends to undermine the charitable psycho-social understanding of unwilling motherhood shown by the courts and English doctors in the late nineteenth and early twentieth centuries. For some, abortion is the one and only rational response to unwanted pregnancy: while for anti-choice activists, all interference with pregnancy and birth is wholly evil and culpable. This ideology connects with emerging jurisprudence on wilful intent outlined in *R. v. McHugh*,[2] in which the concept of "wilful," for the purposes of establishing criminal intent, was defined as an action conducted with bad motive or evil intent. Following *R. v. Smith*[3] in 1976 it was put upon the Crown to prove that the accused acted with this bad motive or evil intent when she killed her baby. So this had the immediate effect of augmenting the Crown's burden: rather than proving mental disturbance it had to establish malevolent aforethought. Ironically, or luckily for the accused women, the disturbance of mind written into law functioned to negate any presumption of wickedness on the part of the mother. However, this presumption is reversed toward the end of the twentieth century. This reversal resonates with anti-choice rhetoric, which articulates a burden of criminal responsibility on mothers who abort unwanted pregnancies. Both conceptualize the foetus as a "human being" with full legal personhood.[4]

Despite the clear intent of the infanticide provision, prosecutors after 1948 faced the same kinds of problems they had always faced in securing the conviction of women who had killed their babies. The important medico-legal questions continued to be those pertaining to evidence and proof required for an indictment, and later conviction, for the serious charges of murder and manslaughter, and now the lesser charge of infanticide. Criminal justice practices continued, unsurprisingly, to be oriented toward conviction for the serious charges, and, as a result, the law continued to be administered in an entirely ad hoc manner. Murder and manslaughter charges continued to be laid along with infanticide, concealment, and neglect.

In the wake of the infanticide provision, legal practices governing the killing of newly born babies at birth became more, rather than less, complicated. The vague wording of the infanticide clause and its complex and specifically gendered psychiatric evidentiary non-requirements made infanticide convictions difficult to prosecute, let alone win. These difficulties, coupled with attempts by Crown prosecutors to secure convictions for murder and manslaughter in preference to infanticide, resulted in few changes from the point of view of those women charged and convicted for the range of crimes covering maternal neonaticide. Some women were tried and sometimes convicted of the more serious crimes, while others were not.

Infanticide-specific difficulties are also to blame for this lack of consistency. The legislative attempt to address maternal neonaticide in terms of women's unique experiences of unwanted pregnancy (and the physiological and psychological effects of pregnancy, childbirth, and lactation) as seen through the lenient and charitable English psychiatric discourse did not work well in the Canadian context. It was soon evident, following attempts at practical application of the statute, that Crown prosecutors would have to prove seven separate elements "beyond a reasonable doubt" in order to sustain an infanticide conviction. These requirements were articulated in *R. v. Marchello* in 1951 and included: "at the time of the wilful act or omission the accused must not have fully recovered from the effect of giving birth to the child [and] by reason of giving birth to the child the balance of her mind must have been disturbed."[5] Because infanticide was adopted as a separate charge in Canadian law, rather than as a means of formally mitigating a manslaughter conviction with psychiatric evidence (as it was within the English framework), the burden was on the Crown to prove each of these elements to secure a conviction. Given the special circumstances of infanticide, and the daunting challenge of proving culpable homicide in these cases, it was unlikely that Crown prosecutors could secure the convictions they sought, especially if infanticide was brought as a single charge in an indictment.

Following the *Marchello* case, a new clause was added to the *Criminal Code* in 1955 aimed at easing the burden of proof on the Crown. The new clause made it necessary for the Crown to prove wilful intent only, and it excluded the requirement that it prove (1) that an accused mother was suffering from the after-effects of childbirth and lactation and that (2) as a result thereof the balance of her mind was disturbed. This peculiar suspension of the need to introduce psychiatric evidence of mental disturbance regarding pregnancy, childbirth, and lactation – the essential mitigation that still lay behind "infanticide" – made convictions significantly more likely and, more important, potentially entirely removed the psychiatric discourse from the adjudication of these cases. Soon infanticide charges became part of the plea-bargaining process in which guilty pleas for infanticide were exchanged for reducing murder and manslaughter charges.

Throughout the late 1980s and 1990s, in the United Kingdom, the United States, and Canada increasing anxiety about child abuse and, in particular, violent child abuse ending in homicide resulted in the infanticide law and its punishment framework coming to be perceived as an obstacle to increasingly aggressive prosecutorial ambitions. Even though infanticide convictions were more easily obtainable in the later twentieth century as a direct result of the 1955 *Criminal Code* amendment, common law had established a punishment framework that only occasionally included incarceration upon conviction. Typically, women convicted of infanticide would be sentenced to a few years probation and/or psychiatric treatment. This seemingly sympathetic and charitable response failed to meet the punitive standards demanded by the criminal justice authorities in the 1980s and 1990s. By the 1980s, a dissatisfaction with the infanticide defence had developed, and Crown attorneys began abandoning the charge in favour of second degree murder.

By the 1980s maternal killing of newborns had begun to be framed in the same terms as were infant killings that were the result of prolonged physical abuse. Both types of homicide were responded to with similar punitive force because, in either case, women were perceived as equally culpable and as acting wilfully. The diminished capacity element of infanticide law slowly disappeared from legal policy discussions, to be replaced by the twin concepts of "rationality" and "will." This is connected to broader developments in law and public policy beginning in the 1980s, when there was a shift away from collective responsibility toward privatization. These governing practices, first used by the conservative governments of Margaret Thatcher in the United Kingdom, Ronald Reagan in the United States, and then Brian Mulroney in Canada, are grounded in the ideological notion that the market is the best mechanism for resource allocation and that the individual should not be interfered with by the state. According to Fudge and Cossman (2002, 3-4), privatization is marked by the reconfiguration of the liberal state's role and its responsibility toward the life chances of its citizens. Well-being becomes a matter of individual responsibility. These developments can also be observed in criminal law, which is increasingly oriented around individual responsibility. As a result, the death circumstances usually described as infanticide in both lay discourse and in law came to be viewed, in the later twentieth century, as the extreme end of the child abuse spectrum rather than as a distinct psycho-social phenomenon.

Canadian Case Law, 1948-52

Rex v. Krueger (1948) (Murder)

In 1948 Lillian Julienne Krueger, an unmarried twenty-eight-year-old woman living in a boarding house in Winnipeg's North End, was charged with "murder" for having committed maternal neonaticide. The court evidence indicated that:

> On Saturday morning, November 6, 1948, William Law, a lodger at 382 Elgin Ave., Winnipeg, found, lying some 18 ins. from a garbage can situated just inside the back fence of the property, the body of a dead female infant. The body was naked but a paper bag had been placed over the head. It came right down to the shoulders and in the bag was the placenta to which was attached the umbilical cord which was attached to the other end of the navel of the infant.[6]

It was determined as a matter of relevant legal fact, by the magistrate court, that Lillian Krueger lived at 382 Elgin Avenue as the baby's body was discovered in a "large brown wax-lined paper bag which contained, amongst other things, a blood stained piece of brown wrapping paper upon which was an Eaton's' delivery slip label with Krueger's name and address on it."[7] This physical evidence was enough to connect the baby's body to the address of the mother, Lillian Krueger. Krueger initially refused to submit to a medical examination intended to determine if she had been "recently confined." This medical evidence was sought by the Crown in order to secure its intended charge of murder.

When questioned by the authorities, Krueger at first denied knowledge of the baby's death, attempting to conceal her pregnancy and birth, but when pressed by the police inspector, and asked again whether she would assent to a medical examination, she admitted that the dead baby was indeed hers. After the police inspector cautioned her that she "might be charged with concealing a birth or some more serious crime,"[8] Krueger voluntarily provided the authorities with the following signed statement:

> On Thursday, or about two-thirty Friday morning, I was in bed, and I felt as though I was having the diarrhoea. Then I went to the bathroom. In a little while I felt as though I had to go again, and someone was in the bathroom,

so I just grabbed the pail in my room. Then the baby passed out and I passed after it. When I came to, there was a pool of blood. Then I grabbed the pyjamas and used them as a pad. I went to bed, and I stayed there all day. I got up and had supper about six o'clock, went back to bed again. A knock came at the door and two girls wanted to see Nettie. I told them Nettie wasn't home and they left. I went back to bed. About 8:30 p.m. I went across to my other room at 382 Elgin. I went back to 382, took the baby out of the pail, put it in a paper bag, carried it out back. I think I put it in the barrel, and went back into the house.[9]

Krueger was then charged with murder, committed for trial, and sent to the Manitoba Gaol for Women at Portage La Prairie under a warrant of committal.

The main question of the case dealt with the defence's appeal of the warrant of committal on the grounds that direct medical testimony regarding live-birth had not been provided to the court at the preliminary hearing. The legal issue was not whether live-birth had been established (this would be a matter for the trial) but whether the police magistrate had the authority to issue the warrant of committal since no physician had provided direct medical testimony at the preliminary hearing.[10] Absent direct medical testimony, Krueger's lawyer argued that she could not be incarcerated indefinitely, and the warrant of committal was set aside. Nevertheless, Krueger remained in custody to await her trial for murder.

Despite the availability of the infanticide provision at this time, and its obvious suitability in this case, the authorities proceeded against Krueger in the old established manner, charging her with murder (having threatened to charge her with "concealing a birth or some more serious crime") and committing her to await trial. Once again, the thorny question of evidence of live-birth was raised, although in this case only in a very narrow and technical sense that was not subject to the rigours of proof required at a criminal trial. The passage of the infanticide provision might have operated to make it much easier to convince jurors that live-birth had occurred, but in this case the technical medico-legal requirement that still-birth be assumed was ignored by both police and the Crown, who brought the charge of murder and requested the warrant of committal.

R. v. Marchello (1951) (Murder)[11]

Any hopes that the infanticide provision would ease the Crown's evidentiary burdens in any significant way and allow for increased convictions under the homicide framework evaporated when, in 1951, the Ontario High Court, as it was then called, dealt with the new infanticide law, albeit in a case where a charge of murder was laid with an acquittal delivered by a jury on account of insanity.[12] The case addresses the legal ramifications of not using "infanticide" as a mitigation in a charge of murder or manslaughter as well as the meaning of "newly born child."[13] The request by defence counsel to find the accused guilty of infanticide rather than murder was rejected because of the narrow definition of "newly born" used by the judge. McRuer J. argued that an infanticide conviction could not be substituted because, at four and one-half months, the child was too old to allow for this. He outlined his reasoning for refusing to instruct the jury that they might find the accused guilty of infanticide in the event they determined that the insanity defence could not be made.

McRuer J. was the first to note that the Canadian act was difficult to apply, in part because it departs from the amended *English Infanticide Act, 1938,* in two significant ways: (1) it fails to define "newly born child" and (2) it makes infanticide a very specific offence defining the perpetrator-victim relationship. Regarding the latter, infanticide can function as a lesser included offence to murder or manslaughter but not in the case of *any* child, only in the case of one "newly born." According to McRuer J.:

In 1948 the offence of infanticide was introduced into the law of Canada for the first time. Four amendments were made to the Criminal Code.

Section 262 was amended [c. 39, s. 7] to read as follows: "(1) Culpable homicide, *not being infanticide and* not amounting to murder, is manslaughter." (The italicized portions were added.)

And the following subsection was added: "(2) A woman who by wilful act or omission causes the death of her newly born child shall be deemed not to have committed murder or manslaughter if at the time of the act or omission she had not fully recovered from the effect of giving birth to such child and by reason thereof the balance of her mind was then disturbed, but shall be deemed to have committed an indictable offence, namely infanticide."

Section 268A was added [c. 39, s. 8]: "Every one who commits infanticide is guilty of an indictable offence and liable to imprisonment for three years."

Section 951 was amended [c. 39, s. 41] by repealing s-s. (2) and substituting therefor the following: "On a count charging murder, if the evidence proves manslaughter *or infanticide* but does not prove murder, the jury may find the accused not guilty of murder, but guilty of manslaughter *or infanticide,* but shall not on that count find the accused guilty of any other offence." (The italicized words were added but no other change was made in the subsection.)

The legislation adopted by the Canadian Parliament is based on the English Infanticide Act, 1922, c. 18, but instead of following the language of the Act, another phraseology was adopted, and instead of providing that one guilty of infanticide might be dealt with and punished as if she had been guilty of the offence of manslaughter of the child, a separate punishment was provided limited to 3 years' imprisonment.

The immediate question that arose before me in interpreting this section was what was meant by "her newly born child."

[...]

I think that the cardinal principle of interpretation of statutes must be applied to this statute and that is that the words used are to be interpreted in their popular and ordinary sense as generally understood in Canada unless a contrary intention is clearly indicated in the statute. I think in no sense could a child four and one-half months old be referred to as a "newly born child." The Act does not clearly indicate an intention that a child within the meaning of the section is to be regarded as newly born as long the mother has "not fully recovered from the effect of giving birth to such child and by reason thereof the balance of her mind [is] then disturbed."

In 1938 a statute [the Infanticide Act, 1938, c. 36] was passed in England which was designed to define more clearly the offence by making provision that where the other facts were present and the child killed was under the age of 12 months the accused might be found guilty of infanticide.

[...]

The Canadian Act as it stands is, I may say with respect, legislation that in its application is difficult.[14]

In effect, then, McRuer's very cautious estimation of what constitutes a "newly born child" had the immediate effect of preventing the jury from substituting a conviction for infanticide on the basis of his idea that a child four and one-half months old is not newly born. Again, there were technical obstacles to the use of the provision, and these had little to do with the *mens rea* element and diminished capacity wrought by pregnancy, childbirth, and lactation. Thus, at the outset in Canadian legal practice a very narrow notion of what was allowable for an infanticide conviction became part and parcel of the Canadian common law framework.[15]

This decision is markedly different from what occurred within the established English context, which allowed for convictions for manslaughter *but within the lesser punishment framework for infanticide* when the child was less than one year of age. Within the English framework, a jury could find a woman suffering from the effects of birth and/or lactation guilty of either manslaughter of a child or infanticide, both of which carried the same punishment framework – up to a maximum of life imprisonment. In Britain non-custodial sentences have been the norm since 1924 (Ward 2002, 268). The difference in the Canadian law would prove to have a significant effect on the success rate of the Crown's convictions for infanticide. Had legislators been more careful and adopted the *English Infanticide Act, 1938* in its entirety, many of the conviction problems faced by the Crown prosecutors might have been prevented and a plausible punishment framework adopted.

This age limit was established in England following *R. v. O'Donoghue,*[16] where a woman was sentenced to death (but reprieved even before appeal) for killing a thirty-five-day-old baby, who, it was determined, was not newly born. This case precipitated the amendment of the *English Infanticide Act, 1938,* to define a newly born child as an infant up to and including the age of twelve months. This interpretation, seemingly liberal when compared to Canadian practice, was, in fact, a compromise. An upper age limit of eight years had been proposed in a 1936 Infanticide Bill that lapsed during King Edward VIII's abdication. According to Walker (1968, 132), this upper age limit "correspond[ed] more closely both with public feeling and with the Home Secretary's use of prerogative of mercy." And the amendment "would have widened the definition of the mother's state of mind to include 'distress and despair arising from solicitude for her child or extreme poverty or other causes.'" In any event, Walker doubts this bill would have succeeded because it stretched the psychological model of capacity to include broadly defined social influences on criminal behaviour. Nothing like this 1936 bill or the amended 1938 version were ever contemplated in Canada. "Solicitude" for one's child or "extreme poverty or other causes" may have been contemplated by juries and judges in individual cases during the early part of the century, but these social factors mitigating responsibility for murder were never part of the official Canadian framework. McRuer J.'s decision not to instruct the jury as to the availability of the alternative conviction for infanticide echoed the concerns of legislators who debated the English infanticide provision in 1922. The infanticide provision was not established to replace an insanity defence for murder. Lord Chief Justice Alverstone, who was opposed to the bill as it was eventually passed because it might provide the opportunity for women who killed older babies to go free, was concerned that the bill would "erode restraints against child murder more generally" (Ward 2002, 258-59). The aim of the infanticide provision was to circumvent the death penalty and its refusal, which resulted in a symbolic rejection of law. The aim of English legislators was to permit a compassionate legal response to those cases that fit the humanitarian trope of seduction (257-58).

More important, from the point of view of obtaining convictions, McRuer J. felt that the onus resting on the Crown to prove each element of infanticide was far too burdensome. This burden "is so heavy as to make it almost impossible to convict an accused person on a charge of infanticide if laid as a single count in the indictment."[17] The seven separate elements required for conviction (described above) were interpreted as both difficult and contradictory. According to McRuer J.,

On the one hand, the Crown must prove a negative, by showing that the accused "had not fully recovered from the effect of giving birth to such child," and an affirmative that "by reason of giving birth to the child the balance of her mind was at the time of the offence disturbed"; while, on the other hand, on such a charge it would be a good defence to show that the accused had at the time of causing the death of the child by wilful act or omission fully recovered from giving birth to the child or that the balance of her mind was not then disturbed. In such a case, if even a reasonable doubt was raised in the mind of the jury she would be entitled to be acquitted on the charge of infanticide and thereafter she could not be charged with murder or manslaughter as an accused person cannot be put in jeopardy twice for the same homicide.[18]

Thus, the infanticide amendment operated less effectively than did the auxiliary charges of concealment or neglect. The effect of infanticide law was that the defence's job was made simple: all that was required for an absolute acquittal was to prove that the woman was of sound mind (or that she acted rationally) when she killed her baby. And proof of rationality could be fairly easily established with the introduction of already established social and economic circumstances. Evidence of single motherhood could operate as proof of rational behaviour since unwed motherhood was viewed, by the courts in any case, as a socially undesirable circumstance for both mother and baby. The killing of the newly born baby, if viewed as intentional or wilful, could be located in a popular, and well established, social discourse that viewed rejection of unwed motherhood as morally virtuous. This could facilitate an acquittal for infanticide and thwart the authorities' attempts to secure convictions for culpable homicide.

R. v. Jacobs (1952) (Infanticide)

In the first county court decision in which a charge of infanticide was brought by the Crown, the defendant was acquitted both of infanticide and of neglect. The defendant, Annie Jacobs, was found not guilty on both charges because the evidentiary requirements to sustain them had not been met. According to the Brennan County Court judge for the United Counties of Stormont, Dundas, and Glengarry, who relied in part on the jurisprudence set out in *Marchello*:

> There is no evidence here that the accused had not fully recovered from the effect of having given birth to the child nor is there any evidence that her mind was disturbed, that the balance of her mind was disturbed. The doctors for the Crown say her physical and her mental health so far as they could determine when they saw her shortly after the birth of the child was very good. There is no evidence, direct or by implication, that her physical

health and her mental faculties were not satisfactory. I cannot see where I can convict this lady on a charge of infanticide. I do not think the evidence would warrant it and I think I would be foolish to convict this woman of infanticide in view of what Chief Justice McRuer says in the Marchello case.[19]

In other words, the Brennan County Court judge refused to convict Annie Jacobs because she did not exhibit the requisite reproductive mental disturbance for a conviction of infanticide, illustrating the problem identified a year earlier by McRuer J. in *Marchello*.

In *Jacobs* a conviction for infanticide is lost because the Crown established through medical evidence that Annie Jacobs was acting rationally: she lacked the requisite reproductive mental disorder and was therefore not guilty of infanticide. The Crown's attempt to secure a conviction for infanticide by introducing expert psychiatric testimony as to her well-being following the incident resulted in her acquittal rather than a conviction, as was intended by the English lawmakers who passed the original infanticide act. The judge in this case could not have known that the Crown prosecutor was absolutely right to charge Jacobs with infanticide and expect a conviction – except that the Crown should have sought to establish the positive rather than the negative (i.e., that Jacobs *was* suffering from a defect of the mind due to the effects of childbirth and lactation). Instead, the Crown attorney did his job as he was trained to do: he sought to establish wilful intent to commit murder, which, in the case of "infanticide," meant an acquittal. This is perhaps the very reason that reproductive mental disturbance would eventually be removed as a requirement for conviction through an amendment adopted in 1955.[20]

Criminal Code Amendment 1953-54 (Bill 7)

As a result of both the *Marchello* case and the likely dissatisfaction of Crown prosecutors like R.P. Milligan, who put Annie Jacobs on trial, legislators moved quickly to amend the *Criminal Code* to prevent these kinds of legally authorized acquittals. A new amendment was debated and enacted as part of a larger revision of the *Criminal Code* in 1953-54, and it included altering the punishment framework for all laws in order "to create uniformity." The new clause, entitled "No acquittal unless act or omission not wilful," was added precisely to ease the burden of proof on the Crown and to ensure convictions in cases such as *Jacobs*, where mental disturbance was not proven. In March 1954, following the final debate recorded in *Hansard*, Parliament enacted the following amendment:

570. Where a female person is charged with infanticide and the evidence establishes that she caused the death of her child but does not establish

that, at the time of the act or omission by which she caused the death of the child,

(a) she was not fully recovered from the effects of giving birth to the child or from the effect of lactation consequent on the birth of the child, and

(b) the balance of her mind was, at that time, disturbed by reason of the effect of giving birth to the child or of the effect of lactation consequent on the birth of the child, she may be convicted unless the evidence establishes that the act or omission was not wilful.[21]

Thus, this amendment removed the requirement to prove the reproductive mental disturbance – an impediment to conviction – to prevent further acquittals such as those secured in *Jacobs*.

During the amendment's debate, Stanley Knowles pointed out that the new section "[was] one not without double negatives," which appeared to him to "[make] it just that much easier for the prosecution to win or just that much more difficult for the accused to be declared innocent."[22] Mainly, Knowles was concerned that the clause itself, replete with double negatives, obscured the real fact that it dispensed with two important evidentiary elements for infanticide convictions. Knowles was further concerned that the provision might place the burden of proving whether the act was wilful on the accused, in the negative, to secure an acquittal, rather than on the Crown, in the positive, to secure a conviction. Knowles stated: "As I read clause 570 it looks to me as though the necessity of proving innocence is on the accused. As I say, double negatives are confusing, but when one reads the clause through one finds at the end that a person may be convicted unless the evidence establishes that the act or omission was not wilful. In other words, it appears that the prosecution does not have to establish that the act was wilful. The defence has to establish that it was not wilful."[23]

Knowles rightly points out that the section could be read as shifting the burden of proof of *mens rea* to the accused, thus reversing the presumption of innocence. The amended clause removed the psychiatric component of reproductive mental disorder for the offence of infanticide, leaving the presumption to "mental disturbance" open to interpretation by judges and jurors but still requiring proof of "intent."[24] Knowles continues:

I ask the minister to note that special circumstances are suggested in the clause itself, but even after allowance is made for the fact that such a person might not be fully recovered or that the balance of her mind might be disturbed, the clause ends up by saying that she may be convicted unless the evidence establishes that the act or omission was not wilful. If we refer to the note on the right-hand page we see that it is just the one word "new." In other words we have a new clause, and it does seem to me to be a case where the burden of proof of innocence is put on the accused.[25]

Mr. Garson, who was head of the Select Committee of Bill 7 respecting the *Criminal Code,* argued that "intent" remained an element to be proven by the Crown. Garson thoroughly reviews McRuer J.'s reasoning in *Marchello,* and it is worthwhile quoting his analysis at length to illustrate Garson's familiarity with the case:

This case deals with the question whether the accused, under a given set of circumstances, is guilty of murder or infanticide. In that connection I should say that one of the first questions the crown has to decide is whether the charge laid against the lady in the case is a charge of murder or a charge of infanticide. Bearing upon that, the language of Chief Justice McRuer I think is relevant, He said:

The onus resting on the crown to prove all these combined elements in the crime would appear to be so heavy as to make it almost impossible to convict an accused person on a charge of infanticide if laid as a single count in the indictment.

That is to say, if the indictment just had the single charge of infanticide in it.

On the one hand, the crown must prove a negative –

We get into this difficulty my hon. Friend from Winnipeg North Centre was describing.

– by showing that the accused "had not fully recovered from the effects of giving birth to the child," and an affirmative that by reason of giving birth to the child the balance of her mind was at the time of the offence disturbed –

The crown has to prove that as well.

– while, on the one hand, on such a charge it would be a good defence to show that the accused had, at the time of causing the death of the child by wilful act or omission, fully recovered from giving birth to the child or that the balance of her mind was not then disturbed. In such a case, even if reasonable doubt was raised in the mind of the jury she would be entitled to be acquitted on the charge of infanticide, and thereafter she could not be charged with murder or manslaughter as an accused person cannot be put in jeopardy twice for the same homicide.

There is a principle in law that if one commits an act, and if a charge is laid in respect of the commission of that act, and the accused is tried on that charge and is acquitted, then no further charge could be laid based upon that act. Under all such circumstances the accused is "home free."

I believe my hon. Friend can see from this careful considered language of Chief Justice McRuer that the subject matter we are discussing here bristles with great difficulties. The problem which arises in every one of these cases from the very beginning is as to whether, upon the set of facts, the charge should be infanticide or murder. Then, as Chief Justice McRuer makes very

clear, when you get into the actual case the crown is up against a very difficult position because it has to prove a negative of one proposition and a
positive of another in order to secure a conviction for infanticide.

I think my hon. Friend can see from this inadequate, and perhaps from
his standpoint unsatisfactory discussion of the subject that the drafting of
the clause he criticizes is a task of no inconsiderable difficulty.[26]

And Knowles replied that Garson proved his point – that if the amendment was passed it would place an "additional barrier in front of the accused, or conversely [make] it easier for the prosecution."[27] Clearly, Knowles
was uneasy with this addition, which, according to him, "changes the situation, and as I have already said makes it just that much easier for the prosecution to win or just that much more difficult for the accused to be declared
innocent."[28]

As this debate illustrates, clause 570 was intended to ease the burden of
proof on the Crown, over the objections of left-leaning members of Parliament. Garson frames the problem firmly in terms of the Crown having to
prove a negative on the one hand (that a woman had not fully recovered
from the effects of childbirth and lactation) and a positive on the other
(that as a result her mind was disturbed). While Knowles fails to agree that
such a requirement is an onerous burden on the Crown, its operation as a
"qualifier" to the infanticide provision might result in an infanticide conviction that is much easier to obtain not because guilt per se is presumed
but, rather, because two of the defining elements of infanticide are removed
entirely from the discursive framework.

Following a short and bizarre question raised by a Mr. Stick, in which he
asks how McRuer J. would handle a case of infanticide in which a person
with a sex change operation was charged with infanticide (!), Mr. Nowlan
concurs with the objections of Mr. Knowles but further complicates and
confuses the debate by shifting the discussion to the question of intent,
which was not at issue in the amendment under consideration but which
was of concern to Knowles. Nowlan comments:

I think the minister will admit that the saving clause at the bottom of clause
570 is really superfluous, and does not affect the situation in any way. It
says ... she may be convicted unless the evidence establishes that the act or
omission was not wilful ... That is elementary, because if it was not wilful it
would not be a crime ... It is not relieved at all by the last part of the clause,
because if it is not wilful it is not a crime; it is not homicide. If a mother
rolls over on her baby at night and the baby smothers, that would not be a
wilful act and she could not be prosecuted for infanticide.[29]

Nowlan goes on to point out that convictions for infanticide are notoriously difficult to secure and that this amendment is unlikely to change the situation:

> Frankly I am not too much concerned about it, as I told my hon. Friend a little while ago in an aside, because those of us who have had any experience in these matters know how difficult it is to get a jury to convict in a case of infanticide. So often there is sympathy for the mother, and often the mother is unmarried in such cases. Ordinarily the jury will lean over backward to avoid a conviction for this offence, and very often properly so. With this other factor in there, why [sic] you charge a jury very learnedly on the law they are going to throw up their hands and say, "I did not know what he was talking about, I do not believe the judge understood it, so I will go out and acquit her."[30]

With that statement the debate is concluded and the clause is agreed to, "on division," by Mr. Knowles.[31]

In addition to the removal of the legal requirement to prove reproductive mental disorder, the bill passed included an amendment to the Canadian *Criminal Code*'s punishment framework in order to create uniformity in the overall punishment scheme. According to Garson, the goal was to establish "five types of penalties, those two years and under, those five years and under and so on,"[32] which meant that the punishment for infanticide, set at three years maximum, either had to be set at "two years and under" or "five years and under." And, according to Garson, "since the present penalty under the existing code is three years, this penalty would fall within the five year group."[33] This augmentation is objected to by Knowles, who argues that such an increase is "rather a severe sentence in view of the definition of infanticide that we have already been given."[34] He argued that the increase was extreme provided the "exceptional or unusual circumstances" outlined in the legal definition of infanticide: "As I understand the definition, there is imported into it exceptional or unusual circumstances. It seems to me that causing the death of a child, in the sense of it being outright murder, is covered in other sections. Causing the death of an unborn child is covered in clause 209. But if I come back to my questions, namely, in view of the fact that infanticide is defined as something that happens under exceptional and understandable circumstances, is it not rather severe to increase the penalty from three to five years?"[35]

Knowles presents the left liberal position on infanticide. By distinguishing the practice from child murder and killing an unborn child, he illustrates the view that infanticide was a special circumstance, not amounting to murder or even manslaughter. Those in law and order circles opposed this view (which incorporated women's social circumstances) since it often frustrated their attempts to secure convictions. Garson explains that the increase was allowed to provide the courts with "leeway" in these matters.[36] Knowles, on the other hand, is concerned that the increase was allowed solely on a mathematical basis and was intended to broaden the courts' powers. He asks Garson whether the select committee considered "reducing it to two years?"[37] Garson attempts to clarify the intent of the commissioners, arguing that the intention was to widen the scope of the offence to include a variety of circumstances:

> Oh no. I think it would be quite wrong to suggest that it was done solely on such a mathematical basis as that. I assure my hon. friend that the decision as to whether the penalty of three years should be cut down to two would be based on criteria which were not mathematical. As I said a moment ago, they would consider a variety of circumstances which had arisen in cases under this section. The question which they would, I think, pose for themselves and answer would be whether, in covering a variety of circumstances, it was desirable to have a penalty of five years or two years. They decided on five years. Now, that decision was reviewed by the other place on two different occasions and by the special committee of the House of Commons at the last session of Parliament, and no change has been made. There is nothing to prevent us from making a change here if it is thought desirable.[38]

With this final statement, the punishment amendment is agreed upon by members of Parliament.

The passage of the elements connected with infanticide law in Bill 7 would have two significant legal effects. First, the increase in the punishment, although intended to simply broaden the scope of the kinds of cases that might be heard under the offence, made infanticide a potentially more serious offence, allowing Crown prosecutors to seek more severe punishments (as is evident from the case law discussed in the next section). Second, the removal of the reproductive mental disorder element made convictions in any case more easily obtainable. Even though the infanticide law framework represented a fairly lenient approach toward these cases, it is very important to appreciate the sentiment advanced by Knowles, whose opinion favoured outright acquittal in cases of maternal neonaticide. But the effect of these amendments was to subvert, to as much a degree as legally possible, the acquittals that had already been rendered by the courts since the passage of the provision. The new goal was to accomplish convictions for infanticide in a manner that addressed the special circumstances of maternal neonaticide while taking into consideration the left liberal sentiment that such a crime was not anywhere near as serious as murder or even manslaughter and, therefore, did not demand as severe a sanction. In addition, recall that the provision itself, and now the expansion of the punishment framework and the removal of the psychiatric elements, was explicitly intended, according to the *Hansard* record, to eliminate the misapplication of concealment and neglect charges (although neither was removed from the *Criminal Code*). The new infanticide provision was clearly perceived as a solution to a range of tensions created in law by the left liberal recognition of infanticide as a "quasi-crime," which called not for punishment but sympathy. The infanticide provision and the amendments, taken together, did not create the reverse onus (which worried Knowles), but the amendment was clearly intended as a prosecutorial aid to empower the Crown.

Those aligned with the criminal justice machinery (e.g., the police and Crown prosecutors) had rarely accepted the degree of socio-economic mitigation that has so influenced jurors. Their allegiance to law and order policy meant that some kind of criminal justice response was necessary, albeit one with a diminished capacity element that could justify a lesser penalty than murder or manslaughter. The newly revised infanticide provision had something for everyone: members of society and government who were left liberal had the psychiatric mitigation of maternal neonaticide retained in the wording of the statute (in that it was now substantially presumed) in order to qualify intent; and the law and order advocates had a reasonable opportunity at securing the convictions they sought in these cases. Following the passage of section 570, the Crown was still required to prove "wilful intent" in order to secure a conviction for infanticide since, without *mens rea*, no person could be convicted of a crime.

Canadian Case Law, 1955-99

R. v. Bryan (1959) (Infanticide and Neglect to Obtain Necessary Assistance in Childbirth to Conceal Birth)

The newly amended infanticide law did not turn out to be quite the solution Parliament and the legal profession had hoped for. In 1959 a case arising from a jury acquittal for infanticide and a conviction for neglect to obtain assistance in childbirth illustrates that juries remained reluctant to convict, while the state persisted in its attempts to convict women on at least one charge vaguely associated with the crime of maternal neonaticide. *R. v. Bryan* illustrates yet again the tension between those forces pressing for acquittal and those pressing for conviction, and it highlights the centrality of proving wilful intent in murder cases.[39] The *Bryan* case arose from an incident that took place in Toronto on 27 March 1958:

> On that day, in the morning, the accused was suffering pains and, according to her evidence, she thought that she was about to have a miscarriage.

However, she was delivered of a child. It was a normal child. The child was conceived before marriage and the marriage had taken place about 5 months previous to delivery.

The accused had no persons present and did not make any provision for having any persons present for reasonable assistance in respect to her delivery. After the birth of the child the accused, according to her evidence, thinking the child was dead, placed the body in a chute which led to a place for burning garbage. The child however, was not dead, and after a number of hours, a person whose duty it was to deal with the refuse from the premises, dumped some refuse into the incinerator, and set fire to it. He then heard the cry of the child. The evidence is – and it is not disputed – that the child died as a result of burns.[40]

The accused was charged with infanticide and with neglect in childbirth. She was, however, acquitted of the infanticide charge by a jury who, according to McGillivray J., "must have come to the conclusion that she was wholly irresponsible at the time and was incapable of forming the intent sufficient to result in a wilful act."[41] She was convicted on the second charge of neglect by the trial judge and sentenced to one month definite and two months indefinite incarceration.[42] The sentence was successfully appealed to the Ontario Court of Appeal, whose decision was delivered by Porter C.J.O.

The appeal court found that the neglect law itself was inapplicable since the baby died not as a result of neglect in childbirth but, rather, as a result of the circumstances following birth, for which Bryan was not culpable. According to Porter C.J.O.: "I do not think that the meaning of the section can be extended to apply to a death that resulted from acts subsequent to the delivery and the death did not result from the failure to have no reasonable assistance in respect of delivery itself. In this case the death resulted from the combined circumstances of the disposing of the child in the incinerator chute and the burning that took place thereafter."[43] Thus, the applicability of the neglect section in these circumstances was featured, and Bryan was acquitted.

This case illustrated how the removal of the psychological components of infanticide law could, paradoxically, compel an acquittal in direct opposition to the intention of the amendment. A jury was now asked only to view the act as wilful and therefore culpable, but it was unlikely to see a woman as fully responsible for such a crime. This was due to the persistence of strong social factors that, within jurors' ethical frameworks, had always been seen as mitigating circumstances. Given this, it would have been difficult for a jury to view Bryan's behaviour as wilful. The allowal of the appeal of the neglect conviction, largely on a technicality relating to the precise wording of the statute, is also quite in line with the earlier period since circumstances in this case failed to conform precisely to the wording of the law (to which the majority of the court stringently adhered).

However, this stringent application of the statute is disputed by McGillivray J., dissenting, who argued that Bryan was, notwithstanding the technical wording of the law, responsible for the baby's death. And, on the evidence, there is no disputing that she *was* responsible for the baby's death – not because she failed to obtain assistance in childbirth but, rather, because she attempted to conceal the fact of the baby's birth (and alleged stillbirth) by putting it in the incinerator, where it was burnt to death by the janitor. McGillivray J. was quite wrong when he argued that the neglect statute covered the circumstances in this case despite the fact that the law declares that a woman is responsible for the death if the baby dies "during or in a short time after birth, as a result thereof."[44] According to McGillivray J., had Bryan had assistance at her delivery, she would not have mistaken the baby for dead and thrown it in the incinerator. Clearly, McGillivray J. wanted a broader interpretation of responsibility placed on the mother (to ensure the well-being of the newly born infant) than did the majority, who followed the strict letter of the law in order to acquit Bryan.

Canadian Cases in the 1970s

There are no other reported cases of infanticide, concealment, or neglect in Canada until the mid-1970s, when there were three reported cases of infanticide: one from the Newfoundland courts and two from the Ontario courts. During this period the courts were becoming more concerned with the establishment of "wilful intent" as it relates (1) to women having acted with evil intent and (2) to rehabilitation (as it relates to the mental condition of the accused). Jurisprudence establishes the importance of the concept of "wilful intent," which is newly defined as "evil intent." This definition of intent, when applied to mothers who kill their babies following unassisted childbirth, results in an acquittal of the charge of infanticide. Courts do not see the action (or lack of action) of a distressed teenaged woman, which results in the death of the newly born baby, as amounting to evil intent. The Ontario Court of Appeal addressed broader sentencing principles when it allowed an appeal of a twelve-month conviction for infanticide. Here, the principle of rehabilitation is of key importance to the case since the accused is determined to be suffering from depression, and imprisonment is believed to be an impediment to her recovery.

R. v. Smith (1976) (Acquittal for Infanticide without Substitution of Concealment Conviction)

R. v. Smith[45] was heard in the district court in the province of Newfoundland by Cummings J. in 1976. The evidence suggested that, following the child's birth, the seventeen-year-old accused placed her hand over her newborn baby's mouth to prevent it from crying and waking her father, who was sleeping in the next room. Her action was attributed not to malice with intent to kill but, rather, to her frightened and "hysterical" condition, as diagnosed by expert testimony, at the time of unexpected and unattended childbirth. In rendering his final decision, Cummings J. describes the case as an irrational act of a mildly deranged girl whose age, family, and social circumstance were partly implicated in the outcome of the pregnancy:

> Reviewing the evidence of this very sad case I find an atmosphere of unreality that would not preclude an irrational act by the accused without consideration of the consequences. She contended throughout that she did not know she was pregnant and her contention is supported to an extent by the fact the members of her family did not know and certainly took no steps to prepare her for the birth of the child. She was only 17 years of age and had just come through the traumatic experience of unassisted childbirth. Her little brother shared the bed with her at the time. When her mother pulled down the bed clothes and revealed a bed full of blood and the body of a baby, the accused irrationally denied she had had a baby. She maintained throughout her sole purpose in putting her hand over the baby's face was to prevent it from crying and if she did tell Mrs. Pardy she put her hand over the throat, which she denies, she still stated the purpose was to prevent the baby from crying.
>
> Considering all the evidence against the background of a disturbed mind, I have a reasonable doubt the act of the accused in causing the death of her child was wilful. I therefore dismiss the charge of infanticide.
>
> I have considered the included offence of concealing the dead body of a child under s. 277. I am satisfied there is insufficient evidence to substantiate that offence.
>
> The accused is therefore acquitted and the case dismissed.[46]

Cummings J. arrived at this decision following a careful review of the relevant statutes and determined that the section added in 1955, now section 590, was not meant to entirely exclude from consideration the psychological elements of the infanticide law:

> Section 590 does not have the effect, in my opinion, of eliminating from s. 216 the words relating to a disturbed mind as a result of childbirth. The two sections are to be read and applied in sequence and not as one section. Section 590 does not have any significance whatsoever if all the elements in s. 216 are proven. But if all the elements are proven except those relating to a disturbed mind, then s. 590 takes effect to prevent a female, who was of sound mind when she caused the death of her child by a wilful act, from going free. This enlargement of the crime of infanticide to cover the more

blameworthy situation, probably explains why the term of imprisonment for the offence was increased from three years to five in the 1953-54 revision. The anomaly mentioned by McRuer, C.J.H.C., may not be eliminated but it has been reduced.[47]

Cummings J. was wrong to assume that legislators intended to include more blameworthy acts when they raised the punishment framework from three years to five years imprisonment. By acquitting the young woman of infanticide, the judge determines that the accused lacked the requisite *mens rea* (evil intent) for a conviction.

Cummings J. carefully reviews the legal requirements for infanticide and determines that, although the child was born alive, it was newly born and that the accused was the mother of the child. He was "satisfied ... that the accused had not fully recovered from the effects of having given birth to the child and that as a consequence her mind was disturbed," and to an extent that went beyond that previously required for an infanticide conviction, so that her action was not wilful. Cummings J. appears to have come to this conclusion despite psychiatric testimony that described the girl as suffering from pregnancy denial – a well established syndrome.[48]

Notwithstanding Cummings J.'s interpretation that proof of disturbance of the mind remained a legal requirement in most cases of infanticide, and that the removal of the necessity of proof was only to apply in cases where mental disturbance was absent or rejected, his ruling indicates how difficult it might be to establish the wilful intent element before a sympathetic judge. Relying on the then binding decision by the Nova Scotia Supreme Court,[49] Cummings D.C.J. defines wilful intent as acting "with a bad motive or purpose or with an evil intent."[50] Indeed, according to Cummings D.C.J. in the case before the court, the circumstances of childbirth and, in particular, the "denial of pregnancy" diagnosed by Dr. Paulse, an expert in psychiatry, made it much harder to prove wilful intent. This flies in the face of the reasoning behind the 1955 amendment articulated by Garson in the *Hansard* report and McRuer J. in *Marchello*, both of whom intended that the revision should facilitate convictions by eliminating the legal requirement for psychiatric proof of a disturbed mind, with the only essential mental element being wilful intent or wilful omission. And the court continued to require that each element outlined in *Marchello* be proven beyond a reasonable doubt; that is, the court wanted it established that the accused had not fully recovered from the effects of childbirth and, by reason thereof, that her mind was disturbed. It was only if the Crown failed to prove the mental elements that the new section was deemed relevant. However, in approaching these cases, the Crown surely could never meet this burden "beyond a reasonable" doubt, which could likely always be established by contradictory psychiatric testimony.

In acquitting Smith, Cummings J. relied entirely on the mitigating psychiatric evidence provided by Dr. Paulse: "Doctor Paulse said pregnant women denying they are pregnant is a well established syndrome. He described it as an hysterical condition. He said he thought the accused would initially have been in a state of shock because she was totally unprepared for the birth of the baby; however, at the time of the interview she had recovered and seemed relatively unconcerned. Clinical tests showed an immature, inadequate girl but no evidence of overt mental illness."[51]

Cummings J.'s decision is clearly articulated and is based on his benevolent interpretation of the mitigating psychiatric evidence. He provided a subtle and interesting interpretation of both sections applying to infanticide, although not one that seems to be in line with the intention of Parliament: judging by the debate reported in *Hansard,* there is no clear suggestion that the amendment was intended to cover cases in which mental disturbance is wholly absent and where intent is clearly established. Cummings J.'s reading of the purpose of the amendment, coupled with his linking of it to the increase in maximum punishment, would eventually have the effect of expanding the infanticide provision to include cases in which the element of violence was more serious and the intent apparently malicious. This view is consistent with the conflation of infanticide with "child abuse homicide," which becomes prevalent in forensic pathological and legal policy discussions from the 1980s onwards. Despite this, Cummings J. applies the infanticide framework in such a way as to allow the complete acquittal of the defendant on the ground that her actions were not wilful – an outcome in direct opposition to the explicit intention of the 1955 amendment. His finding is again consistent with the "left liberal" aspect of the provision, and his acquittal is based on a sympathetic reading of the evidence, which relies on a psychiatric syndrome to mitigate responsibility and which results in an acquittal. The fact of the denial of pregnancy is not interpreted as intent to eventually kill the baby but, rather, as evidence of diminished mental capacity. This assumption was to be reversed in the 1990s.

R. v. Szola (1977) (Appeal of Sentence for Infanticide)

This was a case heard by the Ontario Court of Appeal, and it concerned the appeal of a twelve-month indefinite sentence of imprisonment in an Ontario reformatory following a guilty plea for infanticide. An appeal of the sentence was granted on the basis of mitigating psychiatric evidence, and the question of the punishment's suitability was addressed in relation to the principle of rehabilitation.

In *Szola* the twenty-four-year-old married mother who pled guilty to infanticide had killed her baby by allowing it to drop from her knees to the floor in an effort to get it to stop crying. The case itself may or may not conform to those cases intended to be covered by the infanticide provision.

Here we see the infanticide provision used to secure a homicide conviction without a trial and that results in a carceral sentence. This marks the beginning of a trend in these cases that begins with a charge of second degree murder and ends with a plea arrangement for infanticide. However, given that the baby is killed by accident, the result of the acute stress experienced by a young woman left alone to care for infant twins and a toddler, the infanticide punishment framework is certainly applicable (although, in this case, severe). Even the appeal court noticed the inappropriateness of the infanticide conviction and sentence. Writing for the court, Brooke J.A. noted that each judge was "equally troubled" that there was no appeal of the conviction: "There is no appeal from her conviction, and while each of us is equally troubled in this respect there is no application for us to go behind this plea of guilty and the conviction that was imposed, and so our task lies only with respect to the sentence before us."[52]

The baby killed was the product of a twin birth, and the woman had one other child from marriage that was described as "most difficult" and "strained."[53] Both "marital and social factors"[54] accounted for her severe postpartum depression. Dr. Selwyn Smith, the psychiatrist who examined Szola and provided testimony to the courts, attributed the death to postpartum depression, for which, he argued, the woman should have been hospitalized under the terms of the *Mental Health Act, 1967*, in order to ensure her own safety and the safety of others.[55] This testimony, having had the benefit of hindsight, hints at the lack judgment on the part of medical professionals, family, and friends who would leave a new mother to care for twins and a toddler on her own, especially within the context of a bad marriage. Nevertheless, the discourse used to mitigate the event is entirely psychiatric. Postpartum depression is accused of causing Ms. Szola to have what amounts to "wrong thoughts" about how to quiet the crying twin. The act of dropping the baby on the floor is defined as "wilful" but not as guided by malice aforethought.

Szola's conviction for infanticide flies in the face of the legal principle that persons who suffer from mental illness are not accountable for their actions and, therefore, are not deserving of punishment. Nevertheless, the psychiatric evidence, not required for a conviction in these cases, was likely introduced at the sentencing phase as a means of providing the court with evidence to justify a reduced sentence. On appeal, this evidence is interpreted as proof of non-culpability and justifies a non-carceral disposition and probation.

Szola establishes the punishment framework to be subsequently adopted in cases of this kind. Since the appeal was of the sentence only, the judges were restricted to the question of the length of the sentence and its underlying principle, primarily rehabilitation. According to Brooke J.A.: "Nothing was to be gained in this case from a consideration of deterrence because this woman was very ill, and deterrence obviously was not applicable. What was needed here was to find some solution by which the criminal process, if it was applicable at all, could help this woman, and this could only be achieved through her rehabilitation."[56]

Because the appeal court judges are inclined to reduce the sentence, they highlight the inappropriateness of a carceral disposition. Brooke J.A. concludes:

> This woman has now served some 20 days in jail. This is no place for her and she should not have been sent there. Her children are under the care of a relative. She should be returned to the community immediately so that so far as it is possible her treatment will bring her a cure from her condition, and perhaps one day she can be restored to her family, or her family can be restored to her. My brothers and I have been very seriously concerned about the application of remedies available in this type of procedure. After this anxious concern we have concluded that the proper course would be to set aside the sentence in so far as it requires any term of imprisonment, and to allow a conditional discharge following a term of two years' probation, the terms of which will be in the normal form but the additional terms of which will centre upon the requirement that she continue as long as necessary to have psychiatric assistance.[57]

Even though this case evinces the kind of circumstances legislators likely meant to be encompassed by the new amendment and its provisions, a bona fide source of mitigation operates to remove the homicide entirely from the infanticide framework and, indeed, the criminal legal framework altogether. The events are characterized, much as they were in the late nineteenth century, as a "tragedy,"[58] for which punishment is neither required nor appropriate. Psychiatric testimony regarding postpartum depression operated here much as it did in England following the passage of its infanticide legislation: to mitigate the killing of an infant rather than to secure a conviction. Evidence of postpartum mental disturbance coupled with the difficult mothering conditions experienced by Szola mitigated her responsibility, even though the baby's death was the result not of shame attached to an unwanted pregnancy but, rather, of an irresponsible action on the part of a stressed out woman in a bad marriage. Here we see extra-medical and extra-legal information pertaining to the woman's social circumstances allowing a broadening of the scope of mitigation and being readily picked up on by the courts in order to facilitate a conditional discharge. This is exactly how the provincial courts disposed of earlier infanticide cases. Sociological information qualified the criminal culpability of the defendant in a manner that allowed for her acquittal. However, the deployment of this kind of rationale soon changes when a case is tried before a judge who focuses on the woman's moral responsibility to the baby.[59]

R. v. Del Rio (1979) (Infanticide)

In *R. v. Del Rio,*[60] the Supreme Court of Ontario, as it was then called (Banks 1983), reaffirmed the principles set out in the 1954 amendment establishing its purpose in law; that is, that the psychiatric elements as outlined by McRuer J. in *Marchello*[61] and rearticulated in the *Hansard* record[62] were "not essential" elements for conviction.[63] Here the case illustrates the direct intention of the amendment. All that was required for a conviction was the establishment of wilful intent. *Del Rio* is the final reported case in the 1970s and the first to rely solely on section 590 to justify both a conviction and punishment for infanticide. Unlike in both *Smith* and *Szola*, in *Del Rio* the court entirely rejected any discussion of mitigation based on childbirth or lactation, and concerned itself entirely with the question of the defendant's "will." Unlike the court in *Smith*, where it was argued that both sections must be read in sequence, the court in *Del Rio* considered no psychiatric evidence because it was deemed irrelevant and therefore unnecessary for a conviction (and it is unclear from the decision whether any such evidence was offered by the defence).

Del Rio was indicted on a charge of infanticide following the death of her two-month-old daughter under suspicious circumstances pointing to intentional violence. Neighbours provided evidence to the police suggesting child abuse because they had heard the mother express rage and make comments such as "If you don't shut up I'll kill you" and "shut up you little bitch, you're a bitch all right."[64]

She is described as twice married and twice divorced, with three children from two marriages. The two-month-old infant who died had suffered from a common stomach problem that caused her to vomit and cry more often than usual, and this condition required frequent hospitalization.[65] This evidence appears not to operate in the mother's favour or in the old nineteenth-century manner (i.e., to mitigate responsibility by illustrating dire circumstances). In fact, it appears to perform the opposite, suggesting further culpability given the mother's duty of care owed to a sick child. Evidence of particular interest to the court was provided by the defendant's sister, who suggested that the baby was the result of an unwanted pregnancy. According to the sister's evidence, Del Rio had expressed concern about being pregnant a third time, saying that it was "probably not a good idea to have this baby, that it was dumb to get pregnant and the only reason she got pregnant was to keep her husband."[66] Her sister further indicated that when she looked after the baby she had no trouble feeding her but that when her sister fed her she had difficulty. According to the sister, Del Rio "would become angry [with the baby] and slap her everywhere."[67] Furthermore, Del Rio's sister told the court that Del Rio had told her that "it was a pain to have the baby and that she didn't want it after it was born, and that on occasion when she was wakened up and it wasn't a feeding time and the baby cried, her mother would slap her on the mouth and tell her to go to sleep."[68] Additionally, the defendant at one point, when talking to a public health nurse, described the infant as possibly "retarded." The nurse, however, believed the child to be bright, alert, and active.[69]

Evidence from both a neighbour and the forensic pathologist established for the court that the child had suffered physical and emotional abuse. Dr. Rieckenberg, the pathologist who performed the autopsy at the request of the coroner, discovered bruises on the infant's head and "a small haemorrhage in the white of the right eye and a scratch on the left side of the neck." And x-rays of the skull "showed several fractures, with a major fracture line running from ear to ear, split or forked at each end" – evidence that helped support the Crown's assertion that this was a case of intentional child abuse homicide.[70] The cause of death was determined to be "subarachnoid haemorrage."[71]

The evidence provided by Del Rio's sister, the neighbours, and the report of the forensic pathologist established that the infant died from intentional "wilful" violence and raised the obvious question of the applicability of the infanticide provision. None of the nineteenth-century elements of infanticide is present, nor is there any suggestion of postpartum depression. The difficulties faced by the single mother of three are taken as evidence not of dire circumstances beyond her control but, rather, of both her own culpability and of being a "bad" mother.

In *Del Rio* Judge Cromarty relies on the definition of evil intent outlined in *R. v. Smith* to arrive at the conclusion that the act was wilful and that the Crown had met its burden of proof. Moreover, "wilful" is defined, following *Smith*, as "something more than a voluntary or intentional act. It included the idea of an act intentionally done with a bad motive or purpose or, as it is otherwise expressed, with an evil intent."[72] In direct contrast to the deliberations in *Smith*, in *Del Rio* the issue of childbirth and lactation and its effects are irrelevant to the judgment.[73] Notwithstanding the intention of mid-century legislators, an obviously much broader scope of circumstances is included under the charge of infanticide, facilitated in part by the removal of the requirement to prove distressed circumstances. What is striking about this decision is the absence of discussion about poverty or marginalization. Nowhere is there any discussion of the difficulties faced by a lone mother raising three infants in straitened circumstances. The idea that social forces are somehow implicated in these circumstances and should therefore mitigate the crime is entirely absent.

The removal of the psychiatric elements of infanticide, along with the individualization of maternal responsibility, had the effect of ensuring a conviction. This 1978 context, in which a young mother is socially isolated, certainly fits the contours of the infanticide provision, particularly since, in 1955, the punishment framework was expanded to encompass more blameworthy circumstances. The malicious intentionality ascribed to the woman's actions was derived from a range of mutually reinforcing discursive constructions taken up in law in order to secure a conviction. Del Rio was described as a "bad" mother from the start: because she was ambivalent about the third pregnancy; because she was unable to stay married; because she used foul language toward her baby; and, finally, because she had been physically violent. The socio-economic factors in this case were constructed in such a way as to incline one to believe that Del Rio was capable of child abuse murder precisely because she was a "bad" wife and mother: her poverty and her single motherhood were her own fault. This evidence was buttressed by the forensic evidence of child abuse, with violence being proof of evil intention. Unlike her nineteenth-century sisters, Del Rio could no longer rely on any kind of "sociological imagination" to mitigate her crime. She was found guilty as charged and remanded out of custody until sentencing.

Del Rio foreshadows the concern voiced in the 1990s by the Office of the Chief Coroner for Ontario when it tried to have the infanticide law abolished through legislative amendment. It provides an example of the kinds of deaths of babies, later diagnosed as "shaken baby syndrome," that get taken up by the Coroner's Office for intensive investigation and criminal law response. Taken out of its historical and sociological context, infanticide law certainly operated here to "excuse" the legally wilful and violent actions of the accused, but none of her socially straitened circumstances played an overt role in mitigating her intentionality.

Canadian Cases in the 1990s

R. v. A.P.P. (1992) (Infanticide)[74]

In this case, a twenty-four-year-old Armenian woman killed her newborn baby when she threw it out a window. The infant suffered a fractured skull and hemorrhaging, which resulted in its death. A.P.P. was at first charged with second degree murder, but this charge was reduced to infanticide in exchange for a guilty plea. Here we see a case that entirely conforms to late nineteenth-century and early twentieth-century circumstances of maternal neonaticide, in which the Crown settled on the serious murder charge. While it is not evident from the trial record, this practice conforms with the established practice, in which the more serious charge is laid in anticipation of a plea bargain for a lesser conviction.[75] In keeping with its law and order approach, the Crown requests a carceral disposition to be served in the Ontario correctional system.

The event is framed as "a tragedy for all concerned,"[76] and the defendant is described as suffering from "pregnancy denial" and of fearing being ostracized from her close-knit Armenian community.[77] In part because the report centres on sentencing, it highlights a range of information that relieves, rather than exacerbates, her culpability. For example, psychiatric evidence of pregnancy denial is provided to the court by Dr. Ben-Aron, who examined A.P.P. while she was involuntarily confined to a psychiatric facility under section 7 of the *Mental Heath Act* for two weeks following the baby's death. She is described as of good moral character: she is smart, hardworking, and has strong ties to her family, which is well respected within the Armenian community. Being pregnant and unwed placed her in an untenable position. In fact, the pregnancy denial is, much like the nineteenth-century trope, described in terms of her attempting to maintain her good moral character and by hiding her shame.[78] According to Dr. Ben-Aron's evaluation: "Her need to deny being pregnant, first and foremost to herself and then to her family and friends, was powerfully motivated. Within the tight-knit community to which she and her family belong, the disclosure of her being pregnant and unwed would have been so hurtful to them, would have been socially and emotionally devastating."[79]

According to the presiding judge, Vaillancourt J., A.P.P.'s act was motivated not by evil intent toward the baby but, rather, by virtue and love for her parents:

> A. loved her parents and could not disclose the pregnancy because it would have been so hurtful to them, and she would not have been able to cope with inflicting such pain. Instead, she mentally denied the reality in her own mind – lying to herself, and effectively lying to her friends and family by not saying anything to them about being pregnant. Even after the birth of her child, her denial was so powerful that when asked by the staff at the [hospital] about whether or not she was pregnant, she continued to deny it. This, even in the fact of physical evidence to the contrary. So effective had been the denial that she had obliterated the reality of the pregnancy from her mind.[80]

As in the early twentieth-century infanticide tropes, in which pregnancy is concealed in an effort to hide one's shame, A.P.P.'s actions are portrayed as virtuous and, therefore, criminally excusable. Furthermore, her action is characterized as directed by a "mental force" (both internal and external) that compelled her to kill the baby at birth and that constructed her as "not responsible" for its death. According to the psychiatric evidence adduced at sentencing:

She remembers seeing a lot of blood and seeing the baby, and feeling as if she were functioning under the control of a mental force within her, but which felt distinct from her. She felt as if she were acting under direction when she took the baby to the window and put it outside. There was no sense in her of the reality of what was happening or the true significance of her actions. She felt as if she were doing something that she was supposed to be doing. It was as if there was a force inside her, directing her to put the child outside and, at the same time, giving her permission to do so, reassuring her that what she was doing was exactly what she was supposed to do and that what she was doing was alright.[81]

In this case, the modernized psychiatric discourse of irresponsibility and denial is described in terms of a dissociative episode in which the mother believes her actions are benevolent. Her intent is couched in terms of "good" rather than "evil." On these grounds, and the grounds that neither retribution nor deterrence were necessary, Vaillancourt J. issued a suspended sentence and probation of a period of three years, during which time A.P.P. was required to conform to the standard demands of a probation order and to continue psychotherapy.[82]

R. v. Lalli (1993) (Manslaughter and Infanticide)[83]
This case, heard at the provincial court level in British Columbia in 1993 before de Villiers J., is an instance in which a defence counsel attempts to get his client tried on a charge of manslaughter in the hope that he could secure an acquittal of this serious charge, which, on the principle of double jeopardy, would result in no further action being brought against the defendant.[84] However, de Villiers J. recognized his request as a "ploy on the part of defence counsel" and ordered Lalli to be tried on both charges. De Villiers J. quotes section 662(1) of the *Criminal Code* to explain that manslaughter and infanticide are mutually exclusive charges and that substitute convictions for either are only possible on an initial charge of murder.[85] The judge further concludes, quite rightly, that "the express inclusion of manslaughter and infanticide in the offence of murder, in subsection (3), coupled with the omission of any provision for the inclusion of infanticide in manslaughter or of manslaughter in infanticide in that section, fortifies the conclusion that Parliament did not intend to include infanticide in the offence of manslaughter or vice versa."[86]

Nor, however, did Parliament intend for women suspected of killing newly born babies to be tried on charges of both manslaughter and infanticide. As the debate described above shows, the intention of legislators, particularly with the amendments adopted in 1955, was only partially to widen the scope of circumstances that could be tried under the infanticide provision.[87] The main intention was to deal with the evidentiary burden faced by the

Crown identified in *Marchello*. However, quite at odds with the intentions of Parliament, de Villiers J. ordered Lalli to stand trial on charges of both manslaughter and infanticide on the basis that she wilfully killed her baby and that she should have foreseen the harm caused as a result of her actions.

The circumstances in the case are perhaps the very ones legislators meant to encompass when they augmented the punishment framework and removed the Crown's burden to prove the reproductive mental element. The circumstances here are widened to the extent that the three-week-old baby died from violence at the hands of its mother. Lalli was accused of killing her apparently "unwanted" baby by shaking it and causing it to die from a subdural haemorrhage. The court noted that the accused "did not want [the baby], and contemplated an abortion before the birth." The accused was described as suffering from postpartum depression exacerbated by her domestic circumstances, which were marked by a "callous and indifferent husband." She was treated as a "domestic servant" by her husband's relatives and was characterized as "culturally more refined than they were and she was lonely and without friends in an alien country."[88] None of these social, economic, or cultural specificities was taken as mitigating the circumstances of the death, and Lalli was held fully accountable. According to de Villiers J., none of the psychiatric and medical evidence is relevant to the court (in fact, he indicated that it wasted two days of the court's time, which could have been used to try other people!).

Her action is characterized as intentional and wilful: "the accused knew her actions would cause serious harm to her baby, but she wilfully carried them out."[89] Couched in terms of evil intent, the baby's death is compared to the death in *Smith*, where the accused placed her hand over the baby's mouth to prevent it from crying. According to de Villiers, placing a hand over a baby's mouth to prevent it from crying and, thereby, smothering it is distinctly "unintentional," while shaking a baby to stop it from crying is wholly intentional and preventable. According to his rationale, the mother in the latter instance should have known her actions would cause the baby's death, while the mother in the former instance could not have foreseen the death – so her actions were "accidental."[90] The fact that Lalli is said to have "contemplated abortion" is apparent evidence of her evil intent since contemplating abortion "proves" that the born-alive baby was "unwanted" and expendable, as though, to Lalli, a foetus and a live baby were the same thing. Contemplation of abortion, along with physical violence, operated in this case as culpatory evidence of intentional homicide. Lurking behind this evidence is a strong anti-abortion sentiment that holds that anyone who contemplates abortion is inherently evil and a potential killer. Here we see an absolute reversal of assumption. Now, evidence that the baby is subjectively "unwanted" does not mitigate responsibility, as it did in the late nineteenth and early twentieth centuries. The married woman-mother is assumed to be wholly responsible for the pregnancy, despite familial cultural values, and therefore as acting with malice when she kills the baby. Here again we see the kind of case in which law and order advocates contend that infanticide law allows women to "get away with murder." The circumstances do not fit with the requirements of a manslaughter charge, and it is very likely that an infanticide conviction was secured (although not reported).

R. v. Peters (1995) (Sentencing Manslaughter)[91]

In 1993 the Crown initially responded to this very high profile "murder" case with a charge of second degree murder.[92] The circumstances of this case conformed to early twentieth-century practice of charging infanticide rather than second degree murder. At trial, the murder charge was withdrawn in exchange for a plea of guilt for manslaughter. According to the case report: "The 26-year-old accused was unmarried, lived with her parents and was of low intelligence. She was diagnosed as having serious psychiatric problems. She had no criminal record and had a good employment history. She had spent 21 months in pre-trial custody at a psychiatric hospital."[93] The circumstances of the unattended birth and subsequent homicide also conformed to infanticide: "The offender gave birth, without assistance, to a full term or close thereto child in the family bathroom. Other members of the family were in the house but were unaware of the birth and were said to be unaware of the pregnancy. While unattended in the bathroom for several hours, the offender used a pair of scissors to inflict multiple stab wounds on the newborn. The fatal wounds severed the spinal column."[94]

In contrast to cases in which the events are described as a "tragedy" for all concerned, and in which sympathy for the mother's circumstances are included in the judgment, the death of the victim-baby is central to Donnolly J.'s acutely ahistorical moralistic judgment, which included a two-year period of psychiatric incarceration: "No mitigating factors are found in the crime itself. The killing of a newborn offends the laws of mankind [sic] and nature. It is beyond the outer limits of perversity and shame. Universal denunciation is the instinctive response. The aggravating factors are the gravity of taking a human life and the absolute vulnerability and dependency of the victim."[95]

Undeterred, Donnolly J. further enhances his puritanical response to the infant's death: "This crime against nature bespeaks some type of derangement. The killing is beyond comprehension. The manner of killing is inscrutable. Even if the killing had to happen, the manner of killing adds another dimension to horror. The basic facts of the killing and its mode call for psychiatric assessment and treatment as a condition of any custodial

term. The proposed recommendation for psychiatric treatment is also reasonable, having regard to the offender's seemingly limited capacity to com-
prehend such a foul and abnormal crime."[96]

Constituted as an inscrutable crime against nature beyond comprehension that "bespeaks some type of derangement," the psychiatric evidence in
this case has no relevance to the judge's understanding and does not mitigate the crime itself. The killing is considered acutely pathological, but the
pathology does not, in this case, mitigate culpability for the homicide. In
fact, "society must be protected" from women like Peters, who, although
she served her sentence in a psychiatric facility, is given one of the longest
sentences (twenty-one months plus two years) in the history of cases of
maternal neonaticide.

There is little doubt that the violence inflicted on the body of the infant
is central to the condemnation of this homicide. However, this level of violence is not unusual in cases of maternal neonaticide and has often been
described as a "dissociative mental reaction" to the birth of the child. This
occurs because the pregnancy is denied, as was the case in *R. v. A.P.P.*[97] and
in many of the early twentieth-century cases of maternal neonaticide (prior
to the removal of the requirement to consider the effects of childbirth and
lactation).[98]

The right-to-life rhetoric in the *Peters* case has the particular effect of positioning the infant as a bona fide victim entitled to society's full legal protection, particularly from mothers of "low intellectual capacity." In this
case, the mother's punishment was rationalized as providing protection to
the victim by deterring "like-minded potential wrongdoers" through establishing a "fear of punishment." This despite the many years of judicial decisions establishing that general deterrence is unnecessary in these cases.[99]
Moreover, both the characterization of the crime and punitive response are
couched in terms of a universal moral condemnation of maternal neonaticide
through the legal trope of "perspective of the community." The judicial
appeal to community serves to reinforce a kind of moral order in which
maternal neonaticide is universally viewed as evil. This idea shifts the understanding considerably from a place where maternal neonaticide is viewed
as the consequence of structurally induced social pressures (the united tropes
of the callous rogue, the illegitimate baby, and the single mother hiding her
shame) to a place where maternal neonaticide is perceived as a "crime against
nature." In the late twentieth century maternal neonaticide is constructed,
in certain cases, as universally "offensive" and "perverse," an offence not
just to secular law but to the laws of "nature" and "mankind" as well. Within
this framework the infant-victim is the distinct object of a unique kind of
sentiment: she/he is an individual deserving of all the rights and freedoms
granted by a liberal legal framework. Finally, in some of the cases reported
in the 1990s, we see the emergence of a discursive framework within which

a preoccupation with the protection of victim-baby further replaces an earlier compassion for mothers who find themselves in tragic circumstances and enhances the idea of an infant's inherent right to life.

R. v. Gorrill (1995) (Appeal of Nine-Month Carceral Sentence for Infanticide)[100]

Once again, the facts in this case conform to the late nineteenth- and early twentieth-century legal descriptions of maternal neonaticide, for which the infanticide law was intended. The accused, aged twenty, gave birth unattended in her parents' home. She was described as an intelligent honours student in her last years of high school, and she had won a scholarship to the University of New Brunswick. Following the birth, Gorrill's sister discovered her lying unconscious in the hallway of their home, and the baby was later discovered dead underneath the covers of Gorrill's bed. The placenta and blood-soaked scissors were also discovered in Gorrill's room. The autopsy determined that the baby was born alive, full term, and had been asphyxiated by its mother.[101]

At Gorrill's trial on a charge of infanticide, the jury determined that the baby died from "wilful omission" rather than from a "wilful act"; that, during her pregnancy, the accused demonstrated a "callous disregard for life" (because she wanted an abortion), and that she suffered no mental disturbance requiring hospitalization.[102] In the court's consideration of the appeal of the nine-month sentence, Pugsley J.A., writing for the appeal court, agreed with the trial judge, who emphasized general deterrence by arguing that "*pregnant persons* cannot just let newly born human beings die in these circumstances" (emphasis added).[103] This legally enforced duty of care owed to the newborn stands in stark contrast to earlier cases, in which concern for the infant is entirely absent. In this case, Gorrill is entirely responsible for both the pregnancy and birth (even though the father, some twenty years her senior, knew about the upcoming birth) and is wholly obligated to ensure the infant's continuing survival. Her failure to protect the infant's right to life is part of the broader discursive framework within which the details of the case are narrated. She is described as exhibiting "complete lack of affection for the unwanted child," evidence submitted by the Crown to show her "betrayal of the core behaviour values of the community" and to exacerbate her culpability.[104]

All psychiatric evidence (both psychosis and disassociation are rejected) is put to use not as mitigating evidence but, rather, as evidence of Gorrill's selfishness in concealing the pregnancy and birth from her family. According to the trial judge, Ms. Gorrill was "motivated more by a desire to keep the pregnancy and the birth a secret from her family than any form of disassociation disorder."[105] Pregnancy denial, in this case, no longer operates to mitigate responsibility but, rather, enhances it because the mother is expected to "want" the baby simply due to the inherent value of infant human life. In this case, the scheming woman, whose actions "are that of a determined woman,"[106] replaces the tragic maiden in distress. Rather than viewing Gorrill's desire to hide her pregnancy as the act of a caring woman motivated by a desire to prevent bringing shame upon her family, the appeal court views it as a way of constructing her as an evil, selfish woman who failed to protect the life of her innocent baby. Gorrill is further described as "artful," "manipulative," and an unreliable witness in her own defence precisely because of her "wilful" denial of her pregnancy.[107]

A key feature of this appeal court decision is the distinctive, and highly problematic, distortion of feminist legal academic literature to justify moral concern for the infant-victim. First, relying on Backhouse (1984, 447-48) to support the idea that "society's attitude has changed substantially in the last 80 years"[108] in relation to thoughts about infant life, the judge goes on to highlight an notion taken (out of context) from well known psychiatric and criminological academics who support the claim that psychiatric illness mitigates maternal neonaticide (Maier-Katkin and Ogle 1993, 903). In contrast to their intent, the judge uses their ideas to argue that "infanticide is 'among the most disquieting of crimes, at least to the sensibilities of the modern world, in which standards of civilization are generally associated with the protection of the defenceless and innocent.'"[109] In addition, and to justify the court's affirmation of the nine-month sentence, Pugsley J.A. points to the 1954 amendment raising the punishment from three to five years as evidence of society's moral disapprobation with regard to maternal neonaticide and argues that a failure to impose a carceral sentence would "inadequately reflect society's view of the gravity of this crime."[110] This appropriation of academic research and legal knowledge is not particularly unique for an appeal court decision; however, what *is* unique is the way in which this research is used to advance the rhetorical notion that society as a whole (including the researchers and legislators cited) advocate the kind of right-to-life argument advanced both by the trial judge and the appeal court.

The final two cases reported in the 1990s come from the Quebec courts. In these decisions we see a marked difference in the responses from the Quebec court and in those from the courts of Ontario and New Brunswick.

R. v. Guimont (1999) (Appeal of Conviction for Murder)
The Quebec Court of Appeal allowed the appeal and ordered a new trial in this case, when the lower court judge refused to instruct the jury that it might bring in a conviction for infanticide under section 662(3) of the *Criminal Code*. In this case, an eighteen-year-old woman was charged with murder after she smothered her ten-month-old son with a pillow. The woman, who was living with her parents at the time of the killing, was diagnosed as

suffering from a form of manic depression that was exacerbated by the birth of the child. The jury convicted the woman of manslaughter following a trial during which they heard expert opinion as to the accused's mental state – opinion that likely caused them to find for the lesser conviction. The decision itself deals directly with the procedural issues in relation to murder, manslaughter, infanticide, and mental disturbance as mitigating intentionality.

The lower court instructed the jury that it might only substitute manslaughter and did not allow them to consider the offence of infanticide as a lesser included offence under section section 662(3). According to the judgment, a manslaughter verdict would have required the jury to conclude that mental disturbance negated the specific intent to kill, whereas an infanticide verdict would only have required it to conclude that mental disturbance was present at the time of the killing and that it was related to the birth of the baby.[111] According to the Quebec Court of Appeal,

> The specificity of the offence resides in the fact that a link must be established between the mental disturbance and the birth of the child or lactation: it is not a requirement that the act itself is caused by the mental disturbance, it is sufficient that "her (the mother's) mind is then disturbed" (s.233). It is a question of reduced responsibility on the part of a woman who [translation] "causes the death of her new-born child while she is in the grip of mental disturbance caused by the birth," as professors Fortin and Viau have described. In the same vein, the writers Grant, Chunn and Boyle specify, correctly, that "the only causal connection the section requires is between childbirth/lactation and the mental disturbance. There is an implicit assumption that if a woman with disturbed mind kills her child, the disturbance is what led to the killing."[112]

The legislator presumes in a way that the mental disturbance connected to the birth caused the murder.

The situation is otherwise if the issue of mental disturbance is not raised in relation to infanticide, as in this case. The trial judge refused to put the verdict of infanticide to the jury; the appellant was, however, able to invoke her mental disturbance to negative the specific intention required for a finding of guilty of murder, in support of her claim that the crime was manslaughter. In that case, the mental disturbance must be causative, in the sense that it must be the mental disturbance which prevents the formation of the required specific intention; the mental disturbance might not be related to the birth but is must be causally related to homicide, which, as indicated above, distinguishes it from the offence of infanticide.[113]

In summary, in order to conclude that manslaughter occurred, the jury had to decide that the mental disturbance *affected* the appellant to the point of neutralizing her intention to kill, whereas for a verdict of infanticide, it was sufficient if the jury concluded that the mental disturbance, *present* at the time of the killing, was related to the birth. In this case, even if the jury rejected the thesis of mental disturbance causally related to the homicide, nothing prevented it from concluding that a mental disturbance related to the birth existed and was present at the time of the homicide, without nevertheless being causally connected to the homicide.[114]

Guimont sets out, in the clearest possible terms, the manner in which the infanticide provision is meant to operate in relation to murder and manslaughter, and as a lesser included provision to both. Here we see the development of the prosecutorial strategy of attempting to secure a conviction for the murder and being thwarted by a jury that refuses to convict. Later, the prosecutorial aims are thwarted by the Court of Appeal, when an appeal is allowed and a new trial is ordered. Both the psychiatric evidence *and* the procedural difficulties continue to prevent the authorities from securing the most serious convictions in cases where the circumstances are now deemed more blameworthy than the were in nineteenth-century scenarios.

R. c. *Lucas* (1999) (Infanticide and Concealment of Birth)[115]

In 1999 the provincial court of Quebec acquitted thirty-two-year-old Natalie Lucas of infanticide and concealment of birth for the death of her newly born baby. Madame Lucas concealed her pregnancy from her boyfriend, who was the father of the baby, and their families and friends, and she eventually gave birth alone in the bathroom of her boyfriend's parents' home. She was described as obese, which contributed to the ease with which she concealed the pregnancy from her boyfriend, Pierre Lefebvre. Lucas claimed that the baby was bluish and not moving when it was fully born and that the umbilical cord was wrapped around its neck. The baby did not cry or move. After cleaning the bathroom (with the baby in her arms) she placed it in a plastic bag and then in a backpack but had no intention of hiding its body.[116]

Medical evidence provided by the forensic specialist who conducted the autopsy, Dr. Claude Pothel, indicated that the baby had breathed for a certain time; however, he could not confirm whether the breathing had occurred while the baby's body was still in the birth canal or whether it breathed after the umbilical cord had been severed and once it had proceeded in a living state from the mother's body. There was no evidence of trauma or suffering, but there were signs of cyanosis, suggesting a lack of oxygen.[117]

Psychiatric testimony provided by Dr. Renée Fugère suggested that Lucas lacked the will to live, thus negating any intent to kill. Dr. Fugère argued that Lucas was socially isolated, that her relationship with her boyfriend was in conflict, and that there was little likelihood of any resolution of the difficulties. Lucas had recently experienced the death of her godfather and, at the same time, her professional responsibilities at work had been augmented, which caused her significant frustration. The psychiatrist concluded that these social factors contributed to an emotional detachment that facilitated the concealment of the pregnancy and birth, thus negating her will entirely. The fact that Lucas did not request any assistance before or during the birth, when she was hemorrhaging and near death, suggested to Fugère that she could not have formed the requisite *mens rea* for a homicide conviction. Obstetrical evidence provided at trial by Dr. Donald David indicated that the foetus was poorly positioned at birth and that birth itself was very swift, resulting in very strong and rapid contractions. According to his testimony, this scenario might have caused the baby to be deprived of oxygen during the birth. In addition, the mother experienced placenta previa, which caused her to haemorrage and to become extremely weak.

None of the medical or extra-legal evidence in this case functioned to aggravate suspicions of Madame Lucas's intentionality. As a consequence of her failure to ask for help following the birth, she was understood as being utterly *without will*. Evidence that she had received an abortion when she was nineteen suggested that she had considered what it means to raise a baby as a single parent.[118] Overall, the forensic evidence was inconclusive, and the judge could not find that the baby had died as a result of any intentionality on the Lucas's part since it could not be established that the baby had been born alive. The difficult and unattended birth, coupled with the evidence provided by the accused, did not allow the Crown to meet its burden.

The sociological evidence informally provided to the court, through Dr. Fugère's testimony, allowed the judge to understand Lucas's experience in those terms rather than seeing her as suffering from any psychological or psychiatric illness. The court was convinced that Lucas was taken by surprise by childbirth and that she did not intend either to kill the baby or to conceal its birth. She is acquitted of infanticide on these grounds and is further acquitted of concealment because, for both circumstances, there lacked the required legal evidence (mental disturbance and intent to conceal) for convictions. The death of Lucas's baby was seen as the result of an "error in judgment" rather than as a malevolent or malicious act.[119] The outcome in this case differs from those in many others in large part because the testimony provided to the court by Dr. Fugère helped to put the woman's experience within a social context, thereby mitigating her responsibility for both offences. The outcome in the Lucas case echoes those of the late nineteenth and early twentieth centuries, where infant deaths are understood as the product of misguided actions firmly located within a social context rather than as being the product of an organic mental illness or evil intent.

Through this discussion of legislative debate and reported legal cases I show that, over the course of the twentieth century, responsibility for maternal neonaticide has shifted from an act understood in relation to socioeconomic disadvantage, to an act understood as a psychiatric disorder produced by the effects of childbirth and lactation, to an act understood as being unjustifiable because the infant-victim has a "right-to-life" that the courts must protect.[120] These developments can be located more broadly in a range of social and legal reforms augmenting the status of both women and infants, and they can be viewed as part of a shift from a discourse of "tragedy" (focused on the mother) to a discourse of "humanitarianism" (focused on the baby). The tragedy discourse of the late nineteenth and early twentieth centuries viewed unwanted motherhood in compassionate terms, linking the causes of maternal neonaticide to the limited availability of birth control and abortion, to illegitimacy, and to seduction. While these sociological factors were a part of the psychiatric discourse on the insanities pertaining to pregnancy, childbirth, and lactation, they also functioned to provide an individualized explanation for maternal neonaticide. When the 1954-55 *Criminal Code* amendment removed the necessity to prove reproductive mental disorder, the view of the individual as influenced by her socio-economic circumstances, a product of established psychiatric discourse, was replaced by an overt concern for the infant's right to legal protection as expressed in "right-to-life" rhetoric. The reported legal cases discussed here demonstrate a more or less steady progression toward the "responsibilization" of mothers and an accompanying discourse in which the legitimately "unwanted" baby disappears. As I show in the next chapter, this trajectory of responses is also connected to the forensic medical discovery of "child abuse" and to the broad augment about the valuation of human infant life (partly as a result of a broad right-to-life discourse that regulates maternal neonaticides throughout the 1990s).

5
Vengeance for the Innocents: The New Medico-Legal Designation of "Infanticide" as "Child Abuse Homicide"

This chapter examines cases of infant death investigated by the Ontario Office of the Coroner between 1980 and 1998 in order to analyze the medico-legal processes whereby many, if not most, infant deaths investigated by coroners have come to be regarded as undetected incidents of "child abuse homicide." I show that significant kinds of regulatory practices and categories of deviance emerge from certain historical events that are unrelated to the events or processes subsequently subject to regulation. My approach is closest to what is described as a Foucauldian feminist approach. Here I want to draw attention to the consequences of law and order approaches that resort to criminal law as a means of solving what are essentially problems with broad social antecedents and that defend the use of the infanticide provision despite its apparent medicalization of deviance. One of the central organizing arguments advanced here is that critical criminologists and socio-legal theorists should not be too quick to describe patterns of regulation as inevitable outcomes of patriarchal capitalism. What I show is that these kinds of overarching theoretical formulations are often inapplicable because the development of regulatory categories and criminal law is open and contingent and outcomes are often unpredictable. In the case of the development of the law of infanticide (which governed maternal neonaticide in the early twentieth century) and its current application by the courts, a very complex series of historical events (with ironic outcomes and unintended consequences) can be critically examined from a perspective that attends to the ways in which regulatory categories are operationalized by agents of the state. And it can be further analyzed in terms of the effects of these events on the women to whom the regulatory category applies. In other words, the *effects* of regulatory categories and laws should remain firmly in view, as should the seemingly oppressive historical conditions from whence they came.

In the late twentieth and early twenty-first centuries maternal neonaticide is recast in terms of criminal responsibility requiring punishment under criminal law. A variety of reforms in law and in public sensibility have resulted in the overall elevation of the status of the ex-nuptial infant and its unwilling mother: the reform of inheritance laws intended to prevent illegitimacy and its socially unacceptable counterpart – single motherhood; the decriminalization, and subsequent access to, contraception and abortion; the symbolic rise in the legal status of the infant due, in part, to the political tactics of the anti-choice movement (which displayed pictures of a foetus in utero in order to garner sympathy for the idea that abortion is akin to killing a live-birth human being). Finally, media reports of maternal neonaticide now tend to refer to these incidents as "dumpster babies," implying that the women who put them there think of these unwanted babies as garbage rather than admitting that they are plainly attempting to conceal their sexual activity, pregnancy, and subsequent act of giving birth.

In this context, official responses to maternal neonaticide using the infanticide provision have been broadened to include punishment using family law provisions and harsh criminal charges.[1] This chapter draws attention to the role played by medico-legal authorities, specifically coroners, whose authority to define or reinterpret a cause of death finding can influence police and Crown attorneys in their decisions about whether or not to charge and prosecute persons (typically mothers) with a particular criminal offence.

An analysis of Ontario coroners' case files pertaining to infant deaths shows how coroners, police, and Crown attorneys have come to approach the prosecution of maternal neonaticide within the context of other kinds of homicide typically constructed as child abuse murder, and how, in light of a perceived failure of the criminal justice and child welfare systems to prevent these deaths and to punish the perpetrators, infanticide cases are now responded to in a decidedly more punitive fashion than previously. Within this broader socio-legal context, the *Criminal Code* infanticide provision has become academically unfashionable and is now only rarely preferred as a criminal charge. Infanticide is no longer a popular category since it is now only used to define a baby killed under the narrowest of circumstances. As is seen in this and the following chapter, "plea arrangements" from women charged with second degree murder or manslaughter are typically accepted by Crown attorneys for the lesser charge of infanticide with regard to cases of infant killing that clearly do not conform to the aims of the *Criminal Code* infanticide provision.

I begin by mapping the rise of what is known as a child abuse discourse, from its emergence in the mid-twentieth century, when it was identified as a "new" phenomenon, to its contemporary position as the dominant paradigm through which virtually all childhood suffering, and certainly all child homicides, are apprehended. I thus explore a significant historical shift in the criminal justice regulation of maternal neonaticide. Canadian authorities historically constructed maternal neonaticide as a "device of last resort" for desperate young women, but they now construct it as the wholly willed and wicked act of an abusive violent mother despite the fact that some of the cultural conditions that prompt maternal neonaticide persist. The regulation of maternal neonaticide as child abuse homicide has resulted in a flawed reconceptualization of these kinds of deaths as "child abuse homicide." Infanticide-type deaths bear no social or legal connection to the professional designation "child abuse," which is generally understood by the child protection movement to be a dysfunctional social relation between a caregiver and a small child. Babies killed at birth have not yet had any social relation with their caregivers and generally live no more than a few seconds before they are killed or left to die. Until now, this event, defined as infanticide since the early seventeenth century in England and since the eighteenth and nineteenth centuries in Canada and the United States, has never been considered a form of child abuse. In fact, many infant deaths are difficult for authorities to figure out. They remain without clear causes and are typically classified as "unexplained" or "sudden infant deaths"; but these designations are now often suspected of masking child abuse and, under the Office of the Coroner, warrant extensive investigation and surveillance of single women on the part of social workers, police, and forensic pathologists. Child abuse homicide is targeted for a first or second degree murder charge, with the mothers often the prime suspects, despite the fact that causes of death remain vague. The changes in how cases of infant death are scrutinized by agents of the criminal justice system have had a significant impact on the eventual outcomes of a range of cases caught up in a web of fears about undetected child abuse in North America and elsewhere (Best 1990; Jenks 1996; Scheper-Hughes and Stein 1987).

In the first section of this chapter I describe the discovery and medicalization of child abuse in North America and the United Kingdom in the broadest terms: the identification of child abuse as a significant social problem – one that should be of special concern to forensic pathologists. In the second section I describe the development of the medico-legal concept of "battered baby syndrome" and its variant, "shaken baby syndrome," and the implementation of child death review teams as a means of identifying and/or preventing "missed" incidents of these syndromes. I illustrate Hacking's (1995, 56) point that child abuse is always "discovered" after sensational (or sensationalized) incidents. In other words, vile behaviour toward children, or "child abuse[,] has been with us always" but required "inventing new descriptions [and] providing new ways to see old acts – and a great deal of social agitation" before it became an object of investigation and social action (55). Research conducted at the Office of the Chief Coroner demonstrates how new descriptions/interpretations of infanticide are invented by medico-legal authorities and are then publicized by the press, providing the public with "new ways of seeing old acts" (55).

In the third section I provide an illustration of this process within a contemporary context. Here, I discuss a press campaign mounted in the *Toronto Star* designed to highlight cases of infant homicide that the newspaper columnists considered to be examples of "women getting away with murder." I show how closely this campaign was linked to the activities of the Office of the Chief Coroner. These activities included the establishment of a number of high-profile inquests as well as a broad campaign to influence the public and, especially, legislators and those responsible for child protection policy about undetected and under-prosecuted cases of child abuse homicide. This campaign had its counterpart at the federal level in the establishment of a broad consultation process that included the consideration of amendments to the *Criminal Code* framework governing infant homicides.

Certain law and order advocates have misconstrued infanticide as a kind of child abuse and have consequently responded to the practice as child abuse homicide, resulting in attempts to convict very vulnerable young women for first and second degree murder. This response to infanticide is largely justified in the name of the "innocent" baby, who has emerged as the latest rights-bearing victim in Canadian criminal and family law. The research discussed here shows how a heightened moral condemnation of child abuse resulted in augmented criminal law responses to infanticide, particularly on the part of coroners, police, and social workers. These various agents rely on reports submitted by only a few forensic pathologists who specialize in the identification of child abuse homicide. Many of these reports actually defined child abuse as an official cause of death for infants who were killed or died shortly following unattended labour and delivery, despite the fact that the World Health Organization includes this as an officially recognized cause of death.[2] The research discussed in this chapter further demonstrates how a very public and sensationalized campaign unfolded in Ontario during the 1990s, largely in response to toddlers who died from serious neglect and abuse, and that drew attention to the serious and ongoing problem of child beating. However, the extension of the category of child abuse homicide from these kinds of cases to homicides involving newborns is problematic. This chapter highlights the kinds of problems that result from public policy recommendations that fail to distinguish between two very different phenomena: child abuse and infanticide.

Infanticide and the Medicalization of Child Abuse: The "Discovery" of "Child Abuse" in Canada, Britain, and the United States

The "discovery" of child abuse as a serious social problem, and its subsequent definition as a form of "deviance" requiring medical, legal, and social welfare intervention, is identified by various authors, within different professional contexts (mainly in the United States), as emerging between the 1940s and the 1960s. This attitude developed alongside the gradual disappearance of cultural attitudes sanctioning corporal punishment. Battering first became characterized as an illness and only became characterized as criminal deviance in the 1980s (Pfohl 1977). Hacking (1995, 56) argues that the phrase "child abuse" seldom appeared before 1960, its predecessor being "cruelty to children."

The discovery of child abuse within the academic and professional disciplines is generally credited to J. Caffey (1946, 163-73), a forensic pathologist who, in 1946 in the *American Journal of Radiology*, published his discovery of fractures in long bones of infants who had died from subdural hematoma. Among forensic pathologists interested in child abuse, this is identified as the earliest discovery of what was then known as "Caffey's Syndrome." This was, however, not the first time that violence against children had been discovered. In the late nineteenth century the people involved in the nascent social work industry had identified cruelty toward children as a significant social problem requiring drastic intervention (Pfohl 1977). Caffey's discovery of child abuse in 1946 led to a range of research studies by American forensic pathologists, who ventured to scientifically document and describe whether or not and how babies had died from a range of violent means (usually chronic subdural hematoma). In addition, they raised concerns about the designations "sudden infant death syndrome" and "sudden unexplained death," which they argued were tenuous categories that potentially masked intentional homicides. Underlying the discovery of child abuse was the belief that cases typically referred to as "fatal battered babies" represented only a tiny fraction of the actual occurrences.

In practical, or procedural, terms Caffey's discovery resulted in a range of forensic pathologists being trained to autopsy babies with a view toward determining whether they had been the victims of child abuse. In 1960 Lester Adelson, a forensic pathologist working in Cleveland, Ohio, published *Pathology of Homicide* and influenced subsequent generations of forensic pathologists in the United States.[3] Those who trained under Adelson went on to initiate research that recognized "child abuse syndrome" and "shaken baby syndrome" as bona fide causes of death in infants (see Helfer, Kempe, and Krugman 1997).

Commenting on the British experience, Jenkins (1992, 104) argued that the discovery of child abuse was linked to professional aspirations, mainly among groups such as pediatric radiologists and forensic pathologists who actively published on the subject. According to Jenkins, the *British Medical Journal* is widely credited with publishing the first discovery of the so-called battered-baby syndrome in 1963. Scheper-Hughes and Stein (1987, 339) argue that child abuse and neglect, "long grappled with as a vexing and chronic social problem by generations of child welfare and social workers, was suddenly 'discovered' and expropriated by a more powerful profession: medicine. When C. Henry Kempe and his associates (1962) at Colorado General

Hospital created a new diagnostic entity – the 'Battered Child Syndrome' – the American public finally sat up and took notice."

According to Scheper-Hughes and Stein (1987, 339), the "discovery" of child abuse by the American medical profession led to broader discoveries and to increasing reports of child abuse. A range of national incidence studies, beginning in the 1970s, "reported sharp increases annually in the reports of maltreatment." According to Scheper-Hughes and Stein, this reported rise in incidents had a particular effect:

> Between 1976 and 1981, the total number of reports documented nationwide has more than doubled (the American Humane Association 1983). Social and behavioral scientists rushed in, often with premature causal explanations based on retrospective studies of poorly defined abusers and abused. Research instruments and procedures were designed and implemented for the early detection of "high risk" parents (i.e. *mothers*) at public hospitals. Welfare patients, especially single mothers, were observed throughout labor, delivery, and the hours postpartum for signs of inadequate attachment to their newborns (*see* Kempe and Kempe 1978, 62-63). Based on inferences from this brief period of observation, "problem" mothers were targeted for early intervention programs that included home visits by nurses, clinical social workers, and child welfare workers. (339; emphasis in original)

It is, as Scheper-Hughes and Stein (1987, 339-40) note, not surprising that the development of these interventionist strategies gave rise to the child abuse "expert" in a range of fields:

> the discovery of child abuse and the consequent development of interventionist strategies also resulted in a proliferation of child abuse experts – researchers, educators, clinicians, therapists, and social workers – occupying newly created positions as members of child trauma teams in hospitals, on child abuse "hot lines," as facilitators in self-help "parenting" and stress management groups, and in emergency shelters and treatment programs for the abused. Child Abuse Prevention (CAP) workers visited schools, clinics, and day care programs in order to alert teachers, doctors and child care professionals to the covert signs (i.e. distress and agitation) thought to be symptomatic of "sexually abused" children. In addition, they hold classes to educate even young toddlers, with the use of "anatomically correct" puppets and dolls, about the differences in "good" and "bad" touches by parents and other adult caretakers. This was said to be part of the process of "empowering" children.

And, finally, the media played a role in buttressing the interventions of these experts by publicizing some of the most bizarre and sadistic examples of child abuse. According to Scheper-Hughes and Stein (1987, 340), these narratives played a significant role in justifying the new and unprecedented "public interventions into the private lives of citizens."

One thing that is clearly evident from the definition of child abuse across the different professions is that infanticide, or maternal neonaticide, is usually not included as part of its social relations.[4] Infanticide has generally been viewed as a gender-specific form of homicide within a framework that mitigates women's culpability on either a compassionate or a psychiatric basis. The diminished responsibility lens through which infanticide has been viewed stands in stark contrast to the law and order lens through which many now regulate child abuse and infant homicide as intentional lethal violence perpetrated by parents and caregivers. During this process, infanticide became almost obsolete, subsumed under "child abuse homicide," with its focus on intervention, detection, and punishment.

"Fatal Child Abuse Syndrome" and Child Death Review Teams: The International Context

By the mid-1980s a number of cases in Britain and the United States revealed that children who had been in the care of state child protection agencies and social workers had died. In Britain there were numerous investigations following an inquiry into the death of seven-year-old Maria Colwell in 1973. Maria Colwell had been removed from her home to a foster home and then returned only to be starved and repeatedly beaten before eventually being murdered by her stepfather. The inquest into her death led to intense media scrutiny and to the criticism of individual social workers as well as the child protection agency (Jenkins 1992, 104-5). According to Jenkins, the Colwell case galvanized a range of professional interests, resulting in a range of social and political reactions. Most significantly, the concept of child abuse entered public consciousness in a new way and mobilized a range of experts who came to view it as a problem of crime control rather than as a problem of unmet social welfare needs. According to Jenkins:

> The consequences of the Colwell case have been described as a moral panic over the theme of physical abuse, a topic frequently addressed in book, documentaries, and fictional works during the next three years ... In 1976, a Parliamentary Select Committee on Violence in the Family produced a report with a separate volume on violence perpetrated against children. *Child Abuse* entered public debate as a concept and a term. In 1970, the central problem was *battered babies; nonaccidental injury* came to the fore by 1974; by 1978 *child abuse* established itself as a dominant phrase. The usage was consolidated and popularized by the British publication during 1978 of *Child Abuse,* by R.S. and C. Henry Kempe.[5] (105)

The Colwell inquiry led to a range of procedural amendments for the regulation and administration of the child protection system in the United Kingdom, with the underlying aim of detecting children "at risk" for child abuse in order to prevent possible murders. Interagency coordination was a key feature of this new protection system. Tracking suspected or known child abusers and providing education and training to social workers in order to identify the warning signs of child abuse constituted the focus of intervention and prevention. During this period, the focus on those at risk led to the education of social workers and the development of centralized child abuser registries. The identification of risk factors for infant homicide soon became the holy grail of social workers, police, and investigating forensic pathologists. In addition, feminist movements pressed authorities to recognize and criminalize child sexual abuse.

The first child death review team in North America was established in the late 1970s in the United States. Since that time, child death review teams have been established in most American states and in two Canadian provinces (Wilczynski 1997a, 186). The main objective of these teams has been to re-evaluate forensic medical evidence and to provide amended cause-of-death designations in light of newly acquired knowledge about child abuse homicide. These teams have been established largely without public pressure or support and are the result of concerns by persons in certain professional sectors who have witnessed child deaths and have felt powerless to either prevent them or to actively participate in effecting a punitive carceral response. However, the news media, alerted to the professional concerns, would do their best to generate public interest and concern. In Ontario, in the late 1990s, the *Toronto Star* threw its weight behind the campaign for criminal and civil law reform.

The *Toronto Star* Discovers Child Beating

> They died despite signs of abuse.
> – *Toronto Star*, 18 September 1996, A1.

In 1996 two staff reporters for the *Toronto Star* newspaper wrote that they approached the Ontario Coroner's Office and asked the coroner to review child deaths for a five-year time period – a period that they had already researched. The wanted to find out whether the case files showed "trends similar" to those their own researchers had observed – trends that included the overly lenient sanctions deployed against mothers, fathers, and parents charged in the deaths of their children. Perhaps not surprisingly, given that the Coroner's Office had already identified the problem and a number of inquests were pending, the Coroner's Office investigation following the *Star's* prompt "discovered" the same thing (M. Welsh and C. Donovan, "How the System Failed These Kids: They Died Despite Signs of Abuse," *Toronto Star,* 18 September 1996, A1).[6] The newspaper report characterizes missed warning signs as a serious problem and as a failure of the children's aid societies (CAS). According to the *Star*'s "ongoing ... investigation of 77 child deaths in the past five years" it was discovered that "serious warning signs" existed prior to death in at least twenty-three cases (ibid.).[7] According to the *Star* report: "Of the 23, children's aid societies were involved in hearing of abuse in 15 cases" (ibid., A6). This figure represents a total of 19.4 percent of all cases reviewed over a five-year period. The *Star* further reported that "the coroner's review examined 135 homicide cases in the same time period. That review, which is also preliminary, showed that 22 of the 135 cases were known to an Ontario children's aid society prior to the homicide" (ibid.).

According to the coroner's study, there were slightly fewer children "known to" children's aid societies (16.3 percent) in which the children may have died from parental violence than were found in the study the *Star* claimed to have conducted. In other words, of all the cases reviewed, those children known to children's aid societies were slightly better off than were those not known to them. Nevertheless, the suspicion was that there were many more cases known to children's aid societies that simply remained undocumented. Dr. Jim Cairns, deputy chief coroner at the Toronto office, signalled the potential reality of many more "unknown" infant homicides when he noted that he would only be able to confirm if children's aid was involved if it was written in the coroner's file (M. Welsh and K. Donovan, "How the System Failed These Kids: They Died Despite Signs of Abuse," *Toronto Star,* 18 September 1996, A6). However, the category of "children known to" children's aid societies is a poor one: these are not children who are actually under the care of children's aid societies; rather, they are simply "known to" the societies for one reason or another. These are not children with whom social workers have particularly regular contact, and therefore the idea of social worker accountability in their deaths is usually misplaced.

The *Star* report was timed to coordinate with Dr. Cairns's announcement that a joint task force, in conjunction with the Ontario Association of Children's Aid Societies, would study the causes of child mortality in Ontario with a view toward preventing future deaths and creating a system to evaluate the risk of serious injury or death in each case known to Child and Family Services (M. Welsh and K. Donovan, "How the System Failed These Kids: They Died Despite Signs of Abuse," *Toronoto Star,* 18 September 1996, A1). According to Cairns, "his research found numerous cases where a young homicide victim was known to a Children's Aid Society prior to death, often because of abuse or neglect" (ibid.). Both the proposed Inquest and the newly established Ontario Child Mortality Task Force targeted a range of "long overdue" administrative and criminal legal changes in order to remedy the deficiencies of the child welfare system. These included the eventual implementation of a centralized interactive child abuse registry managed by the Ministry of Community and Social Services. Its purpose would be to track known and suspected child abusers, and it would be accessible to all provincial children's aid societies, police, coroners, and doctors who suspected abuse.[8] This centralized system would replace the poorly managed and ineffectual provincial child abuse registry.[9] In addition, the Office of the Coroner was committed to improving its own investigative procedures. Dr. Cairns noted that "we need to educate all professionals involved with high risk children with a view to learning how to prevent deaths" (ibid., A6).

The first story introduced the readers to a case that involved the death of an eight-month-old infant. The pathologist who performed the initial autopsy missed the signs of abuse and determined that the cause of death was sudden infant death syndrome. The body of this infant was exhumed three years later, when it was discovered that its month-old sibling had been hospitalized with a broken leg, bruises, and a bleeding nose (M. Welsh and K. Donovan, "How the System Failed These Kids: They Died Despite Signs of Abuse," *Toronto Star*, 18 September 1996, A6). In yet another example, a six-month-old died following numerous contacts with health care professionals. A doctor failed to diagnose a broken arm as intentional child abuse, and child welfare workers "didn't investigate Sara's living conditions and accepted denials of abuse by her crack-addicted parents; a Canadian Mothercraft Society worker didn't investigate Sara's room for the obvious signs of neglect and abuse; and the children's aid society did not heed warnings from the parole officer of the baby's father, who had been jailed five years for assaulting his son, Mikey Junior, so viciously that he was left permanently disabled and blind. The parole officer had warned that the father was planning to move back with the family" (ibid.).

The *Star* story attempted to make clear that there were instances in which serious questions were raised about the management of these cases. Sara's case was included to highlight something that had been noticed by the Coroner's Office over the years, which was that the labelling of deaths as sudden infant death syndrome often disguised deaths from child abuse.

"Cry for the Children"
Following the high-profile announcements about the Coroner's Inquests and Cairns's establishment of the Ontario Child Mortality Task Force Joint Task Force, between April and June 1997 the *Star* ran a series entitled "Cry for the Children," in which it described the circumstances of a few especially shocking deaths of babies and toddlers known to children's aid societies. In the first story of the series, which ran on the front page of the paper on 19 April, the *Star* described the infants as "victims of the system," which

"put the rights of abusive parents over the safety of their children" (M. Welsh and K. Donovan, "Cry for the Children," *Toronto Star*, serial report, 18 May 1997, A1). This story, along with others in the series, highlighted the worst examples of child poverty, parental neglect, and abuse. In the discussion of these few cases, it was pointed out that signs of abuse were evident yet nothing was done, thus further violence resulted in death. Sprinkled with photographs of abused and murdered babies and toddlers, the series described in intimate detail the injuries inflicted (often by their mothers' boyfriends and sometimes by their fathers), while pointing out the failures of both the Ontario provincial welfare and Canadian federal criminal justice systems and urging a range of policy changes.

Following a story that had been published six months earlier and had described one or two cases in which infants and toddlers were the victims of domestic violence, this so-called "investigative report" was meant to draw out, for the public, the extent and nature of the problem of child abuse by presenting the material in an individualized and very personalized manner. It is evident from that first story in September 1996, and the ones that followed in the spring of 1997, that the media coverage was aimed at educating the public about the nature and extent of the problem of child abuse homicides so as to prepare it for the administrative and criminal law changes that would reappear in 1998 as inquest and task force recommendations. By the time these recommendations were announced, the readership of the *Star* was already intimately familiar with the kinds of injuries sustained by the few infants and toddlers who died from intentional violence as well as with the frustrations of police who thought they could have prevented their deaths had they been informed of the risk. The readership was also informed, through individual case narratives and the opinions advanced by the Office of the Coroner, that the criminal sentences given to the perpetrators did not reflect the seriousness of the crime. And finally, and perhaps most important, the readership was encouraged to see that something could be done about all this if laws and attitudes were changed.

"A Cop's Crusade"
The second story, "A Cop's Crusade," which ran a week after "Cry for the Children," described the failures of the child protection system from the point of view of the provincial police detective who investigated the death of Tiffani Coville. His personal account of his frustration with failures to protect the infant are used as a narrative device to highlight, once again, the failure of the child welfare and criminal justice systems from the vantage point of the police officer (M. Welsh and K. Donovan, "A Cop's Crusade," *Toronto Star*, serial report, 26 April 1997, A1). The story argues that Tiffani was failed in life and in death by doctors, nurses, and social workers

who had not called the police; by a system that did not track known child abusers; and by a coroner who listed her death as sudden infant death syndrome and allowed her burial even though x-rays would eventually suggest, when read a second time by a senior radiologist, that there was evidence of healing fractured rib injuries – an unusual and suspicious finding in an infant so young. The police officer "hero" is credited with bringing a measure of "justice" to her death by uncovering the sequence of events that led to her demise at the hands of her mother's common law spouse. The story suggests that good police work, along with certain procedural changes in reporting to police, would lead to the detection and prosecution of many more cases of child abuse and murder.

"Getting Away with Murder"

The third story in the *Star* series argued that "most parents who kill their children in Ontario receive little or no punishment for their crimes" (M. Welsh and K. Donovan, "Getting Away with Murder – of Children," *Toronto Star,* serial report, 18 May 1997, A1). These claims are buttressed by quotes from homicide detectives who supported the authors' dismay at the sentences. One officer is quoted as saying: "The life of a child is cheap, very cheap" (ibid.).

According to the *Star:*

> Serious charges like second-degree murder are often plea bargained down because of poor medical and police investigations, the tendency of police, crown attorneys and judges to feel sympathy for the accused parent, and the simple fact that children are so easy to kill that little trace of the crime remains. As a result, parents charged in the death of a child typically receive no jail time or sentences of less than two years. And the younger the child killed, the lower the punishment. Jim Cairns, Ontario's deputy chief coroner, who is making it much of his life's work to change standards for child death investigations, agrees that sentences don't reflect the horror of the crime. (M. Welsh and K. Donovan, "Getting Away with Murder – of Children," *Toronto Star,* serial report, 18 May 1997, A1)

This story frames the issue in terms of a failure of the criminal justice system to adequately address the seriousness of this sort of crime: individual cases are again personalized and highlighted for intense scrutiny. This decontextualized approach makes it appear as though parents were and are in fact "getting away with murder." The story provides the reader with reporter-produced information on sentencing practices in statistical form, thus "proving" that their claim is true. Just in case the point is missed, the authors provide a table of nine cases – entitled "Crime and Little Punishment" – to illustrate their thesis that people are getting away with the murder of children. These cases are detailed in order to educate the reader on the difficulties of gaining "appropriate" convictions, with the underlying message that "appropriate" means either first or second degree murder charges.

What is striking about the presentation of these materials (aside from the absolute failure to provide any kind of balanced assessment of the individual cases within the context of homicide more generally, either by providing Canadian Criminal Justice Statistics on infant homicide or by interviewing sociologists and criminologists) is the way in which the *Star's* sample of seventy cases is presented as seventy cases of *actual* child abuse. The reporters present these cases as though there is no question that these are, in fact, purposeful child abuse cases in which an infant or toddler dies from repeated abuse and that the perpetrators are, in fact, guilty. It is important to note that, contrary to what the reporters claim, the seventy cases in their sample, including the fifty-two that went to court, are *not* all cases of child abuse. This story ignores the possibility that the reason many of these cases did not go to trial (or were plea bargained) is that they were one-time-only events and/or accidental. Nevertheless, the story tells us that "71 percent got off with little or no punishment" and that "in return for a guilty plea, the charge was plea bargained down to a lesser charge in 51 percent of the 41 cases where a parent or caregiver was convicted" (M. Welsh and K. Donovan, "Getting Away with Murder – of Children," *Toronto Star,* serial report, 18 May 1997, A6). We are also told that less jail time is received for killing younger victims, again without any notion of the circumstances of the death, as though the criminal justice response in all homicide cases should simply result in convictions of second degree murder regardless of the circumstances of the individual deaths. Thus, not only does the story not provide the reader with information on how these charging and plea bargaining practices compare with those pertaining to the homicides of adults, but it also fails to provide the reader with a sense of the circumstances in each case (which may well have warranted lesser charges and reduced penalties).

The cases, both in the table and the bold statistical figures, provide the reader with the impression that all of these infants were the victims of child abuse and that all of the perpetrators were guilty of murder. If one explores their data in more depth, even using the numbers they provided, then one discovers that, in 29 percent of the cases that went to court, the accused received sentences of between two and seven years or life. However, of the 71 percent who supposedly "got off with little or no punishment," 30 percent (21 percent of those who went to court) were acquitted or determined to be not guilty. This means that of those who were found guilty (forty-one in all), 63 percent "got off with little or no punishment." We can separate "little" from "no." Twenty-four percent of those found guilty of a criminal offence received no actual jail sentence (but were likely sentenced to years of probation and community service). Those in the "little" category amounted to 39 percent of those who were found guilty. Of these, 19.5 percent were sentenced to jail for one year or less and 19.5 percent were sentenced to one to two years in jail (M. Welsh and K. Donovan, "Getting Away with Murder – of Children," *Toronto Star,* serial report, 18 May 1997, A6). While a number of those found guilty were certainly treated leniently, the suggestion that 71 percent of child murderers in the sample got off with little or no punishment is misleading at best and a gross distortion at worst.

The *Star* provides a similar kind of statistical evaluation for those cases that are plea bargained down to a lesser charge. It does this in order to show the reader that in 51 percent of the forty-one cases in which a parent or caregiver was charged, a plea bargain was accepted for a guilty plea. But this figure is practically meaningless without comparative data, raising the question of whether or not *all* charges are to a certain extent subject to this level of reduction through special plea arrangements. If this were to the case, then not only would the plea arrangements in these cases seem more appropriate but the suspicion that police and Crown attorneys might lay "inappropriately" serious charges in anticipation of this process would also be bolstered.

Finally, the *Star* reporters claim that their research discovered that the age of the victim was related to the jail term received and that the younger the victim the less the jail time. Here, taking "average age" of victim as the category under which to make statements about jail terms is more than meaningless. Their presentation of the material as a bar chart in which a jail term of one year or less for a victim whose average age is fourteen months, and a jail term of more than one year for a victim whose average is thirty-two months, provides the reader with the impression that, if you kill a very young infant, then, regardless of the circumstances, you are unlikely to receive more than one year in jail. Their representation assumes that all the cases in their sample are "like" cases, and it ignores the likelihood that many victims died from differing, sometimes accidental, causes. It also ignores cases in which the perpetrator was found not criminally responsible by reason of insanity or was found guilty of infanticide. In other words, their representation ignores all causes of death and social circumstances other than those pertaining to child abuse.

In the Coroner's database, used to collate and track all deaths by type, the coroners list a "death factor." The death factor is not necessarily the technical "cause of death," something that would have been discovered had the file been examined. Causes of death are medical determinations that describe how a person died. Subdural hematoma, asphyxiation, burns, blunt trauma to the head, suffocation, and drowning are all medical causes of death, some of which *are* listed in infanticide cases as death factors. But death factors often describe a kind of "mediate cause of death," which alerts the coroners to significant types of death, which they may feel deserve special attention. As such, the death factor designation represents an almost textbook example of the kinds of professional classification that can be described as the social construction of a social problem (see Best 1990; Pfohl 1977; Scheper-Hughes and Stein 1987). The actual causes of death in the *Star's* sample were not necessarily the result of intentional and repeated violence, the kinds of violence usually associated by professionals with child abuse. But the Office of the Chief Coroner for Ontario lists child abuse as a death factor in almost all infant deaths due to violence, regardless of whether or not there is evidence of old injuries. Some cases, in which the proximate cause of death is that the babies were shaken, are one-time-only events – not typically considered bona fide child abuse by experts in the field. In addition, the *Star's* sample included a case of maternal neonaticide, which, again, does not conform to the notion of child abuse (and in which, incidentally, the police report indicated that the baby had twenty stab wounds, when in fact, the autopsy listed the wounds as "multiple cuts" rather than "stab wounds").[10] This case in particular illustrates how a failure to provide a social and historical context for criminal justice responses to homicide can provide a misleading picture of the nature of a social problem. The young single mother was initially charged with second degree murder and pled guilty to manslaughter – a much harsher disposition than those that had been handed out in almost all similar cases over the last 100 years.

There were two cases in which fathers were convicted of criminal negligence and manslaughter, respectively, when their infants were shaken to death. The report fails to inform the reader whether these events were one-time-only events or even (possibly) unintentional deaths rather than actual child abuse (which would entail evidence of older injuries). Cases of death from shaken baby syndrome, as they are referred to by the Coroner's Office, can often involve infants who clearly suffered other kinds of violence, but they can also be one-time-only events resulting in death. The difference in the criminal justice response might then reflect a difference in the circumstances of the death and, therefore, in the actual severity of the crime.

"How to Save the Children"
In the final story of the *Star* series the readership is informed about "how to save the children." This front-page story tells the reader that "both laws and attitudes must be changed so that child safety becomes paramount over the rights of abusive parents" (M. Welsh and K. Donovan, "How to Save the Children," *Toronto Star*, serial report, 21 June 1997, A1). Seven individual changes are suggested:

1 Change the law so that children come first.
2 Give watchdog powers to the ministry that funds children's aid.
3 Institute province-wide investigative training of social workers.
4 Create a computer database linking all 55 children's aid societies.
5 Initiate a public information campaign against child abuse.
6 Crack down on doctors and other professionals not reporting abuse.
7 Launch innovative prevention programs province-wide. (ibid.)

The article then provides a detailed explanation of the need for each of these recommendations to solve "the problem" of child abuse. It provides a sense that its recommendations are novel and that, by applying them to the child welfare system (and assuming a criminal justice response to punish abusive parents), "society" can solve "the problem" of child abuse. The story provides no information about the success or failure of these kinds of initiatives in other jurisdictions and adds little new information to the broader debate about the root causes of child abuse per se.

The reporters' discussion does highlight one long-standing anxiety about juvenile delinquency. Child psychiatrist Dr. Steinhauer provides the *biological* ideas necessary to logically justify administrative and criminal law intervention strategies in preventive terms. According to Dr. Steinhauer: "With brain development, the first three years is critical. We have huge numbers of children who live in chronic conflict and tension, and that impacts on the areas of the midbrain that cause rage, anxiety and a predisposition to violence" (M. Welsh and K. Donovan, "How to Save the Children," *Toronto Star,* serial report, 21 June 1997, A1). In addition, the story cites an American study as authoritative evidence that child abuse eventually leads to juvenile delinquency: "A U.S. study published this week by the Child Welfare League shows abused and neglected children are 67 times more likely to become juvenile offenders than those who are not abused" (ibid.).

What the report fails to tell its readers is that this old idea has its roots in nineteenth-century reform movements that sought to save society from juvenile delinquency by removing children from "bad" homes. Rather than aim their responses "at ameliorating abuse or correcting abusive parents," the late nineteenth- and early twentieth-century reform movements sought to remove children from their corrupt environments and put them in institutions, or "houses of refuge," on the grounds that "they could learn order, regularity and obedience" (Pfohl 1977, 311). Unlike the reform movement of the late nineteenth and early twentieth century, however, the *Star* suggests institutionalizing *both* child and parent. Its solutions would institutionalize the suspected abused child under the care of Child and Family Services and the suspected abusers, being efficiently prosecuted by the criminal justice system, would be incarcerated in jails. This new approach varies only slightly from the older one in that it seeks to focus more directly on the process by which perpetrators of abuse can be more efficiently prosecuted. However, like the earlier reform efforts, the *Star's* recommendations would have the effect of expanding the scope and intensity of professional interventions in the lives of identified "bad parents" and children deemed "at risk," and would correlatively require the expansion and enhanced training of a range of professional groups.

Speaking for the Dead:
The Coroner's Inquest and the Ontario Child Mortality Task Force
In April 1998 the Ontario Child Mortality Task Force (OCMTF), working for the Ontario Association of Children's Aid Societies (OACAS), published a final progress report on the implementation of the broad changes suggested by the coroner's juries regarding child welfare agencies, the Coroner's Office, and the government (Ontario 1998b). In addition, the OACAS prepared a collation of Coroner's Inquest recommendations according to topic, released in February 1998. *Inquest Recommendations by Topic* (Ontario 1998a) is, for our purposes, the more important document because it addresses the prevention of, and response to, child abuse homicides in much greater detail and includes careful consideration of the *Criminal Code* options. The OCMTF report is consistent with the Coroner's Inquest recommendations, but its focus is on the role of the Coroner's Office, the establishment of a pediatric death review process, and the implementation of child welfare reforms.

By the time these reports were issued, the *Toronto Star* had done its best to prepare the public to receive its recommendations as both reasonable and long overdue. Indeed, what is striking is the similarity between the framework for response developed in the *Star* series and that produced within an entirely different context by experts on child abuse and child welfare, by the Coroner's Inquest jurors, and by the OCMTF (as well as by those who contributed to a federal Department of Justice consultation paper, "Child Victims and the Criminal Justice System," [Canada 1999] produced years later). These reports are uniquely connected to the *Star* series because the cases upon which their argument for change is built came from the Ontario Chief Coroner's Office and the comments of the deputy chief coroner, Dr. Jim Cairns. Cairns had been much in evidence in the *Star's* reports, and he was professionally involved in both inquests as well as being a member of the OCMTF. The newspaper's recommendations and the technical professional recommendations that followed were, then, of a piece, and the problems of child abuse and child abuse homicide were already a part of the public consciousness and were, in any event well established within the social work and criminal justice community well before they were announced as formal recommendations by the inquest jurors and the task force members.

Coroner's Inquest Recommendations
In the fall of 1996 and the winter of 1997, shortly after the announcements in the *Toronto Star*, the Office of the Chief Coroner of Ontario began its inquests into the deaths of eight "children"[11] known to children's aid societies in Ontario. By February 1998 it had conducted and completed six inquests and the OACAS issued its report on its findings. The following is a summary of each inquest conducted:

- Shanay Johnson died at age 2 years of a head injury on October 6, 1993 in Toronto. The mother has been convicted in this death. The Metropolitan Toronto CAS was involved in providing services. One hundred and seven recommendations were made by the Coroner's jury.
- Wilson Kasonde died at age 10 and Margaret Kasonde died at age 8 in Ottawa as a result of gunshot wounds on May 25, 1995. Their father has been convicted in their deaths. Ottawa-Carleton CAS was involved at the time of their murders. Seventy-four recommendations were made by the Coroner's jury.
- David Dombroskie died at age 4, Angela Dombroskie died at age 8; Devin Burns died at age 3; and Jamie Lee Burns died at age 4 in a house fire in Kitchener on June 11, 1996. Waterloo F&CS was working with the mother and children at the time of their deaths. Forty-six recommendations were made by the Coroner's jury.
- Lisa Marie MacLean died at age 18 months in Sault Ste. Marie after being released from police custody. She was a Crown Ward of the Algoma CAS. Five recommendations were made by the Coroner's jury.
- Kasandra Shepherd died in 1991 at 3 years of age. Her stepmother has been convicted in this death. A physician was acquitted on appeal of obstructing justice in the investigation into Kasandra's death. Peel CAS was involved with the family at the time of the child's death. Seventy-three recommendations were made by the Coroner's jury.
- Jennifer Koval's'kyj-England died at age 6 as a result of injuries received during an attack by her father. The Metropolitan Toronto CAS was providing services at the time of Jennifer's death. One hundred and twenty-four recommendations were made by the Coroner's jury. (Ontario 1998a)

The seventy-one-page OACAS report groups all of these individual jury recommendations by topic, and fifty-eight individual recommendations are discussed in detail. The jury's recommendations add technical detail to the framework introduced in the *Star* series. In particular, the jury sets out, in painstaking detail, the ingredients of the "innovative prevention programs" the *Star* had demanded. All this added up to an enhancement of the investigation, monitoring, and reporting practices for children at risk – virtually a new and very detailed blueprint for professional involvement in these cases. At the same time, the OACAS was calling for increased funding to welfare programs in Ontario.

While many of the inquest recommendations had to do with amending practices, policies, and family law, there were certain recommendations that had an impact on the disposition of instances of maternal neonaticide. Chief among these was the recommendation for the creation of criminal offences involving child abuse and neglect, and the specific recommendation that "infanticide" be removed from the *Criminal Code* and be replaced with "death by child abuse/neglect," which would not require proof of "intent" (Ontario 1998a, 17). This recommendation came from the two inquests held in Toronto. The first was into the death of Shanay Johnson, aged two, whose mother was convicted of manslaughter and sentenced to four years in jail. The second was into the death of six-year-old Jennifer Koval's'kyj-England, who died after being attacked by her father. Therefore, the only case in which infanticide law might have appeared relevant was that of Shanay Johnson, although Shanay was in fact too old to be covered by the infanticide provision.[12]

According to a newspaper report at the time when the jury announced its recommendations, Shanay Johnson's mother, Patricia Johnson, "had been beating Shanay, depriving her of food, burning her with scalding water and leaving her in a crib for hours unattended – all while the family was under the [children's aid] society's supervision" (*Toronto Star*, 8 May 1998, A3). The living conditions into which Shanay Johnson was born were horrific. In 1996, shortly before the inquest recommendations were made public, the *Toronto Star* reported the following details:

> Shanay Johnson's mother was a crack addict with four other children in a house that smelled of urine and feces. In 1991, the first of her two children were taken from her by the Metro Toronto Children's Aid Society, but returned a month later. After Shanay was born later that year, the society took the three children away. Then, in 1993, deciding again that she was now a fit mother, they returned them to her. Five months later, Shanay, 21 months old at the time, was dead. Her mother had whipped her with a belt or coat hangers; she was punched and kicked; three of her teeth were knocked out; her body was black and blue.
>
> Five days before Shanay's October, 1993 death, there was a final warning sign. Shanay's mother called 911 to say the child had scalded herself by turning on the hot water tap in the bath. She was allowed to keep her children and five days later Shanay was dead. The pathologist found that her tiny buttocks were dunked in scalding water. The mother, Patricia Johnson, was sentenced to four years in prison. (M. Welsh and K. Donovan, "How the System Failed These Kids: They Died Despite Signs of Abuse," *Toronto Star*, 18 September 1996, A6)

No doubt due to the severity of the abuse suffered by the deceased toddler, the fact that she had come into contact with the Toronto Children's Aid Society, and the high-profile reports in the newspapers about this case, the jury's response to her death was particularly fraught with emotion, resulting in a high-pitched response couched in terms that, even in a case of this severity, appear melodramatic. The "Opening Statement" of the Verdict of the Coroner's Jury outlining the recommendations set the moral tone for the extensive recommendations:

> We the Jury on behalf of the citizens of Metropolitan Toronto wish to express our sympathy for the lost life of Shanay Jani Johnson.
>
> When we say the word mother we think of someone who provides unconditional love, keeps us safe, and provides a happy home. This didn't happen for you. For a part of your short span of life you were loved, safe and happy with your Foster Family. Then you were returned to your birth family through a system that did not recognize your rights and needs as an individual, and that failed to recognize your danger. Four short months later we lost you forever.
>
> Shanay, be assured, with these recommendations implemented, the large cracks in the child protection system will surely be filled by the people, Government of Ontario and agencies responsible for the safe keeping of our children.
>
> Shanay, the final chapter of your short life now comes to an end. Little one, you can now rest in peace knowing that society has benefited from your death even though it did not have the opportunity to benefit from your life and what you would have contributed. Your memory will never be lost to any of our hearts and minds.[13]

The jurors made their recommendations to alter the policy and practices at the federal and provincial levels of government. They recommended amendments to the *Criminal Code of Canada,* to the concept of "best interests of the child" in family law, and to the *Child and Family Services Act* itself. Jurors recommended procedural and policy changes to the Ministry of Community and Social Services, children's aid societies, and health professionals' reporting practices.

With respect to the *Criminal Code,* the jurors recommended both the repeal of the infanticide law and a new category of homicide – one that would not require the Crown to prove intent. This suggestion is based on the rationale that the "innocence" of a child deserves a strong punitive response. Below are their recommendations and rationale for same:

> 1. We recommend the Federal Government of Canada amend the Criminal Code to include an offense of Death by Child Abuse/Neglect which does

not require specific intent to kill with a minimum term of imprisonment without eligibility for parole to be classed as second degree murder.

Rationale: The death of one of society's most vulnerable members must be seen as being, at least, if not more than equal to the death of an adult as in their innocence they are unable to defend themselves or escape from danger.

1. We recommend removal of Infanticide from the Criminal Code.

Rationale: It would be replaced with sections under Death by Child Abuse/ Neglect.[14]

Child Victims: The Federal Department of Justice

The Toronto inquests' suggestion that the federal government add "child abuse/neglect" to the homicide law of Canada and remove the infanticide law was taken up by the Family, Children and Youth Division of the Department of Justice as part of a broader consultative project addressing various questions about child victims and witnesses within a context of heightened recognition of "the true scope and extent of child abuse, neglect and exploitation and the harms they cause" (Canada 1999, 3). The Department of Justice's background paper describes events that have given rise to a range of recommendations aimed at protecting children from various kind of harm: "there have been a number of alarming incidents that have given rise to concern about the safety of children. Adults use various means to approach and have sex with children, as well as those fourteen years of age or older, who are over the general minimum age of consent to sexual activity. Adults have killed children in a number of jurisdictions by direct physical attacks and through the most horrendous forms of neglect. Children have also been the victims of severe, long-lasting, and often permanent physical and emotional harms and injuries" (ibid., 5).

The Department of Justice notes in this paper that these events have given rise to a renewed interest in child protection and to a call from certain professional sectors for criminal law and child welfare reforms: "The issues and suggestions for reform come from a wide range of sources in response to reported cases of grievous injury and death of children. Those recommending greater protection for children include judges, Crown prosecutors, defence lawyers, police, health care workers (including those active in the mental health field), hospital child abuse teams, public health nurses, academics, social workers and others directly concerned with child protection. Suggestions also include recommendations from judicial inquiries, coroner's inquest juries, child fatality review committees, and other review bodies" (Canada 1999, 5).[15] The paper only "focuses on extreme forms of conduct and injury that can never be justified or defended ... its object is to help ensure that there are child-specific criminal offences available which accurately reflect the horrendous types of conduct involved and make successful prosecutions possible" (ibid., 6). It is within this context that the removal of infanticide is considered.

In light of the paper's careful definition of its purpose, the consideration of the removal of infanticide is awkwardly positioned. Infanticide has never been considered an extreme form of abuse or homicide, and it operates as a specific kind of defence to murder. Nevertheless, its removal is considered within the broader context of child-specific criminal offences, specifically, child homicide, which includes the removal of "intent."

I show how concerns over the nature and extent of child abuse have become connected to the investigation and prosecution of women suspected of killing newly born babies, drawing authorities toward more intensive investigation, supervision, and risk management regimes. Within this context, the Canadian infanticide law has been challenged on a number of troubling fronts, not just on the ground that it represents an inappropriate medicalization of the actions of rational women in difficult circumstances but also because it provides insufficient retribution for heinous crimes committed by fully responsible and wicked individuals. This claim is grounded in the generalized concern about child abuse and neglect as serious, widespread, and even horrifying problems. In fact, certain law and order advocates have been quick to appropriate the feminist critique of the medicalization of women's deviance, seemingly represented by the infanticide provision, for their own purposes (see, for instance, Bauman 1997, 149-51; Pearson 1997, 78-79).

Without in any way suggesting that the medico-legal category of infanticide is unproblematic, the extension of the category of child abuse/neglect homicide to cover maternal neonaticides that conform to the established infanticide scenarios is especially troubling. Such a designation allows for little mitigation and indeed operates to flag a particularly heinous and blameworthy crime. The suggestion that this new offence would not require intent in order to be proven is undemocratic and unlikely to survive Charter scrutiny. While it might be argued that, in cases of death following long-standing serious abuse, the gross failure to fulfill parental responsibilities amounts to intent, where such a category is made to cover homicides in which there is no evidence of previous abuse and which were carried out in traumatic circumstances that gave rise to the possibility of some level of diminished culpability, the removal of an intent requirement amounts to rendering crucial evidence all but legally irrelevant. In such cases, evidence can be indicative of a partial absence of intent, with the mother often acting at a moment of acute distress. To remove the intent requirement is to make an end run around the due process rights of the accused. In short, the infanticide provision creates a framework for mitigation, which, despite the conceptual weaknesses of the category, is entirely fair. Simply repealing the infanticide law at a time when a new offence of child abuse/neglect homicide is enacted would remove the opportunity for appropriate mitigation. This is quite different from reading mental disturbance into the amended infanticide provision: in the former case, the defendant is denied the opportunity to make full answer and defence; in the latter case, the defendant is granted an unproven mitigation (albeit as a means of enabling conviction).

6
Retributive Justice:
The Disappearance of Infanticide

Mission Statement
We speak for the dead to protect the living.
The Office of the Chief Coroner for Ontario serves the living through high quality death investigations and inquests to ensure that no death will be overlooked, concealed or ignored. The findings are used to generate recommendations to help improve public safety and prevent deaths in similar circumstances.[1]
– Office of the Chief Coroner for Ontario,
the Ministry of Public Safety and Security

Like the case of the Brampton teenager charged with second degree murder for killing her newly born child after a denied pregnancy and unexpected birth, other cases investigated by the Office of the Chief Coroner for Ontario sometimes result in murder charges prior to plea bargains for infanticide. The cases of maternal neonaticide are among a range of others kinds of infant killings (e.g., shaken baby syndrome, battered baby syndrome, and sudden infant death syndrome). Like the situation in *Del Rio*, the infanticide charge continues to exist, for some, as a barrier to retribution. This occurs in cases where it is implied or evident that the mother acted wilfully and with evil intent.[2] In these cases we see the infanticide charge operating much as did the concealment charge in the nineteenth century. Infanticide is seen in some quarters as allowing for a lesser penalty for violent killings when the mothers might, or should, be convicted for murder.[3]

This chapter reviews coroner's investigations into deaths of infants in Ontario between 1986 and 1998.[4] My research reveals a discernible shift, on the part of coroners, police, and Crown prosecutors, toward a more punitive approach to cases of maternal neonaticide. I describe a range of outcomes that conform to the established infanticide scenario, from indictments and sometimes convictions for first and second degree murder to infanticide convictions, including cases where infanticide is the result of a plea bargain. There are even cases in which the old recourses of concealment and neglect charges are deployed. Thus, while the shift in official attitudes toward maternal neonaticide, and the infanticide law in particular, is significant and may result in *Criminal Code* amendment, the patchwork of individual cases continues to be as complex as ever, and governance continues in an entirely ad hoc manner.

The large sample from which these cases are drawn consists of all deaths of infants less than one year of age in which the death was ruled a homicide by any one of the regional Coroner's Offices in Ontario between 1986 and 1998. The incidents themselves were investigated by the Coroner's Offices because foul play was suspected, requiring investigation to assist the police and the Crown prosecutor in building their prosecutions.[5] It should be emphasized that this broad sample of homicide cases, from which my sample of maternal neonaticide cases is drawn, is the result of a complex sifting process wherein deaths considered "suspected murder" by the coroner and the police were drawn from all infant deaths investigated by the coroner, most of which were deemed not suspicious. Nevertheless, the question of what kinds of details make a case suspicious can be linked to broader questions of social inequality and poverty among single women on welfare. Many of the mothers investigated for murder were "welfare mothers," whose personal and sexual conduct was scrutinized and later connected to intentionality and/or responsibility for murder.

Although the Coroner's Office is careful to state that the question of culpability is a matter for the police, a cause-of-death finding essentially determines which course of action the police will then take. Similarly, Crown prosecutors will claim that it is up to the police to lay charges, which they then simply prosecute. However, the police will almost invariably determine whether or not a criminal charge will be laid based on the autopsy report from the forensic pathologist.[6] And, a police officer will sometimes consult with the Crown Attorney's Office about a particular charge before it is laid.

A total of eighty-eight cases were provided by the Coroner's Office, representing all cases between 1986 and 1998 in which the death of infants under one year of age was determined to be a homicide. When mothers were present at the time of the death, they were almost always considered suspects, especially when they were young, unemployed, and single. However, the overwhelming majority of the infants were suspected to have been killed by a father or a male common law spouse (stepfather). As we shall see from the police reports, the women are subject to intensive investigation.

Child abuse was coded in the Coroner's database system as a death factor in sixty-seven, or 76 percent, of all cases. "Death factor" is a quasi-medico-legal category that allows the coroner to comment on the background or context of the death; it is not the same as the formal medico-legal category of "cause of death," under which the immediate physical cause of death (e.g., asphyxiation, subdural hematoma, etc.) is recorded. This coding of death factors by the Coroner's Office is misleading because it makes it appear as though all of the cases in which child abuse is listed as a death factor are, objectively speaking, cases typically described by experts in the field as child abuse; that is, cases in which there is evidence that a child experienced prolonged or repeated physical violence in the home.

A few examples are useful. In 1988 a mother jumped from a downtown building with her baby in her arms. Both were killed instantly. The death factor of the infant was coded as child abuse. A baby sitter shook a crying baby who died from the injuries it sustained; there was no evidence of old injuries, but the death factor was listed as child abuse. A mother smothered a crying baby who died of suffocation; there was no evidence of old injuries, but the death factor was listed as child abuse. Those cases investigated by the Coroner's Office in which infants died from intentional violence at the hands of their parents *and* in which there was evidence of old and healing injuries to the body that could be attributed to non-accidental injury are small compared to all other cases listed as child abuse (and that certainly deserve further attention). However, without a careful review of autopsy reports to determine if there were old intentionally caused injuries, those cases in which child abuse is a legitimate concern are indistinguishable from those in which it is not. Nevertheless, there are a few cases in which old healing injuries are evident and where child abuse may therefore be an entirely appropriate finding (although not as a medical cause of death). These findings are in sharp contrast to those of Greenland (1973, 2), who examined the coroner's files and found that "'battered child syndrome' in the classical sense was rare in Ontario." His study concluded that the physical abuse of children in Ontario was not limited to very young children, it was just that the young were more likely to die as a result of it. Of the files examined (359 cases in 1970) by Greenland and his colleagues:

> More than one third of the children received only bruises or welts, and fully ten per cent had no apparent injury. A minority suffered serious injuries such as burns, bone or skull fractures, brain damage and internal injuries. Fifteen per cent were injured sufficiently to require hospital admission. More men than women were reported as verified as having abused their children. Injuries were unintentionally inflicted in most cases by the natural parents or other adult caretakers. Excessive use of discipline was the most apparent cause of injuries, not deliberate or malicious abuse or neglect. Many children were victims of physical assaults expressed in a context of child rearing.

These findings are striking given the kinds of claims now being made by the Office of the Chief Coroner for Ontario. A follow-up study, like that conducted by Greenland and his colleagues, is required for an accurate picture of the nature and extent of child abuse in Ontario (see Greenland 1987).

According to June Frank (Manager, Coroners Information System, Office of the Chief Coroner for Ontario), child abuse is recorded as a death factor in these cases in order to facilitate a report to the province's Child Abuse Registry.[7] Once the case is determined to be the result of child abuse, the coroner has a duty to report the incident to the Ministry of Community and Social Services, Child Abuse Registry. Presumably, once this report is provided to the ministry, it allows social services to monitor other children in the household with a view to preventing future harm. However, this vast overrepresentation of child abuse in the death factor category only makes sense if the aim is to subject individual suspects to enhanced surveillance by the child welfare authorities. The Child Abuse Registry in Ontario is maintained by the provincial government and contains information about individuals investigated by agents of the regional children's aid societies. It contains information, which is governed by confidentiality regulations, about the child abuser. It can be accessed by child welfare authorities, the coroner, the children's lawyer, persons providing counselling or treatment to the alleged abuser, researchers, physicians, the abused child, and the registered person or her/his agent. One does not have to be convicted of a *Criminal Code* offence to be named in the province's child abuse register.[8]

Infanticide and the "Child Abuse Death Factor" in the 1980s

In the 1980s (1986-89) twenty-seven cases of infant homicide were investigated by the Ontario Coroner's Offices, and child abuse was listed as the death factor in all but three. Of all cases in which homicide was considered the "death type," 90 percent were attributable to child abuse – regardless of whether the infant had old injuries. In come cases the coroner and pathologist determined neonaticides to be child abuse, but they were prosecuted as infanticide. For example, in 1987 and 1988 two cases were investigated in which the death factor was considered to be child abuse but the medical cause of death was considered to be neonatal asphyxiation. In one case the pathologist considered the asphyxiation to be of "undetermined origin," and in the other an x-ray examination found no evidence of fractured bones. Both mothers were charged with infanticide, and one mother was also charged with failure to seek assistance in childbirth. In both these cases the women and the infants were brought to the attention of the authorities when the women showed up in an emergency department with vaginal hemorrhaging. Emergency doctors suspected a recent full-term delivery and notified the police, who would have notified the coroner once a body had been discovered. Both babies were determined to have been born alive on the grounds that there was air in their lungs and that they were full-term. In both cases the coroner sent a letter to the Child Abuse Registry indicating that the deaths had been classified as infanticide. In both cases the mothers either denied they were pregnant or denied knowing they were pregnant. They told the authorities either that they thought the babies were dead when they were born or that they died shortly afterwards. Neither woman confessed to an intentional killing of these infants.

In the case of Baby R (1987),[9] witnesses told the investigating police officers that they saw the mother-suspect give a green garbage bag to her fourteen-year-old brother and tell him to throw it in the garbage bin across the street at a donut shop. The brother admitted to having thrown the bag in the garbage and took police to the Tricil garbage bin, where they found the body of an apparently full-term baby. At that point the police notified the coroner, who pronounced the baby dead and took the body to the morgue for an autopsy to determine if it had been born alive. Police officers examined the suspect's apartment and took photographs, blood samples, and other evidence at the scene. Eventually, the police laid a charge of infanticide against a seventeen-year-old single woman.

Dr. Chitra Rao of the Regional Forensic Unit, Hamilton General Hospital, performed the autopsy and, on the basis that air was present in its lungs, declared the infant to have been born alive.[10] The medical cause of death was determined to be asphyxia. The Chief Coroner for Ontario at that time, Dr. R.C. Bennett, sent a letter to the registrar of the Child Abuse Registry, Ministry of Community and Social Services, advising of the death of the newborn, indicating that charges had been laid against the mother and that the coroner had classified the death as due to infanticide.

Murder Convictions for Maternal Neonaticide during the 1990s

In the 1990s the death factor determinations become more accurate in cases of neonaticide, and the items listed are the medical or proximate causes of death. Child abuse was no longer listed as a death factor. At the same time, however, a noticeable change in charging practices occurred, in which infanticide was no longer laid as the preferred criminal charge. There had been a shift toward a more punitive charging framework, in which second degree murder charges were laid, sometimes in conjunction with the usual infanticide, concealment, and neglect charges. It would appear that these cases were being pursued as though they were child abuse homicides, even though the Coroner's Office was now reporting the causes of death more accurately. From 1990 to 1998 there were four cases that clearly fit the model for maternal neonaticide and that showed no evidence of old injuries, and yet second degree murder charges were laid. The death factors were listed as "cuts and stabs," "asphyxia," and "drowning."[11] In all four cases the women and the babies were brought to the attention of the authorities because the women required medical attention for vaginal bleeding.

Baby B: Dumpster Baby

In the case of Baby B, found in a garbage bin beside the garage of the suspect-mother's residence, it was determined, again by Dr. Charles Smith, that the baby was full-term and had died from asphyxiation. Smith determined that the baby had been born alive on the basis that there was air in the lungs and stomach. The Coroner's Investigation Statement indicated that the full-term infant had been born at home and that the single young mother had failed to properly resuscitate it following birth. It was noted that this young woman did not attempt to get help and concealed the body of the infant. The police laid three charges: second degree murder, concealment, and neglect. The suspect told the doctors and the police that she believed she may have miscarried a foetus of approximately one month gestation and that she had flushed it down the toilet. It was only after the police threatened to pump out the septic tank to retrieve the foetus that she confessed to giving birth to a stillborn baby and took the police to the garbage bin at the rear of her residence.

Baby S: The Question of Live-Birth

A murder charge was also laid in the case of Baby S. The police were called to a residence where a young, single woman had given birth unattended and required emergency medical assistance when her parents came home and found her in the bathroom, unconscious and covered in blood. The baby was found dead in the toilet bowl and the coroner determined that it had drowned. The autopsy, again performed by Dr. Charles Smith, indicated that the infant had been born alive (there was air in its lungs) and that it had died from "asphyxiation (infanticide)." The mother was subsequently charged with second degree murder and remanded to custody.[12] The twenty-three-year-old woman eventually pled guilty to manslaughter. A newspaper report at the time of the trial stated:

> CM, a first year university student, pleaded guilty to manslaughter in the death of her newborn son, found in a toilet shortly after his birth on a bathroom floor ... M has maintained she didn't realize she was pregnant until she gave birth in 1992. M's parents were out when she delivered the baby. They returned home to find her on the bathroom floor, dazed and covered in blood, court heard [sic] Initially, M told police the infant was born in the toilet bowl and she hadn't touched him. She later admitted he was born on the floor and that she put him into the toilet. M was in shock and a semi-comatose state when she was found, her lawyer Bernie O'Brien said. The baby, who was no more than a few minutes old, had

been asphyxiated. Experts suggested either the umbilical cord caught around the baby's throat or he drowned, said O'Brien. He said the woman's family and friends didn't suspect she was pregnant. The lawyer said she gained and lost only 10 pounds before and after birth.[13]

Again, we see the ad hoc approach to investigation and prosecution resulting in a forced guilty plea to manslaughter. The outcome of this plea in this instance highlights the move toward more punitive responses, especially when, if the woman had had access to a good defence lawyer, scientific evidence that a nuchal cord might have been the cause of death should have been enough to establish reasonable doubt. In addition, the practice of remanding the accused in custody between the time of the laying of the charge and her first appearance in court is unusual in cases of infanticide since offenders are not considered any kind of threat to the public.

Baby O and Baby J: Violence to the Body

In the case of Baby O, the body of the infant was discovered by police officers and was eventually connected to the twenty-four-year-old single mother, who had gone to seek medical attention at a hospital emergency ward. According to the report, the autopsy, again conducted by Dr. Charles Smith, indicated that there was some external violence to the baby's body (stabbing in chest, neck and head fractures) and that the cause of death was attributable to these injuries. The mother was charged with murder.

In the final neonaticide case in which murder was charged, the circumstances of the case are similar to those in each of the other cases. A twenty-four-year-old single woman was taken to the emergency department of a hospital with vaginal bleeding and was charged with second degree murder after the body of the infant, Baby J, was discovered by police with multiple stab wounds to the head and neck. The mother had given birth alone in the bathroom of her home. The court ordered a mandatory thirty-day psychiatric assessment and the suspect was confined to the London Psychiatric Hospital. The evidence of violence to the infant's body played a role in the subsequent public reaction aspect of the case, as reported in the newspapers at the time. This case was also included in the *Toronto Star*'s sample cases of child abuse and was mentioned in the story entitled "Getting Away with Murder – of Children" (M. Welsh and K. Donovan, *Toronto Star*, serial report, 18 May 1997). The *Star* reported that the infant was stabbed twenty times and that the mother was sentenced to two years imprisonment.[14] The *Star* presents that case as one among many, including child abuse homicide cases such as the death of Shanay Johnson, in which the punishment for the crime is characterized as "too little." According to the *Star* report: "Barbara Peters, a 24-year-old London woman, stabbed her newborn baby 20 times with a pair of scissors, piercing the spinal cord. Peters was sentenced to two years less a day in a psychiatric hospital when she pleaded guilty to manslaughter. She originally was charged with second degree murder. The judge, in his ruling, said Peters was of low intelligence and suffered from psychiatric problems" (ibid., A6).

However, according to a report in the *London Free Press*, the baby was stabbed only twice.[15] The actual autopsy report indicated that the baby had indeed been stabbed, although it did not indicate how many times or the depth of the wounds. There were, however, many small lacerations to the head and neck in addition to the likely fatal stab wounds.[16] Such a finding is typically consistent with pregnancy denial and unassisted births. It has never operated as legal proof of intentionally inflicted violence and certainly not as an indication of evil intent as defined by *R. v. McHugh*.[17] In fact, in most cases in the early twentieth century it was assumed that such injuries were likely the result of shock or the woman's attempts to hide the deceased baby. While the injuries in this case were certainly severe, the *Star* report, which indicated that *both* the outcome of the case and the excuse of psychiatry were somehow out of proportion with the facts of the case, responded in a way that is typical of the late twentieth century. As I have shown, it is only in terms of severity of response that this case is out of proportion with any other case of infanticide over the last century; the violence was certainly no more severe than that in many cases of maternal neonaticide that were treated leniently during the early twentieth century.[18] In the present case of Baby J, the accused woman spent twenty-one months in pre-trial custody, both in jail and at the London Psychiatric Hospital, and was diagnosed as psychotic and in need of long-term psychiatric care.[19] And, as the *Star* reports, she was later sentenced to a further two years in custody following her plea of guilt for manslaughter (M. Welsh and K. Donovan, "Getting Away with Murder – of Children," *Toronto Star*, serial report, 18 May 1997, A6). The reaction, in the form of the murder charge, the manslaughter conviction, and the tone of the newspaper reports, as well as the length of time spent in custody (both psychiatric and jail), stands in sharp contrast to the kinds of assumptions that influenced legal practices in the early twentieth century.

Today in Ontario evidence of violence amounts to a conviction and harsh punishment. In the early part of the century, violence to the body was explained first in relation to unattended birth (even though the circumstances of unassisted childbirth today are exactly the same as they were eighty to 100 years ago). Earlier, intentional violence was explained as the outcome of either lactational insanity or, subsequently, of a dissociative mental state brought about by giving birth following a denied pregnancy. In these earlier cases, the shock of the birth is seen as the factor that precipitates the intentional violence: the violence is not viewed as merely the product of some kind of inherent, undefined evil. Moreover, the contemporary idea that violence perpetrated against the baby's body in an attempt to dispose of it is evidence of evil intent used to be discounted by criminological experts who characterized this practice as *méthode cuisinaire*. This was viewed, under the circumstances, as rational, normal behaviour. Lacassaigne explained this practice not in terms of evil intent but in terms of women attempting (legitimately) to conceal their shame through secretly disposing of the babies' bodies. Today, the idea of shame has disappeared because there is no longer a strong moral stigma attached to unwed motherhood and illegitimacy per se, and violence is constructed only as evidence of evil intent. In contrast, those cases adjudicated in Quebec and discussed in Chapter 4 reveal an approach to mitigation that allows evidence of pregnancy denial to mitigate intentionality. In some jurisdictions women's experiences of denial and concealed pregnancy, along with the shock of unexpected childbirth and its intense pains, excuse criminal culpability for maternal neonaticide.[20]

Punitive Overkill: The Marginalization of "Infanticide"

I have shown how, within the context of a widespread professional concern about child abuse (perhaps best described as a "moral panic"), a number of cases have been responded to as cases of murder. These were cases that fit with the kinds of circumstances that, for well over 100 years, have been considered infanticide, and in which the system failed to respond according to the clear intent of legislators and judges who were involved in the passage of the infanticide act. They were cases in which newborns were killed by their mothers more or less immediately after birth, sometimes as a consequence of unattended birth, and where there are clear questions about mental capacity arising from the denial of pregnancy. In all four cases, circumstances that would have suggested powerful mitigation to early twentieth-century coroner's inquest juries and grand juries, and which would have been seen as appropriately eliciting an infanticide indictment, are, by the 1990s, seen as indicating an especially heinous crime requiring retribution.

1990s "Infanticide" Convictions

There were, however, also cases during the 1990s that resulted in infanticide convictions but in which the circumstances were quite different from those found in the traditional infanticide scenario. Indeed, the circumstances of the 1990s might well have prompted a much more punitive response than would have been the case in an earlier time. Each of the cases in this section differs significantly from those in the early part of the century (as well as from the other cases discussed in this chapter) in a number ways. First, while at ages five months and eight months, respectively, the infants are well within the age range covered by infanticide law, charges are more typically laid in cases involving much younger babies. In addition, both babies were born to married and not particularly young mothers. In both cases the infant's cause of death is clearly agreed upon, but questions of mental capacity do cast doubt (in the eyes of the law) on the mother's criminal culpability for first or second degree murder. The women are considered mentally compromised by either postpartum depression (although in this case the diagnosis is contested because there is evidence of child abuse) or severe and long-standing psychosis at the time of the killing. And in each case the psychiatric evidence was forced to fit into the infanticide framework when defence attorneys and Crown prosecutors agreed upon an infanticide conviction in exchange for a guilty plea.

Baby D: Sudden Infant Death Syndrome and the "Murder of Innocents"

In the death of Baby D in 1996 the mother was suspected of smothering it and was initially charged with first degree murder. However, she was committed to trial on second degree murder and pled guilty to infanticide. At first, this case was considered to be an instance of sudden infant death syndrome (SIDS); however, the investigation changed its focus when a pre-autopsy x-ray revealed fractured bones. This particular finding fuelled suspicion of the mother who, in addition to having other children out of wedlock with a different father, was considered to be "cheating" welfare because, in order not to violate the "spouse-in-the-house" rule, she claimed that her current boyfriend did not live with her and the children (when, in fact, he did). In addition, by this time an initial finding of SIDS had become more broadly reviewable because of a widespread anxiety among forensic pathologists and coroners that such findings often concealed murders.

SIDS, or "cot death" as it is referred to in Britain, was officially defined in 1969 at the Second International Conference on Causes of Sudden Deaths in Infants, attended by twenty-seven pathologists, pediatricians, and epidemiologists from the United States, Canada, and Europe (Firstman and Talan 1997, 199). At this conference J. Bruce Beckwith, a pediatric pathologist and leading researcher at the Seattle Children's Orthopedic Hospital, introduced the definition of sudden infant death syndrome as a broad diagnostic category in the unexpected deaths of young children for which no explanation could be found at autopsy (Firstman and Talan 1997, 195). Kirschner (1997, 249)[21] defines a negative autopsy as: "An autopsy in which there is no significant disease processes or injuries and in which the cause of death cannot be determined after the gross dissection, microscopical examination, and all laboratory tests have been completed."

Since SIDS is a diagnosis of exclusion, the chief difficulty in SIDS deaths lies in eliminating other causes of death that may leave little trace and, especially, in distinguishing between intentional and unintentional asphyxiation.

According to Kirschner (1997, 277), "asphyxiation of the young infant usually produces no distinct pathological changes observable at autopsy. This is true of both accidental and homicidal suffocation." He further notes that a range of findings at autopsy suggest possible intentional asphyxiation but are not conclusive evidence of homicide:

> Punctate petechial hemorrhages may be observed on the head and neck, and in the sclerae and conjunctivae. This variable finding is suspicious of, but not diagnostic of asphyxiation. The infant who has been febrile or septic may show similar petechial hemorrhages at postmortem examination. Some pathologists place emphasis on the presence of significant numbers of intrathoracic petechiae (on the thymus, epicardium, and pleural surfaces) as characteristic of SIDS, and few or absent petechiae as suspicious of suffocation. In my experience, approximately 50 percent of documented SIDS cases will show only minimal to moderate intrathoracic petechiae, and their absence is not predictive of asphyxiation. (ibid.)

The fact that forensic medicine is unable to prove with certainty whether an infant died from intentional asphyxiation frustrates those in the medical community reviewing these cases as medical proof is the basis upon which a homicide charge must proceed. If there is any doubt about the cause of death, then convictions are unlikely since the uncertainty in the diagnosis can operate as "reasonable doubt" in murder trials. Therefore, certain *social* markers are appealed to by forensic pathologists in order to frame a death as homicidal. According to Kirschner (1997, 277): "Any previous family involvement with a child protective services department is cause for concern when a child dies suddenly or unexpectedly. A caretaker with a history of psychiatric disorders, marital difficulties of the child's parents, frequent visits of the child to emergency rooms, signs in the child of nonorganic failure to thrive, and reports of previous apneic episodes witnessed by only one parent are all warning signs of possible abuse. In most large metropolitan regions, the prevalence of SIDS within census tracts varies inversely with average income and other indicators of good quality of life."

Therefore, in the absence of other medical indicators of child abuse, indicia of homicide in SIDS cases relate to the class and marital status of the mother and include questions about her mental capacity. Any previous contact with children's aid (whether it is for suspected child abuse or simply for economic reasons), marital stability, and frequent visits to emergency wards by children who are diagnosed as developmentally abnormal or who have had episodes of sleep apnea reported only by one parent are likely to be the objects of a homicide investigation. Moreover, if more than two infants die in one family and the autopsy is negative, then it is to be considered a homicide. According to Kirschner (1997, 279), "if a previous unexplained infant death, including SIDS, has occurred in a family and no further evidence of metabolic disorder is forthcoming, the unexplained death of a second infant should be classified as undetermined ... Should a third infant death without an obvious natural disease process occur in the same family, the cause of death should be identified as asphyxiation, and the manner of death classified as homicide."

This diagnosis of homicide in multiple SIDS deaths was revised in the 1980s when it was discovered by team of investigators in upstate New York that five babies, originally diagnosed with SIDS, had been murdered by their mother, Waneta Hoyt.[22] The "H babies," as they were known in the medical community, had been the subjects of Alfred Steinschneider's research on SIDS and sleep apnea (Steinshcneider advanced the notion that SIDS was a familial trait) (Firstman and Talan 1997). This case led to the psychiatric model of Munchausen syndrome by proxy in order to explain serial infant homicide by mothers. In fact, Kirschner (1997, 279) now argues that "the diagnosis of Munchausen syndrome by proxy is appropriate" in multiple incidents of SIDS, given the extremely low probability of SIDS occurring multiple times in one family (1 in 10,000,000). In England Sir Roy Meadows, a pediatrician who acted as an expert witness for the Crown, was at least partly to blame for the wrongful murder convictions of a number of women who, he testified, suffered from Munchausen's syndrome by proxy. Meadows, who is a retired pediatrician, is the author of a 1977 article entitled "Munchausen Syndrome by Proxy: The Hinterland of Child Abuse" and published in the British medical journal *The Lancet*. Meadows famously claimed that, "unless proven otherwise, one cot death is tragedy, two is suspicious, and three is murder."[23] On the basis of the theory that SIDS deaths are really hidden murders – and on the expert testimony of Roy Meadows – Sally Clark, Trupti Patel, and Angela Canning were each convicted of murdering their babies. It was subsequently determined that each of the women's infants died from SIDS.[24] In April 2002, Angela Canning was sentenced for the murder of her two sons, seven-week-old Jason in 1991 and eighteen-week-old Matthew in 1999, but in December 2003 the conviction was overturned by the Court of Appeal in the UK.[25]

Because of the discovery of a single case of multiple deaths attributable to intentional asphyxiation which was initially diagnosed as SIDS, the SIDS category now includes possible filicide as one cause of death. In the 1960s Stuart Asch, a New York psychiatrist, had published a paper discussing the question of whether infanticide at the hands of mothers suffering from extreme postpartum depression was really SIDS death (Firstman and Talan 1997, 200). By the 1990s this possibility had been all but reversed: the finding that SIDS determinations have masked some intentional homicide was a well established idea in the forensic community. All cases of SIDS are inevitably subject to some kind of suspicion, particularly when coupled with the kinds of social markers identified by Kirschner.

When investigators found evidence of long bone fractures (and possible child abuse) in the death of Baby D in 1996, the initial determination of SIDS death was reversed.[26] Even though the baby's mother claimed the infant died of SIDS, investigators had good medical evidence that the infant's death was in fact a homicide, and the body was transferred to the Toronto Hospital for Sick Children to be autopsied by Dr. Charles Smith. Along with the discovery of a fracture on the left leg near the ankle, the autopsy listed findings consistent with previous head injuries and asphyxiation. To buttress these findings, police noted that the suspect was an "unwed mother" who lived with her common law spouse in a basement apartment and that he had fathered the deceased infant but not the eighteen-month-old surviving sibling. The relationship between the suspect-mother and the common law spouse is described as immature and unstable. Highlighted in the case file are notations that suggest the mother, a high-school dropout, was cheating welfare because she collected mother's allowance while the father of one of the children shared the apartment with her. Neither of the parents of either the mother or the father of the deceased infant approved of the union. The suspect is described as having a difficult relationship with both her own parents and with the parents of the father of the deceased baby. At a visit to the scene police paid special attention to conditions that are suggested in the Coroner's Office directive concerning SIDS, and they noted that there were very few signs of alcohol consumption and no signs of smoking. The apartment was described as very messy and humid, with a distinct odor "consistent with an unclean apartment."

Police investigators noticed that the eighteen-month-old sibling had been brought to the local emergency department on nine occasions. On three occasions in the past nine months the infant had either a forehead or a dental injury after a fall, as revealed in visits to the emergency department of a local hospital. This infant was eventually taken into custody by Children's Aid. They also note that the mother was brought to the emergency department about a month before the infant's death by her own mother when she explained that she had almost killed her baby by smothering it. The baby, it was learned, was prone to long bouts of crying that the mother was unable to prevent. Various witnesses interviewed by the police confirmed that the suspect-mother had a difficult time with the baby and that she was unable to care for it or to provide it with comfort. During a hospital visit in 1995 a doctor who treated the baby for congestion, dry cough, vomiting, and diarrhea noted that the "parents look[ed] very stressed, not listening, immature."[27] The baby was described as crying twenty-four hours a day and the mother herself was described as unable to get any sleep because of this. There is some concern that mould in the basement apartment might have been the cause of the baby's irritability. The fact that the baby seemed fine when it was with its grandmother generates suspicion not about mould but about the mother's "caregiving" skills. Shortly before the infant's death, the suspect-mother complained of depression and was prescribed the anti-depressant medication "Zoloft" and was asked to fill out the Beck Inventory Depression Scale and return it later in the week, a task that she failed to accomplish.

While the medical evidence in this case points to the possibility of intentional violence being the cause of death, the details of the mother's income, marital status, hospital visits, and mental capacity played an important role in constructing her as culpable for murder. She was in fact charged by police with first degree murder, which was reduced to second degree at trial, and she ultimately pled guilty to infanticide. Throughout the investigation the mother denied having had anything to do with killing the baby and pointed instead to the mould growing in the apartment, which she had had inspected by a city building inspector because she was concerned that it might be having an adverse affect on the infant's health and well-being. The mother was certain that the mildew was contributing to the baby's irritability. The city inspector looked at the problem and advised the mother to wash the mildew off the walls and move some furniture that was blocking an electric heater in the baby's room. These doubts about the possible cause of death, coupled with the medical uncertainties surrounding it, the difficulty in proving both that the mother had "exclusive opportunity" at the time of the infant's death and that it was she who caused the fracture to the baby's leg, and the suggestion that she may have been suffering from postpartum depression and sleep deprivation probably all contributed to the final finding of guilt for infanticide.

The circumstances surrounding the case pressed both for and against this kind of murder conviction. The above-noted factors made a murder charge very difficult to sustain, particularly for a jury that might be reluctant to sentence an obviously troubled and likely grieving mother to prison. In fact, it would appear that psychiatry played a particularly significant role in the outcome of this case, even though the circumstances of the killing did not *necessarily* conform to the kinds of circumstances legislators intended to be covered by infanticide. As I show, the fact that a murder charge was initially laid in this case was a relatively new phenomenon – one that followed from developments surrounding SIDS determinations. And, given the range of difficulties faced by Crown prosecutors in proving culpability, it is not surprising that an ungrounded plea of guilt for infanticide was accepted.

Baby P: Cult Death Madness

In another very high-profile case the coroner determined that the death factor was child abuse, with the medical cause of death classified as asphyxia. The forensic pathologist, again Dr. Charles Smith, determined that the baby had died from being strangled. There was no finding at autopsy of any external marks of violence (save for some tiny scratch marks on the body), and the osseous system was considered normal, with no evident fractures. Regional Chief Coroner Dr. Keith Johnson wrote to the Children's Aid Society to inform it of the death of the five-month-old and the fact that the mother, who was psychotic at the time of the homicide, was convicted of infanticide. He further stated: "Since the death of a child is obviously a severe form of child abuse this report is to be considered as formal notification to your agency."[28] The death of the infant is further described in the radiology report from Toronto's Hospital for Sick Children as "sudden death of a baby while family was involved in cult-like activities."[29]

News reports also hinted at the "cult-like" flavour of the case by presenting commentary from local police confiding that blood had been found at the scene of the crime "but it was not the baby's or the mother's." The police, however, refused to elaborate, saying only that "no one else required medical attention."[30]

The Coroner's Investigation Statement provides comprehensive details of the circumstances surrounding the death of the infant, pointing to a history of serious mental health and capacity issues with respect to the mother charged with murder. It is noted that the mother, a southern European immigrant, had been described by her mother as having dreams and visions of Our Lady of Fatima (Virgin Mary) since age five. Once in Canada, the mother married and later gave birth by Caesarean section. The pregnancy is described as "unplanned" and the birth as upsetting because she considered Caesarean birth to be unnatural.[31]

On the weekend of the homicide, the mother told her co-workers that they should pray because a miracle was about to happen. She also told her mother that she had had a vision of Our Lady of Fatima and requested that she assemble the family to pray for peace and salvation. According to the Coroner's Investigation Statement:

> On Saturday May 22 the [name] family had a barbecue at the residence of [sister's name] who was a sister of [mother]. Sister had a two year old [name] who was born with liver and heart problems and was basically not well. At the barbecue on May 22 [Mother] requested that the family gather at her mother's residence at [address] to pray together to Our Lady of Fatima for salvation and peace. [Mother] and her husband went to prepare the house by covering all of the furniture and windows with white sheets and linen. Herbs were placed at the doorways and candles were obtained and lit beside

pictures of Our Lady of Guadeloupe (Virgin Mary). [Mother] directed that the family should be dressed in white and [parents] then began praying in the bedroom with their five month old son [name] dressed in white and laying in the centre of the bed. At approximately six PM on May 22 nineteen family members gathered in this small house on [address] and proceeded with an evening of prayers. Through the evening hours many of the family members decided to leave or were asked to leave by [mother] and finally at 10 pm, mother asked that they all leave and that included her mother and her sisters. They were asked not to return until the next day. Her husband and sister stayed with mother and at approximately 10:30 PM [mother] directed [father] to take [sister] home and as well not to come back as [mother] intended to stay there and continue to pray with [baby] and [niece]. Her efforts were to obtain assistance for [niece]'s health. None of the family members returned to the residence at [address] that night or the next morning.

The next day due to some concerns of [sister]'s health she was taken to the [local] General Hospital and later committed to the London Psychiatric Hospital as being mentally unstable. This was approximately 1000 hours on May 23, 1993.

After this the family became concerned because they had not heard from [mother] so between 1400 and 1430 hours [name] the husband, [name] a neighbor, and the grandmother and [a sister and her daughter] returned to [the house]. They found [mother] sitting in the middle of the bed holding [niece 2 yrs old] and she had a blanket wrapped around [niece] and she was rocking back and forth. [Baby] was lying on his back in the middle of the bedroom floor on a pillow still clothed in white but he was motionless and he appeared to be blue. [Mother's] face around her mouth was covered with dried blood as well as her clothes and hands. [Mother] had a rosary in one hand and a piece of broken glass in the other. [Grandmother and sister] picked up [baby] and he was cold to touch. Attempts at mouth to mouth resuscitation were made to no avail. [Grandmother and sister] took the baby [name] and [niece] and drove directly to Woodstock General Hospital. They arrived at 1511 hours and despite attempted resuscitation [baby] did not respond. It was felt that the child had been dead for a number of hours[32]

In a chronology of events detailed in the local newspaper it is reported that family members returned to the house to find the infant dead, with the mother covered in her own blood and clutching a rosary and piece of glass, which she used to cut her own tongue. Later the police added the charge of infanticide to the second degree murder charge, and the mother pled not guilty to both charges. The local newspaper mistakenly defines infanticide as including "neglect": "Infanticide is a charge laid against mothers who willfully *or through neglect* cause the death of their own baby."[33]

Once the trial was over, newspaper reports headlined the finding of guilt for infanticide. In addition, the reports outlined seven separate elements for infanticide alongside the detailed story of the baby's death. According to one report a jury found the mother "not guilty of second degree murder ... after psychiatric testimony indicated she was 'clearly psychotic' when she obeyed voices that said her five-month-old baby was an evil dog that must be suffocated. But the jury did convict the 26-year-old married mother of a lesser charge of infanticide in the death of her son on the joint recommendation of the defence and crown attorney."[34]

The details of this case fit uneasily with those of late nineteenth-century and twentieth-century cases of neonaticide in which infants are killed after childbirth and where social factors are more likely to make up the convincing mitigating framework. The infant in this case was not an unwanted baby, nor was it killed within hours of its birth. The mother had a history of mental health issues manifesting themselves typically as religious visions and dreams and had never been diagnosed with any form of depression prior to the homicide. Nevertheless, strenuous attempts were made to make this case fit with the requirements of both an infanticide charge and a finding of guilt. At trial Dr. Gurpreet Sidhu, a forensic psychiatrist, testified that the mother "suffered from severe depression most of her life and sought comfort in religion."[35] He also testified that her condition worsened with the so-called unplanned birth of her son and that she had trouble nursing and was upset the baby had to be delivered by Caesarean section. Sidhu testified that the mother was suffering from "psychotic hallucinations" the night the infant was killed.[36] Nothing in Sidhu's testimony, or indeed in the details of the case provided by police, the coroner, or the defence itself, indicates either that a charge of infanticide is appropriate or that a finding of guilt is suitable.

Infanticide Plea Bargains

In both of the above cases the circumstances seem inappropriate for a finding of infanticide. In the first, there is some evidence of earlier abuse. In the second, the mother's long-standing psychotic condition is quite inconsistent with the underlying "psychiatric" rationale for infanticide, which suggests a reactive mental illness following pregnancy and childbirth. It may be these kinds of very violent and disturbing infant deaths that have prompted those involved in the development of criminal policy to advocate the repeal of the infanticide provision in the *Criminal Code*. The case of Baby D, whose death was initially ruled as SIDS but later amended to child abuse, with its evidence of previous violence is certainly suggestive of the proposed category of child abuse/neglect homicide. However, the outcome of the Baby P case can be thought of as a just, if poorly grounded, judicial finding. The mother's psychosis might have better suggested a finding of not criminally responsible by reason of mental disorder but, in any case, there are powerful reasons for mitigation.

Infanticide

Five cases in the 1990s conform to the established parameters of infanticide, and they were dealt with by the criminal courts as cases of infanticide. In all but one instance the Office of the Coroner listed child abuse as the death factor rather than a standard medical cause of death.[37] In the case of Baby A, who drowned in the bathtub, the Office of the Coroner listed the death factor as child abuse, without evidence of old injuries or a history of the mother abusing other children.[38] In this first, apparently accidental, death case the baby's body was discovered when the infant's mother called 911 for help. In three of the remaining four cases, the infants' deaths were discovered when women were reported to police following treatment at a hospital emergency department. Further investigation by police in each case turned up the bodies of the infants. In the fifth case, only the body of an infant was initially discovered, and police eventually tracked down a fifteen-year-old girl who, it was determined upon examination, had recently given birth.

In one case the child was a few months old, but the case conforms to infanticide requirements because it was agreed that the mother, who was in her twenties, was suffering from postpartum depression at the time she drowned the child.[39] The remaining four cases are straightforward instances of infanticide, where the infants were killed either intentionally, following secreted and unattended childbirth at home, or unintentionally as a consequence of unattended childbirth. These four young women were less than eighteen years of age and all of them lived with parents who had no knowledge of their pregnancies. Causes of death were "asphyxia," "suffocation," "blunt trauma – beating," and "cuts and stabs." In all but one of these four archetypal infanticide cases, multiple charges were laid along with infanticide, including neglect to obtain assistance in childbirth, failure to provide the necessaries of life, and concealing the body of a child. In the last case of the four, a single charge of infanticide was laid. All charges were laid on the basis of a pathologist's autopsy indicating "live-birth" and "infanticide-like" symptoms such as petechial hemorrhaging of the eyes and/or cyanosis of the nailbeds, indicating possible intentional strangulation and/or unintentional asphyxiation.

In contrast to the early part of the twentieth century, findings of live-birth are now the norm. For the purposes of a homicide investigation, it is now assumed that infants are born alive rather than stillborn. This assumption stands in sharp contrast to that outlined in Boys's (1905) *Handbook for Canadian Coroners* discussed in Chapter 1. By the 1990s, 95 percent of all births take place in hospital, which has the effect of normalizing live-birth.

In the early part of the century, when infant mortality rates were high and the majority of births took place at home, it was normally assumed that a baby discovered dead shortly after birth had died as a consequence of birth rather than as a consequence of violence at the hands of its birth mother. Today, this assumption is completely reversed. In each case reviewed the babies were considered to have been born alive. This determination of live-birth was the key finding that led to the laying of criminal charges and it was necessary in order to sustain any charge of homicide. More important, there were no cases in which stillbirth was the finding, even though the number of stillbirths today is not trivial.[40] All of the autopsies were performed by one of only two Ontario pediatric forensic pathologists – Drs. Chitra Rao (Hamilton) and Charles Smith (Toronto).[41] In each case, the weight and size of the baby established its gestational age, with all cases falling in the full-term range. This finding seems to have had the effect of confirming live-birth. Both forensic pathologists performed the floating-lung test, which had been discredited by European experts such as William Hunter in 1784 and, in Canada, by Boys in 1905. This test continues to be used to support a charge of homicide. Robert Kirschner, the contemporary American expert, cautions forensic pathologists not to assume live-birth, and he discusses a range of birth injuries that can lead to death from natural causes, accidental or intentional injury, and abandonment. According to Kirschner's (1997, 285) instructions: "The pathologist should start with the presumption of stillbirth and then attempt to establish sufficient evidence of live birth to reach that conclusion with a reasonable degree of medical and scientific certainty. In cases of alleged trauma to the pregnant mother, the specific maternal factors that contributed to fetal demise should be identified. When the identity of the infant is unknown, or parenthood disputed, blood and other tissues should be preserved for maternity/paternity testing."

Kirschner (1997, 285) subsequently instructs pathologists on the proper evaluation of the lung test in order to determine live-birth: "Signs of live birth must be evaluated. If the lungs or sections of lungs (in the absence of attempted resuscitation or decomposition) float in water, it is *probable* that the infant was live-born. If the lungs sink, this is indicative of, but does not prove, stillbirth. Lungs of live-born infants that are atelectatic or congested may not float. Milk or colostrum in the stomach is proof of live birth. Meconium or squamous alveolar debris does not indicate live birth, but lungs with alveolar hyaline membranes are characteristic of a living infant" (emphasis added).

In addition, Kirschner (1997, 285) outlines a range of *natural* causes of death shortly after live-birth that can be confused with foul play: "Infants may be live born but die shortly after birth because they are lethally malformed, of previable gestational age, or septic. The child may be full term and live-born but be nonresuscitatable due to perinatal asphyxiation from a variety of causes, including placental abnormalities, nuchal cord, and meconium aspiration." And, finally, Kirschner offers a clear medical definition of neonaticide: "A diagnosis of neonaticide requires that the live-born infant would still be alive but for abandonment or neglect, purposeful asphyxiation, inflicted trauma, or intoxication or poisoning" (285).

Given the incredible difficulty science has in proving live-birth, and since so many abnormal findings can be attributable to natural causes, Kirschner (1997, 286) argues that forensic pathologists must place "greater emphasis ... on nonlaboratory aspects of the investigation, including the development of multidisciplinary multiagency death review teams." The forensic investigator or coroner must then integrate his or her medical findings at autopsy with the investigative findings of police, child protection agencies, and Crown prosecutors when making a final determination. Therefore, the circumstances of the infant's death are just as important as is the medical evidence in determining when death was due to natural, accidental, or intentional causes. In addition, unassisted birth, as a possible cause of death, has completely disappeared as a possible accidental cause of death, even though today many babies would die if born at home with no help.

This combination of both medical and investigative evidence perhaps explains the practices of Dr. Charles Smith, who uses the term "infanticide" as a cause of death finding in his autopsy reports – including both social and legal circumstances as well as clinical findings. For example, in the case of Baby K (one of the two cases in this group that, in order to avoid unnecessary repetition, I have chosen not to describe in detail), who died of asphyxiation, Dr. Smith conducted an autopsy at the request of the regional pathologist. In this autopsy he notes the following: "Anatomical diagnosis: 1. Infanticide. 1.1. Full term gestation. 1.2 Liveborn female. 2. Asphyxia, with 2.1 Petechial hemorrhage of thoracic viscera 2.2. Congestion of the lungs. 2.3. Cyanosis of nailbeds."[42]

In his discussion, Smith notes that "the presence of air in the lungs and stomach indicates that she survived for a period of time following delivery; the pattern of alveolar distention does not suggest that the aeration was of external origin e.g. resuscitation or ventilation."[43] So while Smith's conclusion of "live-birth" appears to have relied on the test conducted on the lungs, this test alone, according to the experts, is insufficient in and of itself to conclude live-birth. The medical finding of infanticide, therefore, likely relied on the investigative efforts of police to determine if the death could be ruled homicide. This practice clearly has the effect of turning a clinical examination into a criminal investigation by substituting social and legal claims for inconclusive medical evidence. Due to the unconvincing nature of the medical evidence, we see an expansion of the investigative efforts of police, coroners, Crown attorneys, and even doctors and social workers, who attempt to provide complementary evidence of immorality as proof of guilt for murder.

Baby L: Intensive Medical and Social Investigation to Prove Murder[44]

In recent years the scope of police investigations into infant deaths has widened considerably, partly in response to the inability to secure convictions solely on the basis of live-birth findings. In the case that follows, these investigative efforts are detailed in order to illustrate how social factors are deployed to support a medical and legal finding of homicide rather than to mitigate culpability. In the case of Baby L, the investigating pathologist determined that the infant had been born alive, and charges for infanticide, concealment, neglect, and failure to provide the necessaries of life were laid against a very young unwed mother who denied and hid her pregnancy from friends and family. According to the Coroner's Investigation Statement, Baby L was a newborn baby, with the umbilical cord still attached, who had been found in a dumpster by two young children playing in a strip-mall parking lot. At autopsy Baby L was determined to have been alive at birth, and it was further determined that there were bruises on the chin and lip and petechial hemorrhages in the eyes, which indicated that the child was asphyxiated. The mother, who was eventually located through a police investigation, was described as a fifteen-year-old attending Grade 10 at a Roman Catholic high school when charges of neglect to obtain assistance in childbirth, infanticide, concealment and failure to provide the necessaries of life were laid.[45] The police discovered physical evidence in the form of a placenta in bloody bedsheets at the young woman's home. The young woman claimed that the baby quit breathing shortly after its birth and that, as a result, she took it to the garbage wrapped in her shirt and covered it with a stuffed animal. The fact that she was sexually active, unwed, very young, and attending Catholic school were the key indicators of infanticide. One can speculate that concealment of birth, neglect in childbirth, and failure to provide the necessaries of life were included in the response framework to ensure a criminal conviction through plea bargaining.

Baby T: Minor Mental Disturbance[46]

In a similar case the following year in a different jurisdiction, Baby T was discovered after a very high-profile search of a neighbourhood by homicide detectives who, following notification from an emergency room physician who had treated a young woman for vaginal bleeding, suspected that a baby had been born at home. The physician, cognizant of the young woman's right to privacy, contacted the Canadian Medical Protective Association, the Chief Executive Office of the hospital, and the Children's Aid Society of that region. The social worker contacted at the Children's Aid Society informed the doctor that she would be contacting the police. The physician noted that he had been advised by the Canadian Medical Protective Association that he was required to maintain patient confidentiality but that, under the *Child Protection Act,* he was obligated to notify the Children's Aid Society. At that point a hospital social worker was assigned to the patient and she was admitted to hospital, where she underwent an obstetrical procedure to remove placental tissue from the uterine cavity and to repair vaginal lacerations.

In addition to the obstetrical procedure, the patient was subject to a wide range of medical, psychiatric, and psycho-social evaluations by nurses, residents, psychiatrists, and social workers assigned to the case. The case file itself contains detailed notes of every communication between the nurses and the patient, the social worker and the patient, as well as various reports by physicians who evaluated her mental and physical condition. Nurses' notes repeatedly describe the patient as "sad and tearful" but "no postpartum depression." Another nurse describes her as "pale, sad and tearful" and notes that the patient told her she was in shock after giving birth alone in the bathroom because she had no knowledge of the pregnancy and that she was not sexually active, except for one time when a condom was used. The patient claimed that the baby was born not breathing and that afterwards she cut the umbilical cord. At one point during her stay in hospital, the patient was visited by a priest. The social worker assigned to her case made it clear in his "Plan-Goals" that he intended to "assist CAS and police with their assessment, to support the family and to assist with funeral arrangements as needed."[47] He was very concerned that neither the teenager nor her mother had become properly attached to the baby since neither seemed concerned about making proper funeral arrangements for it. On 24 January 1995, nurses' notes state that the patient: "continues to be compliant, cooperative, anxious and sad about the recent events. No signs of psychosis, no signs of organic brain syndrome, no signs of major depression, not suicidal. Continues to gain insight into her situation, understands that she will be charged by police when they arrive."[48]

Once it was made clear by the autopsy, conducted by Dr. Chitra Rao, that the baby had been born alive, the young woman was charged with infanticide, and the regional police sent a guard from the detention centre for young offenders to the hospital. This police guard shackled the patient to her bed and insisted on keeping "eye contact" with the suspect at all times. When nurses, doctors, and the patient's parents expressed concern about the requirement of a leg shackle, they were told by the supervisor of the detention centre that both the twenty-four-hour guard and the shackles were standard policy and that they would have to contact either the investigating homicide detective or the individual at the detention centre responsible for young offenders if they wanted that changed. The patient remained shackled to her bed until she was arraigned some days later.

An examining psychiatrist described the patient as "dysphoric, frightened and anxious, as she began to realize the implications of her pregnancy and the death of the newborn infant."[49] The psychiatrist administered a range of psychiatric and depression tests and offered the following diagnosis:

> Throughout her admission, there were no signs of major psychopathology, no psychotic symptoms, no delusions or hallucinations, no signs of organic brain syndrome, no signs of major depression, nor was she suicidal or homicidal at any given point in time. A complete psychiatric assessment including the Schedule for Affective Disorders and Schizophrenia (SADS) current, to generate Research Diagnostic Criteria (RDC) as well as several rating scales, confirmed the absence of any major AXIS I psychiatric diagnosis.
>
> Her score on the Hamilton Rating Scale for Depression was 7/52, on the Carroll Self Rating Scale for Depression – 10/52 and on the Edinburgh Postnatal Depression Scale was 7/30, all indicative of absolutely no evidence of major depression.
>
> Throughout her stay in the hospital, she and her family continued to receive intense support and counseling. She was discharged to the custody of the police who escorted her directly to the court bail hearing and we subsequently learned that indeed she was released on bail.[50]

At the time of the discovery of the infant, newspapers reported that the dead baby was discovered at the young woman's home address and that the seventeen-year-old suspect could not be identified but that she faced a charge of infanticide. Even though this case involved a young offender, the reports made every effort to identify the parents of the young mother and the location of their home.[51] The papers followed the case throughout its duration. The *Hamilton Spectator* headline on Wednesday, 21 August 1996, read "Secret Baby Killed by Mother" and highlighted the concealed nature of the pregnancy and birth and the fact that the teenager denied knowledge of the pregnancy. The report was also careful to list the details of the violence inflicted on the healthy newborn baby. A report in the *Toronto Sun* following the young woman's sentencing for a guilty plea to infanticide framed the event in typical tabloid fashion; that is, in terms of the teen's "responsibility" for a "violent death" for which she received only 100 hours of community service and a two-year probation term.[52] On the same day the *Hamilton Spectator* reported: "Teen Who Killed Her Baby at Birth Sentenced to Community Service." It went on to describe the young woman as "a panic stricken teenager who killed her newborn and hid the body in the basement of her family home." According to the *Spectator*, the judge had not wanted to "'compound the tragedy' by imposing a custodial sentence, Judge Bernd [sic] Zabel ordered the distraught 18-year-old to continue living with her parents, to attend school and take any psychological counseling requested by her probation officer."[53] While this report does not explicitly state that the teenager got away with murder, it was careful to note the judge's statement about infanticide law: "Without the infanticide section of the Criminal Code, this young person would be facing a charge of murder. In this particular case, justice is statutorily tempered with mercy." Although the judge was validating the use of the statute in this circumstance, his comment indirectly highlights the more severe punishment that would have resulted if the infanticide provision had not been in the code. The story further explains that the "offence ... carries a maximum punishment of five years imprisonment in adult court, [and] covers the rare circumstances where a woman who has just given birth and, while in a disturbed state of mind, causes the death of her child by a deliberate act or omission." The defendant's mental disturbance was described through the testimony of the psychiatrist, who "indicated that the teenager had no pre-existing mental illness, but went into a dissociative mental state at the time of the killing due to panic and extreme anxiety." The psychiatrist was noted as saying that "the teenager poses no threat to the public and strongly urged against imposing a custodial sentence" since "she is 'already terrified' of jail and would become suicidal."[54]

The questions of mental capacity and responsibility in relation to the killing – a killing constructed in the *Toronto Sun* as violent and in the *Hamilton Spectator* as possibly accidental – speak to the broader question of how this event is conceptualized at various discursive sites. The psychiatrist's report clearly indicates that the mother does not suffer from any major depressive illness but that she did suffer a dissociative episode when experiencing the shock of unexpected childbirth. Others, however, are not as sympathetic to her circumstances or experience and are unwilling to mitigate culpability on the grounds of mental disturbance. At one point during the investigation a medical doctor (apparently with no psychiatric specialty) provides a letter to the regional coroner indicating that the teenager's overall mental capacity was somewhat impaired not by comparison to the "reasonable man" but by comparison to "fellow taxpayers":

> I think that you and I would agree that this young woman is not really a well-grounded, mature and adult human being. She, of course, is now biologically competent to bear a child but, in terms of her adultness and her soundness in character, as a full grown, mature woman – she is obviously not anywhere near being truly competent to join the general citizenship of the community – certainly not as another good fellow taxpayer. If

we are agreed on this, for me anyway, I can see how logically it becomes inevitable that her thinking, at the time of the delivery of her child, became as ill-formed and as bizarre as it was.

The other point of note is that I have no doubt, at all, that [name] was one of these women who carried her pregnancy, from day one, and was totally unaware of it. This phenomenon is recorded in any textbook of obstetrics – the woman is pregnant and she does not know because the pregnancy is not obvious and, on top of that, she continues to menstruate – everything is just normal.

As for the matter of her Diabetes, one has to wonder how the blood sugars may have shifted during the time of the acute crisis and, as you know, it may have even exacerbated her loss in being able to maintain any form of coherent logical thinking.

It does not make sense to me that, when your child is coming, and you're bleeding, that you do not cry for help. There is no sense to this.[55]

The physician's inability to make sense of this event is understandable. He likely had not come into contact with any cases of this nature and he was not an expert in psychiatry. Despite his lack of expertise, he described a feeling that others connected to the case might have expressed – feelings that frame the woman's action in terms of moral competency and character. Her lack of character and immaturity affects her ability to make a rational decision at the time of childbirth, resulting in a decision that is "ill-formed" or "bizarre." This blatantly condescending evaluation of the young woman's entitlement to "citizenship of the community" operates to mitigate her consequent culpability in the death of the baby, in part because the doctor just could not make sense of the event. It is difficult for him, and indeed for many others, to rationalize how a teenaged woman could hide, deny, and eventually kill her obviously unwanted baby. In the words of the doctor "there is no sense to this."

This lack of a rational framework within which to locate the event of maternal neonaticide has the effect of making a psychiatric explanation relevant to the question of legal responsibility. The fact that the teenaged mother scored very low on the standard diagnostic scales for major depressive illness does not have any real bearing on the outcome of the case since the killing is *already* filtered through a kind of weaker psychiatric framework that exists in order to mitigate culpability. However, the existence of this psychiatric framework is viewed as problematic to those in the law and order community who feel that infanticide law allows women to escape from a murder charge. The lack of punishment for inexcusable murder contradicts the rule of law. Many in this camp believe that "if you kill someone, you kill someone."[56]

Baby A: Postpartum Depression[57]

The case of Baby A fits, albeit a little uneasily, into the established Canadian legal meaning of infanticide law in that it allows for leniency in cases where a mother suffering from postpartum depression kills her newly born child (i.e., someone less then twelve months old). In this case, Baby A drowned in a bathtub at home. Her mother called 911, saying that she had "killed her baby." The police arrived at the woman's home to find a baby face down in eight to ten inches of water still wearing its night clothes but without a diaper. The police attempted cardiopulmonary resuscitation (CPR) but were unable to revive the infant. The Coroner's Investigation Statement indicated that the mother had recently given birth to twins and had been discharged from the psychiatric unit at the Queensway-Carleton Hospital two days earlier, where she had been treated for postpartum depression. There was no history of depression prior to the childbirth and there were no external marks of violence on the child, yet the coroner classified the death factor in this case as child abuse. The police occurrence report noted that the woman called 911 and "advised she had murdered her daughter." Police subsequently charged the woman with second degree murder, likely on the basis of what they took to be her murder confession (although there is, of course, a difference between saying "I killed" and "I murdered"). The woman was eventually allowed to plead guilty to the separate charge of infanticide. This outcome raises the obvious question as to the kind of policy established by Crown prosecutors in cases such as these. Are they merely handled in an ad hoc manner, with certain women being sentenced to imprisonment for manslaughter, others pleading not guilty by reason of insanity, and others pleading guilty to infanticide? Although the evidence of postpartum depression has crept into the framework for infanticide, postpartum depression might also have operated to mitigate culpability at sentencing for manslaughter, although such an outcome might not be desirable from a mental health perspective since it would result in an apparently ill person being sent to jail.

The case of Baby A is unusual because of the somewhat advanced age of the six-month-old infant. In Canada, section 2 of the *Criminal Code* sets the age limit of a "newly born" child at twelve months. In law, the age limit for a charge of infanticide is set at under the age of one year, but in practice it usually applies to an infant under the age of three months.[58] Britain is one of many jurisdictions in which the age limit for infanticide has long been set out in law: in 1938 it was set at one year. In New Zealand the age limit is set at ten years of age or under (Oberman 1996, 3). Thus, while Baby A was a little older at death than were the victims in usual Canadian infanticide cases, her age was not outside the legal range for Canada and comparable jurisdictions.

The postpartum depression in this case places it squarely in the class of powerfully mitigated homicides, of which infanticide is the paradigmatic case. Postpartum depression leading to the killing of apparently *wanted* babies constitutes a very small but well established field of research and treatment in both Britain and the United States, particularly since the 1980s (see, for example, Hamilton and Harberger 1992). However, this field of research is less well established in the Canadian context, and this is perhaps why a case of this nature seems, on the surface, to fit more uneasily within the legal framework of infanticide. Postpartum psychosis is very rare, but it is well documented. According to Maier-Katkin (1992, 278), one of the leading experts in the field, "postpartum psychosis is a rare disorder occurring in fewer that 2 per 1,000 births." Furthermore,

> these women experience terrifying delusions and hallucinations. There is personality change; mood swings occur very quickly. Sometimes voices are heard; sometimes there are overwhelming impulses. This is not a new phenomenon; the syndrome was described by Hippocrates and again by Galen in the earliest medical treatises. A comprehensive study of postpartum psychoses was published by the French physician Louis Victor Marcé in 1858. Epidemiological studies conducted in several nations have confirmed the characteristics and the steady incidence of postpartum psychoses in the intervening years. (Kruckman and Asmann-Finch cited in Maier-Katkin 1992, 278)

In the United States, where there is no infanticide provision, cases of postpartum psychosis tend to mitigate responsibility for murder and manslaughter.[59] According to Maier-Katkin (1992, 279), who observed the outcomes in a small number of cases, one-third of cases such as these tend to be disposed of by way of not guilty by reason of insanity verdicts. And, in sixteen cases of conviction, four were sentenced to probation, three to a term of incarceration less than five years, seven to terms of incarceration between five and twenty-five years, and two were given life sentences (279). These results included a wide range of cases involving women who had killed more than one child, those who had fabricated stories about their babies being kidnapped, and those who had suffered severe forms of psychosis.

Maier-Katkin and others have argued that circumstances similar to those in the death of Baby A deserve humane treatment by the courts (see Brockington 1999 [1996]). This approach recognizes that leniency is justified when "a defendant has committed an offence under circumstances that indicate mental illness of lesser severity than the legal standard of insanity" (Callahan et al. 1987, cited in Maier-Katkin 1992, 280). With this idea in mind, the outcome in the Baby A case is not outside the boundaries of the kind of response called for by Maier-Katkin in the United States. And, indeed, this outcome is similar to responses in Britain, which, as I have noted earlier, allows for leniency when a woman is convicted of killing a child less than twelve months old and there is evidence of postpartum depression.

It is important to note that the authoritative mitigation frameworks governing these cases are now either entirely psychological or intentionalist. The social conditions of the mothers, their specific and/or unique situations, are no longer *formally* relevant.

In Chapter 5 I described a shift in official attitudes regarding child homicide cases toward a harsher punitive framework, and I located this shift within broad concerns about child abuse. In this chapter we have seen some evidence of this shift in the individual files for cases of maternal neonaticide taken from coroners' offices in Ontario. During the late 1980s, the earliest period for which the case files were available, the designation of "child abuse" had become prevalent as a "death factor" in many cases of infant homicides. The Office of the Chief Coroner made a conceptual error in listing all of these death factors as child abuse. Child abuse is a descriptor for social relations determined by a range of factors usually ascertained through child welfare investigation of family case histories. One has to ask why a case in which the victim dies from a shaking but has no history of old injuries would be considered child abuse, while a case in which a father shoots his entire family would be listed as a "shooting." Overall, the vast majority of cases investigated by the Office of the Chief Coroner are listed as child abuse regardless of whether or not autopsies indicate old healing injuries. The practice of recording child abuse as a death factor grossly misrepresents both the nature of the cause of death and the social circumstances within which some of these deaths took place. These determinations have the effect of overrepresenting the seriousness of child abuse and the incidents of death attributable to intentional and sustained parental violence against children.[60]

During the 1990s this practice all but ceased; however, I have been able to show that an especially aggressive response to some events, which previously would have been viewed as infanticides and even earlier would have been seen as almost excusable homicides, is now in evidence. Cases do continue to be dealt with as infanticide, either as a conviction resulting from a plea bargain or as *bona fide* infanticide cases. The plea bargain infanticide cases may be precisely the kinds of cases that have prompted various criminal justice professionals to advocate for the repeal of the infanticide law. However, the cases dealt with as infanticide, even the plea bargain cases, appear to require a more sympathetic and lenient response than would be likely should infanticide law be abolished. Historically, infanticide cases involve very young mothers in straitened circumstances acting during a time of mental distress, mild mental disturbance, or even full blown post-partum depression. Most of these cases involve deaths occurring at the moment of birth. (There was a reversal in presumption concerning live-birth and stillbirth on the part of forensic pathologists in that there was little difficulty in proving live-birth, despite reliance on a not wholly reli-able forensic pathological test and despite the continued occurrence of un-attended childbirth.) Given its dubious constitutionality, the proposal that the infanticide provision be replaced with a generic child abuse/neglect homicide offence, especially where the new offence would not require proof of intent, seems hardly appropriate or even likely. Even plea bargain cases would not be handled appropriately under such a provision. I observed that in one of these cases there was some evidence of earlier abuse but that in another (where the mother suffered from a long-standing psychosis) there was no evidence of such abuse. A case of this kind cannot be appropriately dealt with as a child abuse/neglect homicide. All of the cases continue to be investigated and prosecuted in a wholly ad hoc manner.

Live-birth and specific causes of death are now more provable than they were in the past, the latter because of improvements in forensic pathology, the former because of a change in attitude on the part of coroners.[61] And the investigative tools of forensic pathology have now been augmented by an array of social investigation techniques. The mother suspected in the death of her infant is now very intensively investigated by a range of profes-sionals: police, social workers, nurses, physicians, forensic pathologists, and Crown prosecutors acting in a coordinated and concerted fashion. I have even shown how coroners and other medical professionals have joined the exercise, providing their opinions of the social circumstances and personal qualities of suspects even though their expertise is biomedical rather than sociological or psychiatric. Of course, a crucial change in attitude has ac-companied this mobilization of investigatory reinforcements; it is not just a matter of resources. Coroners now direct teams of investigators in a sharply focused effort to identify and prove wrongdoing on the part of mothers. A full range of information has become available to the coroner regarding the infant-victim and its mother, all of which is refracted through the prism of retribution, deterrence, and invasive prevention. So it is no accident that coroners and forensic pathologists have led the campaign for a more puni-tive response to maternal neonaticide and, specifically, for the repeal of the infanticide provision. The advocacy of such measures is entirely consistent with their new professional position as leaders of the forces charged with identifying, avenging, and preventing infant homicides.

Conclusion

I have described the development pattern of criminal justice responses to the killing of newly born babies in Canada during the twentieth century. Prior to the passage of the infanticide provision in 1948, there is a distinctive tension-filled discursive field, the principal elements of which are a complex legal framework that provides offence categories that vary greatly in their seriousness; a marked reluctance on the part of grand juries to indict and petit juries to convict; pressure from police and Crown prosecutors to obtain indictments and convictions on the more serious charges; and severe legal and medico-legal evidentiary obstacles to indictment and conviction.

This was the background to the 1948 passage of the infanticide provision in Canada. Legislators were exclusively concerned with consistency in securing convictions for homicide in cases where they had previously been rare, absent a confession. The infanticide provision mitigates the maternal homicide of neonates on the basis of a presumed diminished capacity as a result of mental disturbance consequent upon pregnancy, childbirth, and lactation; however, this was hardly the chief concern of Canadian legislators. They merely hoped that the mitigation framework would facilitate conviction and rationalize an unsatisfactory application of the criminal law. Contrary to the more recent feminist critique of the individualization and depoliticization of bio-psychiatric exculpatory models, seen as the defining element of the infanticide provision, the legislative intention was more purely legal-administrative. What is more, the forensic psychiatric model underlying the provision was attentive to the socio-economic forces behind infanticide, which were seen as precipitating the "distress of reason" in infanticidal mothers.

Once passed, the provision was not without its problems, these largely having to do with the need to prove the biological and psychiatric elements "beyond a reasonable doubt." Parliament moved quickly to eliminate the evidentiary burden on the Crown by allowing infanticide convictions without proof of mental disturbance. This left only the requirement to prove that the baby had been born alive and that the mother intended (by wilful act or omission) to kill it. The amended provision provided for mitigation in cases of maternal neonaticide, ostensibly based on psychiatric grounds but formally established merely on the basis of the biological relationship between the perpetrator and the victim.

Almost as soon as this legal matter was settled, the Canadian courts and other legal authorities began to countenance a much more punitive response to maternal neonaticide, at least in certain instances. By the end of the twentieth century presumption of stillbirth and, therefore, innocence was replaced with a presumption of live-birth and, therefore, guilt. More broadly, the developing forensic pathological and legal policy discourse concerning child abuse became central to the response framework within which infanticide was understood and litigated. A developing discourse of the infant-victim as an "innocent" deserving protection – and, failing this, justice – further shifted the ground toward a retributive response. These discursive formations are connected to broader developments in the valuation of the baby. With the availability of contraception and abortion, as well as the emergence of feminist theories of agency that repudiate paternalistic medico-legal understandings of feminine frailties, pregnancies carried to term came to be seen as "willed" and "wanted" by the mother. The corollary is that mothers who kill their babies do so with evil intent. Indeed, the concept of the legitimately unwanted baby, central to the charitable and lenient dispositions of the early twentieth century, was itself undermined by the progressive feminist advancement of women's reproductive freedom. Within this context certain law and order advocates, sometimes drawing on the feminist medicalization critique of the infanticide provision, have called for its repeal and replacement. They have suggested a new criminal offence of child abuse/neglect homicide, in which the duty parents, and particularly mothers, owe to their children is absolute, so that in cases of child death, homicide can be proven without the legal burden of proving intent. The suggestion is that cases now covered by the infanticide provision would be prosecuted under the new law.

My argument challenges existing feminist approaches to infanticide law in a number of ways. I suggest that the medicalization critique was both simplistic and short-sighted. This obligates me to provide at least some ideas for a tentative feminist framework for understanding and responding to maternal neonaticide in law. This must include a feminist understanding of the conditions in which adolescent women, often teenagers, kill their denied and unwanted babies in circumstances that are similar to those found in what I have been calling the traditional infanticide scenario. Of course, such an account would look very different from the sympathetic story that informed jurors and judges in the early part of the twentieth century. Still, it would include many of the same socio-economic, and we would now say political, factors used to mitigate infanticide at that time – most particularly, an understanding of these adolescent women's actions informed by a grasp of their situation as vulnerable female adolescents who find themselves especially disadvantaged within a society marked by gender and economic inequalities and, more specifically, often abandoned by the men who share responsibility for the pregnancy. This involves understanding the network of social relations within which, and in response to which, these women acted as at least partially mitigating in both the legal and the social contexts. Contemporary law and order advocates accuse their opponents of being bleeding heart liberals who "always blame society" for the wrongdoing of individuals. It is important that we *do* blame society, at least to some extent, in those cases that involve women who find themselves at the sharp end of the stick. While we may view the actions of these women as unethical and react strongly to the resultant deaths of newborn babies, a feminist framework of reproductive rationality is particularly unhelpful. And, given that the current law positions the women not as abstract legal subjects but, rather, as *subjects* located within a nexus of mitigating circumstances (be these youth, poverty, or mental illness), the infanticide law provides for a democratic legal response in these cases.

A more vexing question remains. How should feminists regard the element of mental disturbance that has been seen as part and parcel of the story of maternal neonaticide? The problem with the medicalization critique of infanticide does not lie with its suspicion of psychiatric discourses, of their tendency to individualize and objectify human suffering, particularly when taken up in law; rather, the problem lies with how these discourses result in a dichotomy between rationality/social circumstance on the one hand and mental disturbance/deficiency on the other. These are presented as alternatives – feminist politics versus psychiatry – with everyone required to take sides. The adolescent women I have discussed frequently commit maternal neonaticide in the most constrained circumstances, seeing themselves, with considerable insight, as having few viable options. They understand the impact that the infant will have on their lives and the lives of their families. However, these same women do not necessarily act coolly, without mental distress and confusion at a time when they are experiencing extreme pressures, not the least of which are the immediate pains of childbirth (especially in cases where the women may have denied the pregnancy not just to others but to themselves). The discourse of rationality and circumstance is very easily appropriated by law and order advocates, who simply drop the circumstance. And, in any case, it always results in oversimplification. To understand these women's actions as a product both of individual circumstances and of a general structure of inequalities, and to also see them as being emotionally charged and unwise, is not to abandon either feminism or the women themselves.

Indeed, there is little prospect that criminal law will soon find itself able to reflect upon its core feminist principles of social justice. At a time when strategically positioned law and order advocates are pushing for the repeal of the infanticide provision and the adoption of a new child abuse/neglect homicide provision (in which homicidal intent will not need to be proved), the retention of the peculiar psychiatric mitigation underpinning the amended infanticide provision may be the best we can hope for. The idea that infanticide has disappeared or is disappearing as a direct result of the elevation of the status of women in law and society is, at best, overstated. Infanticide cases will continue to come before the courts, and many will be best dealt with through the existing mitigation framework.

Appendix: Current Legal Framework Governing Maternal Neonaticide

Murder, Manslaughter, Infanticide

Culpable homicide is either murder, manslaughter, or infanticide, with the distinction largely dependent on the intent accompanying the conduct.[1] Murder is either first degree (when it is planned and deliberate) or second degree. Murder is reduced to manslaughter when the act is committed in the heat of passion caused by sudden provocation.[2] The minimum punishment for both first and second degree murder is life imprisonment:

235.(1) Punishment for Murder – Every one who commits first degree murder or second degree murder is guilty of an indictable offence and shall be sentenced to imprisonment for life.
(2) Minimum Punishment – For the purposes of Part XXIII, the sentence of imprisonment for life prescribed by this section is a minimum punishment.[3]

The punishment for manslaughter is set at between four years (minimum) and life imprisonment:

236. Manslaughter – Every person who commits manslaughter is guilty of an indictable offence and liable:
(a) where a firearm is used in the commission of the offence, to imprisonment for life and to a minimum punishment of imprisonment for a term of four years; and
(b) in any other case, to imprisonment for life.[4]

233. Infanticide – A female person commits infanticide when by a wilful act or omission she causes the death of her newly-born child, if at the time of the act or omission she is not fully recovered from the effects of giving birth to the child and by reason thereof or the effect of lactation consequent on the birth of the child her mind is then disturbed.[5]

Punishment for Infanticide
237. Every female person who commits infanticide is guilty of an indictable offence and liable to imprisonment for a term not exceeding five years.[6]

There is *no minimum* sentence for this offence.[7]

Other Child-specific Offences

Abandoning Child
218. Every one who unlawfully abandons or exposes a child who is under the age of ten years, so that its life is or is likely to be endangered or its health is or is likely to be permanently injured, is guilty of an indictable offence and is liable to imprisonment for a term not exceeding two years.

Synopsis
This section creates the indictable offence of abandoning or exposing a child under 10 years of age so that the child's life is or is likely to be endangered or the health of the child is or is likely to be permanently injured. The accused must intend to expose or abandon the child.[8]

Neglect to Obtain Assistance in Childbirth
242. A female person who, being pregnant and about to be delivered, with intent that the child shall not live or with intent to conceal the birth of the child, fails to make provision for reasonable assistance in respect of her delivery is, if the child is permanently injured as a result thereof or dies immediately before, during or in a short time after birth, as a result thereof, guilty of an indictable offence and is liable to imprisonment for a term not exceeding five years.[9]

Synopsis
Section 242 makes it an indictable offence to *neglect to obtain help in childbirth* if the act or omission is done with the requisite intent, and the consequences to the child are as specified in the section. The *pregnant woman is liable as a principal* if she is about to give birth and fails to make provision for reasonable assistance for the delivery. This liability only attaches if the woman fails to get assistance *with the intention that the child should not live or to conceal the birth* and certain result follow. The *consequences* which must be proven are that the *child dies* immediately before, during or in a short time after the birth or is permanently injured *as a result of the woman's failure to obtain assistance*. The maximum sentence on conviction for this offence is five years' imprisonment.[10]

Concealing Body of Child

243. Every one who in any manner disposes of the dead body of a child, with intent to conceal the fact that its mother has been delivered of it, whether the child died before, during or after birth, is guilty of an indictable offence and liable to imprisonment for a term not exceeding two years.[11]

Synopsis

Section 243 creates the indictable offence of *concealing the body of a child*. The physical act of disposing of the dead body of a child whether the child dies before, during or after its birth. It must be shown that the disposal was intended to conceal the fact of delivery. This offence is punishable by not more than two years' imprisonment.[12]

Killing Unborn Child in Act of Birth/Saving

238.(1) Every one who causes the death, in the act of birth, of any child that has not become a human being, in such a manner that, if the child were a human being, he would be guilty of murder, is guilty of an indictable offence and liable to imprisonment for life.

(2) This section does not apply to a person who, by means that, in good faith, he considers necessary to preserve the life of the mother of a child, causes the death of that child.

Synopsis

This section creates the indictable offence of *killing an unborn child in the act of birth*. This offence applies in circumstances where the death was caused in such a way that, had the child become a human being (see s. 223), the crime would have been murder. The maximum sentence upon conviction is imprisonment for life.

Section 238(2) provides an exception to liability for such acts dealing with cases in which the act, resulting in the death of the unborn child, was done to save the life of the mother. The person doing the act must consider *in good faith* that such act was necessary for that purpose.[13]

215.(1) Duty of person to provide necessaries of life – Every one is under a legal duty

(a) as a parent, foster parent, guardian or head of a family, to provide necessaries of life for a child under the age of sixteen years.[14]

Definition of Human Being

Section 223(1) defines "human being":

When a Child Becomes Human Being/Killing Child.
223.(1) A Child become a human being within the meaning of this Act when it has completely proceeded, in a living state, from the body of its mother, whether or not
(a) it has breathed;
(b) it has independent circulation;
(c) or, the navel string is severed.

(2) A person commits homicide when he causes injury to a child before or during its birth as a result of which the child dies after becoming a human being.[15]

Psychiatric Assessment Order

Assessment Order:
The psychiatric underpinnings of the infanticide offence are reflected in its inclusion in section 672 of the *Criminal Code,* allowing for court ordered assessment of mental condition with respect to infanticide, specifically section 672.11 (c):

672.11 A court having jurisdiction over an accused in respect of an offence may order an assessment of the mental condition of the accused if it has reasonable grounds to believe that such evidence is necessary to determine:
(a) whether the accused is unfit to stand trial;
(b) whether the accused was, at the time of the commission of the alleged offence, suffering from a mental disorder so as to be exempt from criminal responsibility by virtue of subsection 16(1)
(c) whether the balance of the mind of the accused is disturbed at the time of commission of the alleged offence, where the accused is a female person charged with an offence arising out of the death of her newly-born child;
(d) the appropriate disposition to be made, where a verdict of not criminally responsible on account of mental disorder or unfit to stand trial has been rendered in respect of the accused; or
(e) whether an order should be made under subsection 747.1(1) to detain the accused in a treatment facility, where the accused has been convicted of the offence.[16]

Evidence and Intent

No Acquittal Unless Act or Omission Not Wilful

Despite the explicit provision for an assessment order, an amendment to the infanticide provision in 1955 renders psychiatric evidence unnecessary to secure an infanticide conviction. Section 663 of the *Criminal Code* includes a provision that prevents an acquittal on a charge of infanticide if the Crown *fails to meet their burden of proof* with respect to the psychiatric evidence of disturbance of mind:

663. Where a female person is charged with infanticide and the evidence establishes that she caused the death of her child but does not establish that, at the time of the act or omission by which she caused the death of the child,

(a) she was not fully recovered from the effects of giving birth to the child or from the effect of lactation consequent on the birth of the child, and

(b) the balance of her mind was, at the time, disturbed by reason of the effect of giving birth to the child or of the effect of lactation consequent on the birth of the child,

She may be convicted unless the evidence establishes that the act or omission was not wilful.[17]

Double Jeopardy

Infanticide, as a specific form of homicide, is completely integrated into the *Criminal Code* scheme for culpable homicide. First, double jeopardy, in relation to both murder and manslaughter, attaches to culpable homicide in which an indictment for infanticide is possible:

610.(2) Effect of previous charge of murder or manslaughter – A conviction or an acquittal on an indictment for murder bars a subsequent indictment for the same homicide charging it as manslaughter or infanticide, and a conviction or acquittal on an indictment for manslaughter or infanticide bars a subsequent indictment for the same homicide charging it as murder.

610.(4) Effect of previous charge of infanticide or manslaughter – A conviction or an acquittal on an indictment for infanticide bars a subsequent indictment for the same homicide charging it as manslaughter, and a conviction or acquittal on an indictment for manslaughter bars a subsequent indictment for the same homicide charging it as infanticide.[18]

Jury Verdicts

Section 662(3) allows for a substituted verdict for manslaughter or infanticide on a charge of murder. Section 662(4) allows for conviction of concealing body of child where murder or infanticide is charged but only partly proved.

Offence Charged, Part Only Proved

662.(3) Conviction for infanticide or manslaughter on charge of murder – Subject to subsection (4), where a count charges murder and the evidence proves manslaughter or infanticide but does not prove murder, the jury may find the accused not guilty of murder but guilty of manslaughter or infanticide, but shall not on that count find the accused guilty of any other offence.

662.(4) Conviction for concealing body of child where murder or infanticide charged – Where a count charges the murder of a child or infanticide, and the evidence proves the commission of an offence under section 243 but does not prove murder or infanticide, the jury may find the accused not guilty of murder or infanticide, as the case may be, but guilty of an offence under section 243.[19] *(Martin's Annual Criminal Code 2005)*

Notes

Introduction

1 Sarah Schmidt, "Baby Death: Doctor Didn't Notice Girl, 15, Was Pregnant," *National Post*, 19 March 2002, A2.

2 *Ibid.*

3 Sarah Schmidt, *National Post*, 1 February 2003, A8.

4 *Ibid.*

5 RG 22-392-2210, Container no. 51, Ontario Archives.

6 Until 1955 neglect to obtain assistance in childbirth, with the intent of the neglect being that that child should die, was punishable by life imprisonment. If the intent was only to hide the pregnancy, the punishment was imprisonment for seven years.

7 Maternal neonaticide is defined as the killing of an unwanted newly born baby immediately following, or within a few months, of its birth by the biological mother.

8 *Criminal Code*, R.S.C. 1985, c. C-46, and Amendments, s. 233. A "newly-born" child is to be interpreted under s. 2 as a person under the age of one year.

9 See Appendix: "Legal Framework Governing Maternal Neonaticide." Concealment of birth carries a maximum sentence of two years imprisonment, while "neglect" and "infanticide" carry a maximum sentence of five years imprisonment. In practice, probationary dispositions are the norm.

10 Grand jurors could also substitute indictments for "concealment" or "neglect in childbirth," determined by the factual evidence, when the prosecuting authority failed to meet its evidentiary burden.

11 Neglect to obtain assistance in childbirth is not integrated into the scheme of "lesser included" offences.

12 In addition to the criminal laws regulating infanticide, abortion, birth control, and illegitimacy, Smart (1992) is referring to the *Infant Life Protection Act, 1872;* the *Marriage Act, 1752; Offences against the Person Act, 1861;* and the *Contagious Diseases Acts* of 1866 and 1869.

13 Smart is referring to *An Act to Prevent the Destroying and Murthering of Bastard Children*, 1624, 21 Jac. I, c. 27. This was the first "concealment of birth" provision and was the historical precursor of the nineteenth-century English and Canadian infanticide provisions. In 1803 England reorganized the prosecution of infant murder but retained the concealment provision to allow for an alternative verdict of concealment should the Crown fail to prove murder (see Jackson 2002b).

14 The analysis has difficulty explaining both the practice of maternal neonaticide by married and widowed women (and their prosecution) when these women had means to support the babies and who suffered no shame in their births, but who killed them anyway.

15 Other contemporary examples are battered woman syndrome and premenstrual syndrome, but these are qualifications of the jurisprudence on self-defence and provocation.

16 Even though this critique is heard outside legal circles, it is primarily promoted by legal scholars. This is due to the pattern of legal analysis in which specific *legal rationales* are

extrapolated from their legal context for critical analysis. This pattern of analysis tends to neglect the specific effects of the law in the context of the legal arena itself. For a discussion of the limits of criminal law from a feminist legal perspective, see Busby (1993, 1999).

17 During the late 1940s and early 1950s in many areas of government there were initiatives, organized around a preoccupation with liberal legal rights and due process, to curtail discretionary, sometimes abusive, power.

18 The plight of both the baby and the mother was shared. Later, humanitarian sentiment for the mother disappears and is framed around the baby; ostensibly, this is the rationale for enhanced prosecution and punishment.

19 "Wilful" is eventually defined as acting with a "bad motive" or "evil intent," as in *R. v. Smith* (1976), 32 C.C.C. (2d) 224, resulting in an acquittal and further limiting the possibility for conviction. See Chapter 4 below.

20 *Criminal Code*, R.S.C. 1985, c. C-46, and Amendments, s. 663, "No Acquittal Unless Act or Omission Not Wilful." This section prevents the acquittal of the defendant charged with infanticide if she had a greater *mens rea* that that defined in s. 233.

21 The infanticide section is unique in that it defines a biological relationship between the perpetrator and the victim as mother and child.

22 These cases surely conform to the requirements of the Canadian insanity defence and are not the sort intended to be covered using the infanticide law either by Canadian legislators or by English medical experts.

23 For Smart, this is apparently linked to ideological notions of responsible motherhood, although perhaps not in quite the way she has described. Women's responsibility is diminished because they were conforming to ideological notions governing femininity and motherhood.

24 Ontario 1998a. "Inquest Recommendations by Topic" on file with the researcher.

25 "Shaken baby syndrome" is a phrase used by forensic medical authorities to describe the deaths of infants due to physical force. Usually, death results from subdural hematoma caused by the forceful shaking of the baby. The term "syndrome" does not refer to a medical condition experienced by the baby but, rather, to a set of associated causes of death (or symptoms).

26 This has also led to an unfortunate alliance between some feminist discourses and victim politics (see Roach 1999).

27 For example, in June 1996 Brenda Drummond was charged with attempted murder after she allegedly pointed a pellet gun into her vagina and shot her near-term foetus in the brain. The foetus was subsequently born alive two days later, and the pellet was removed from his brain. Judge Inger Hansen dismissed the charges later that year because Canadian law does not accord the foetus the legal status of personhood (*R. v. Drummond* [1996], 143 D.L.R. [4th] 368). Nevertheless, the case provided the opportunity for the assertion of foetal rights claims both inside and outside the courtroom (*Ottawa Citizen*, 24 December 1996, A1-2). Similarly, a twenty-two-year-old Winnipeg woman who was pregnant and addicted to glue sniffing was ordered by a Superior Court judge "to be placed in the custody of the Director of Child and Family Services and detained in a health centre for treatment until the birth of her child" (*Ottawa Citizen*, 24 December 1996, A1-2). Under Manitoba family law, the grounds for this apprehension order was the court's *parens patriae* jurisdiction over the unborn child. The original order was later stayed and set aside on appeal. According to the final judgment of the Supreme Court: "The Court of Appeal held that the existing law of tort and of *parens patriae* did not support the order and, given the difficulty and complexity entailed in extending the law to permit such an order, the task was more appropriate for the legislature than the courts." See *Winnipeg Child and Family Services (Northwest Area) v. G. (D.F.)*, [1997] 3 S.C.R. at 925. This case was later framed as a question of legal protection for foetuses from abusive parents requiring legislative action from Parliament (see "The Unborn and the Law," *Globe and Mail*, 23 June 1997, A10).

28 By 1965 Ontario was one of only two provinces in Canada that maintained the grand jury system of indictment, which had been abolished in other parts of the British Commonwealth by that time. This system of indictment was abolished in Ontario following the

recommendation by the *Royal Commission Inquiry into Civil Rights* (hereafter referred to as the McRuer Report) (Ontario 1968), which recommended that the grand jury system of indictment be abolished and that this power of review be given to the Supreme Court. See section entitled "The Grand Jury" (Ontario 1968, 770-82).

29 A court may still order an assessment order under s. 672.11(c) to determine "whether the balance of the mind of the accused was disturbed" when she committed the offence of infanticide. However, this provision is all but irrelevant since the infanticide law delivers the defence within the charge itself. In practice, the Crown might pursue an assessment order to determine if the accused is fit to stand trial for infanticide and/or to determine whether or not it could secure a conviction for second degree murder rather than infanticide.

Chapter 1: Regulating Infanticide through Concealment of Birth

1 The death penalty was mandatory up to and following the passage of the infanticide law in 1948. The death penalty for murder was eventually abolished on 14 June 1976. See http://www.amnesty.ca/deathpenalty/canada.htm.

2 In some cases, the Crown failed to prove intent (to conceal, neglect, or kill) and was thus prevented from achieving the indictments and/or convictions by the jurors and or judges in these cases.

3 Section 569(3) allowed for conviction for concealing the body of a child (where murder or infanticide is charged) when the evidence does not prove murder or infanticide. *Criminal Code*, S.C. 1953-54, c. 51, s. 569(3).

4 *Criminal Code, infra* note 9. The legal framework for dealing with cases of maternal neonaticide prior to the enactment of the infanticide provision was essentially as it is today (with certain amendments to the punishment framework), except for the addition of infanticide and the crucial fact that murder was a capital crime until 1976.

5 These Class 1 offences were later alphabetized in the 1930s, when the reporting format was altered.

6 In July 1999, Canadian Centre for Justice Statistics (CCJS) reported that in Ontario from 1993-94 to 1997-98 there were only three charges for the offence of concealment of birth. And in 1997-98 there were no charges. Of the three persons charged, two were convicted and received probation as a disposition, and the third was sent to Superior Court. The disposition in this third case is unknown since the CCJS does not maintain data on the Superior Court. These data are significantly different from the criminal statistics discussed in this chapter, which reported *convictions* rather than police-laid charges.

7 Jac. I c. 27. Within this sex-specific statute the act of the concealment of death rather than death itself operated as presumption of guilt of murder if the child was illegitimate.

8 Beattie's (1986) research shows that two-thirds of the women brought before the Surrey assizes under the 1624 statute were servants. Similarly, Malcolmson's (1977, 202) research shows that approximately 70 percent (thirty-five out of sixty-one cases) of the women brought before the Old Bailey between 1730 and 1774 were employed as servant maids. Table 1.1 below shows that about half of all women convicted of concealment of birth in Canada (1912-19) were engaged in domestic service.

9 *Criminal Code*, R.S.C. 1985, c. C-46, and Amendments, ss. 243 and 662(4).

10 Backhouse (1994, 276n2) has shown that abortion prosecutions did proceed at this time, although the number of prosecutions doubtless reflects only a very small proportion of the abortions that occurred. A penalty of two years imprisonment was available for those who advertised abortion services, and a life sentence was available for those who carried them out. Women who had abortions could be sentenced to up to seven years imprisonment. There seems to have been pressure neither for increased prosecutorial activity nor for the repeal of the sections of the *Criminal Code* governing abortion.

11 According to Boys (1905, 129-30), the murder of a child en ventre sa mère could be considered manslaughter (*Rex v. Senior*, 1 M.C.C. 344; 1 Lewin C.C. 183), where a midwife was convicted of manslaughter when a child died of birth injuries following live-birth. "It was held to be manslaughter although the child was en ventre sa mère at the time when the wound was given" (Boys 1905, 130). Here Boys is discussing an English case. It was later established in Canadian common law (Re: *Sloan Estate*, [1937] 3 W.W.R. 455 (B.C.S.C.))

that a child had to become a "human being" before homicide could be charged. In Canada, the child en ventre sa mère is a person for the purposes of the acquisition of property so long as it is born alive. This legal fiction is not, however, applicable when the result of the inheritance would be detrimental to the child. In addition, a child en ventre sa mère can be chosen to form part of the time period in the rule against perpetuities.

12 Archives of Ontario: Kathleen Whalon 1932 (murder), Jean Gruintel 1935 (murder), Edna Damonde 1935 (manslaughter), Lucy Hawley 1945 (murder), and Mary-Ellen Thatcher 1949 (murder).

13 Archives of Ontario: Dora S. Chase, RG 22-517, no. 51, 1932; Leslie Sheardown, RG 22-517, no. 51, 1935; Emma Passarello, RG 22-517, no. 53, 1941; Vivian Hodge, RG 22-517, no. 53, 1945 (Supreme Court of Ontario Registrar Criminal Indictment Files RG 22-517, 1930-1977).

14 See the McRuer Report (Ontario 1968, 771-82). At the time of the publication of the McRuer Report grand juries in Ontario had three remaining functions: (1) as an instrument of indictment (i.e., to review the evidence of the Crown witnesses to determine whether there is sufficient evidence to put the accused on trial before a petit jury); (2) as an instrument of inspection (i.e., to inspect the jail and institutions maintained in whole or in part by public money); (3) as an instrument of jail delivery (i.e., to determine that all persons who have been committed for trial and are in custody are brought before the next court of competent jurisdiction).

15 See Kains (1893), who lists twenty-two objections to the grand jury system.

16 This test is making it even more difficult than the common law rule seemed to require. This is because a baby could be considered alive if it were outside the mother but not yet breathing.

17 This case was heard in 1871 by the judge of the County Court in the County of Carleton, Ontario. Judgment was reserved for the Court of Appeal, which affirmed a conviction for concealment.

18 Years later, "denial of pregnancy" operates to mitigate responsibility on an infanticide charge. See especially, *R. c. Lucas* below.

19 All cases are referred to by the *Pichè* court without the year of the decision provided.

20 See also Garland (1985, 112), where he argues that the development of criminology was connected to three main conditions, of which "the development of statistical data, produced by surveys, institutions, government and private research" is one. This collection of statistical data, "on births, deaths, marriages, crimes, migration, incomes, etc.," coincided with the "growth of the modern centralised State and its increasing desire to regulate its subject population."

21 Statistics are available for 1917, but it is not possible from the archival summaries to determine which government agency was responsible for their production.

22 Statistical information is aggregated on a yearly basis for each province in Canada, but it is also disaggregated by provincial county. It is therefore possible, by looking at these records in close association with provincial county assize indictment case files, to determine the outcomes in certain cases of maternal neonaticide. For example, where there is only *one* indictment for concealment of birth in a provincial county, one can reference this county in the statistical tables and determine what the outcome was for that particular case. There is, of course, the potential for error here since the case referenced in the indictment series might not be the same as that appearing in the *Criminal Statistics* (Canada 1912-16; Canada 1917-48). For this reason, I have not attempted to "match" the indictment case files for Ontario with the individual returning county recorded in the criminal statistics. Nevertheless, inferences are inevitable since it is possible to determine the "outcome" of concealment indictments by referencing the *Criminal Statistics*.

23 Records were generated in statistical format for every class of offence in the *Criminal Code*. Here I only describe those falling under the category of "Offences against the Person," committed by persons over the age of sixteen years.

24 Abortion and concealing birth of infants are disaggregated in the statistical tables, with concealment falling ahead of abortion (Canada 1917-48, *Statistics of Criminal and Other Offences*, 1920).

25 Abortion and Procuration are aggregated in the statistical tables (see *Criminal Code, supra* note 9).
26 These were disaggregated on a yearly basis and included: Carnal Knowledge, Bigamy, Incest, Seduction and Indecent Assault (Canada 1917-48). By the 1930s these categories had expanded to include, in alphabetical order: Abortion, Abortion and attempt; Assault, aggravated; Assault, common; Assault on females; Assault on wife; Assault, indecent; Assault on and obstructing police; Bigamy; Blackmail; Carnal Knowledge; Cause injury by fast driving; Concealment of birth; Desertion and cruelty to children; Endangering life on railway; Incest; Libel; Manslaughter; Murder; Murder attempt to commit; Non-support of family; Procuration; Rape; Rape attempt to commit; Seduction; Shooting and wounding; Wife desertion; Other offences against the person (*Indictable Offences*, Table 1.2, Dominion Bureau of Canada, 1939).
27 See, for example, Canada 1912-26, *Criminal Statistics*, 1920, sessional paper no. 10d, Dominion Bureau of Statistics.
28 A range of research projects on infanticide in England during the sixteenth, seventeenth, eighteenth, and nineteenth centuries relies solely on the official statistical and court records to provide information about the extent and character of this phenomenon (see Malcolmson 1977; Hoffer and Hull 1981; Rose 1986; and especially Jackson 1997a for a critique of positivism and infanticide).
29 *Criminal Statistics* (1912-26), Minister of Trade and Commerce: Ottawa; *Statistics of Criminal and Other Offences* (1926-48), Dominion Bureau of Statistics: Ottawa.
30 The data for religious affiliation were recorded, although the figures for the proportions of the general population affiliated to each religion are not provided, so it is impossible to determine whether any particular group was over- or underrepresented. The proportion of accused who were Roman Catholics may appear, at first glance, to be very substantial, but it is not as great as a cursory reading of these data may make it appear. The disaggregation of Protestant groups makes it appear as though there are more Roman Catholics than there really were. If Protestants had all been lumped together, then the "typical" offender would have seemed to be a Protestant.
31 These infanticide cases would likely have been cases conforming to what I have described as maternal neonaticide scenarios and are part of the same conviction problem described by the legislators in the *Hansard* debates (1948). The problem is even more evident in the infanticide statistics since a conviction was registered in only one case.
32 The practical outcome of a finding of guilt for concealment of birth would be much less serious than would be the outcome for a finding of "insanity," which would likely result in a long-term psychiatric disposition. An obvious defence strategy in cases where women were charged with murder or manslaughter, however, would be to advance an insanity defence since the consequences of a successful insanity finding might well have been much less serious than would a finding of guilt for murder or manslaughter.
33 *Hansard Parliamentary Debates*, vol. 2, 12 January 1954, 1026-27.

Chapter 2: Unwanted Babies
1 Library and Archives Canada (hereafter LAC), RG 13-1419, no. 174A.
2 These statistics are not used here to suggest increasing incidents of maternal neonaticide or even of concealment of birth, only as evidence of at least a willingness to convict in these cases.
3 See "Introduction" to Archives of Ontario, RG 22-392, Criminal Assize Clerk Indictment Case Files (1853-1929).
4 Personal communication, staff, Archives of Ontario.
5 In 1858 Catherine Graham of Middlesex County was charged with "killing illegitimate child." One has to wonder if the inclusion of the qualifier "illegitimate" was a way of signalling to the grand jurors that hers was a less serious case of murder.
6 These outcomes were, of course, recorded in *Statistics of Criminal and Other Offences*, discussed in Chapter 1. Unfortunately, there is no way of systematically connecting these two sources of data to confirm the outcomes in the cases discussed here, although in individual cases of concealment it might be possible to infer the likely outcome from the county-specific data contained in *Statistics of Criminal and Other Offences*.

7 During this period, the *Criminal Code* allowed for the substitution of a concealment charge when the Crown failed to secure a conviction for child murder. Section 569(3), conviction for concealing body of child where murder or infanticide charged: *Criminal Code*, S.C. 1953-54, c. 51, s. 569(3).

8 Archives of Ontario, RG 22-392-495, no. 13, 1901.

9 *Ibid.*

10 *Ibid.*, RG 22-392-4890, no. 116, 1904.

11 *Ibid.*, RG 22-392-4891, no. 116, 1904.

12 *Ibid.*, RG 22-392-5519, no. 140, 1902.

13 *Ibid.*, RG 22-392-9312, no. 285, 1926.

14 *Ibid.*, RG 22-392-9311, no. 285, 1926.

15 *Ibid.*, RG 22-392-2210, no. 51, 1926.

16 In two instances, the retrieved indictment files referred to a charge of concealment and indicated that a finding of no bill was issued, but there is no other information in the file.

17 Archives of Ontario, RG 22-392-5535, no. 140, 1911.

18 See Canada 1912-26, *Criminal Statistics*, and Canada 1926-48, *Statistics of Criminal and Other Offences*, discussed in Chapter 1.

19 Archives of Ontario, RG 22-392-8749, no. 262, 1900.

20 LAC, RG 13-2700, no. CC124.

21 Provocation is a necessary element for a manslaughter conviction.

22 Annie Rubletz is described as a nineteen-year-old single Ukrainian girl whose religion was Greek Catholic at the time of the appeal of her death sentence.

23 LAC, RG 13-1627, no. CC522.

24 *Ibid.*

25 *Ibid.*

26 *Ibid.*

27 *Ibid.*

28 *Ibid.*

29 The indictment of Annie Flavelle, more than the conviction of Annie Rubletz, illustrates this point.

Chapter 3: The Insanities of Reproduction

1 Prior to the passage of s. 663, "No Acquittal Unless Act or Omission Not Wilful," in 1953-54, the elements of the offence were outlined in *R. v. Marchello* (1951).

2 Geoffrey Clarke (1913), Senior Assistant Medical Officer, London County Asylum, Banstead, uses this term for forms of mental disorder associated with childbirth and pregnancy.

3 Dr. Cyril Greenland, University of Toronto, Queen Street Mental Health Archives and Canadian History of Medicine Society, personal communication at Society for the History of Medicine, Annual General Meeting, York University, Toronto, 1999. Telephone conversations and personal communications occurred between 1998 and 1999.

4 W.C. Sullivan was one of England's leading medico-legal experts on "insanity" and "inebriety."

5 Here Sullivan refers to Lombroso's claim that infanticide does not belong to a criminal class that one could categorize according to discrete types of individuals or racial or constitutional differences. His reference to "anthropological factors" refers to Lombroso's criminal anthropology, which famously attempted to classify human criminal types, guided by the assumption that science can identify the "born criminal." See also Garland (1988).

6 This is not to suggest that anthropologists did not participate in racialization; rather, I only want to show that discussions of anthropological accounts of infanticide do not serve as useful illustrations of racialization because infanticide was generally seen as motivated by social arrangements rather than as evidence of Aboriginal ignorance or immorality.

7 I am referring here to the idea that the woman is not "fully recovered from the effects of giving birth to the child and by reason thereof or the effect of lactation consequent on the birth of the child her mind is then disturbed" (Section 233, Infanticide, *Criminal Code*, R.S.C. 1985, c. C-46, and Amendments).

8 Hungarian physician Ignaz Semmelweis is credited with having introduced one of the first clinical trials of infectious disease when he introduced antiseptic practices (such as washing the hands with a diluted solution of chloride of lime before performing obstetrical examinations) to the wards of Viennese hospitals, thereby reducing the mortality rate of puerperal fever from 13.6 percent to 1.5 percent (Wilson 1976).

9 Maternal neonaticide was popularly thought of as a quasi-criminal act since there was a range of social and economic prejudices that very strongly mitigated individual responsibility. In addition, a woman's "irrational" behaviour or "impulses" were seen as motivated not by "evil" but by "morally pure" intentions. Since women were conforming to society's moral standards, they were viewed as acting "irrationally" but "properly." The "irresistible impulse" to sometimes kill the unwanted or illegitimate baby had its roots in the preservation of society's moral standards and was therefore viewed with compassion. Men who failed to live up to society's moral standards were, therefore, the real "criminals."

10 I have already shown the very considerable extent to which this last claim is true.

11 The act read: "Where a woman by any wilful act or omission causes the death of her newly-born child, but at the time of the act or omission she had not fully recovered from the effect of giving birth to such child, and by reason thereof the balance of her mind was then disturbed, she shall, notwithstanding that the circumstances were such that but for this Act the offence would have amounted to murder, be guilty of a felony, to wit of infanticide and may for such offence by dealt with and punished as if she had been guilty of the offence of manslaughter of such child" (Walker 1968, 131).

12 See also *Criminal Code*, S.C. 1953-54, c. 51, s. 434. Infanticide carried the lesser of all culpable homicide penalties, including "killing an unborn child" (governing mainly abortion), which carried a penalty of life imprisonment and thus creating the anomalous situation where infanticide actually carried a lesser criminal sanction than did abortion. In this respect, then, it was "safer," both medically and legally, for a woman to commit neonaticide.

13 For example, one member raised the issue of peace officers killing fleeing suspects, feeling that such an instance should be dealt with as another separate kind of killing, with reduced or no punishment. Another member raised the issue of the killing of children by motorcars, particularly by drunken drivers, and suggested that this kind of killing be dealt with more harshly in order to deter the large number of vehicular homicides of children. During this period in both Canada and the United States there was widespread concern about the high numbers of children killed by the new motorcars, resulting in public health campaigns to teach children not to play in the streets (but, rather, in newly developed "playgrounds") as well as in criminal justice measures aimed at deterring drivers from so-called reckless driving (see Zelizer 1985).

14 For a discussion of the historical development of partial defences in another English colony, see New South Wales (1993). Technically, Canadian law contains no formal diminished responsibility provision, although "infanticide" essentially operates as such.

15 At the time, J.G. Diefenbaker (PC, Lake Centre) was not yet prime minister, but the Conservative Party's justice critic. Diefenbaker was a defence attorney who privately opposed the death penalty. As justice critic, he was centrally involved in debates surrounding the abolishment of the death penalty.

16 Moves to abolish the death penalty were well under way in England during this time.

17 In fact, in Canada it was not until the 1970s that psychiatrists were occasionally called upon to testify for the defence to support a claim of "diminished capacity" on the basis of postpartum depression in cases of infanticide. See, for example, *R. v. Smith* (1976), where the testimony was aimed at establishing the "wilfulness" of the act. In the 1990s, use of psychiatrists to help the Crown's case by testifying *against* the defence's claim of "diminished capacity" on the basis of postpartum depression seems to have been more typical (see *R. v. Gorrill* [1995]).

18 The doctors' concern with ameliorating these social stressors makes this psychiatric discourse distinctly "humanitarian," in Lacquer's (1989) sense.

Chapter 4: Unwilling Mothers

1 For a discussion of the shift from home-based to hospital-based birthing practices, see Comacchio (1993).

2 *R. v. McHugh,* [1966] 1 C.C.C. 170, 50 C.R. 263, [1965-69] 5 N.S.R. 515.

3 *R. v. Smith* (1976) (Nfld. Dist. Ct.).

4 Petchesky (1984, 343) argues, contra the anti-abortion argument, that the "classical definition of personhood leaves no way to distinguish between infants and fetuses and therefore would allow infanticide"; rather, she argues for a "concept of personhood [that] would avoid biological reductionism yet include newborn babies, as well as allowing for the developmental variations in the fetus at different stages." Petchesky advances a relational theory of personhood that focuses on the interactive and social contexts, or *processes,* in which human beings acquire consciousness and self-awareness. The foetus becomes a person only when it is regarded as such by the mother. This position might have difficulty accounting for those cases in which the relationship between mother and foetus is subjectively and objectively "unwanted" but the foetus is nevertheless carried to term and subsequently killed or allowed to die. If foetal personhood is defined by a humanization process in which the formation of the "person" depends on "the subjectivity of the pregnant woman, her consciousness of existing in a relationship with the fetus" (1984, 343), then infanticide might not be homicide since a "denied pregnancy" has none of the essential conditions for "relational personhood." Although this position is not articulated by Petchesky, it is the logical conclusion of a relational theory of personhood.

5 *R. v. Marchello* (1951), 100 C.C.C. 137 at 141.

6 *Rex v. Krueger* (1948), 93 C.C.C. at 247.

7 *Ibid.*

8 *Ibid.*

9 *Ibid.* at 247-48.

10 The main legal requirements to sustain the charge of murder were live-birth and recent delivery of the baby. If the Crown had sufficient evidence of both then, it was likely it could proceed with a trial for murder. At trial the Crown would have to prove both intent and live-birth in order to gain a conviction. For the purposes of the preliminary hearing, all the Crown had to establish was that there was sufficient evidence of recent childbirth and live-birth to proceed to trial.

11 *R. v. Marchello* (1951), 100 C.C.C. at 137.

12 An interesting corollary of the murder charge in this case was the deployment of the insanity defence. This defence tactic would have been unnecessary had the Crown brought an infanticide charge to court and would have likely resulted in a conviction, albeit on a lesser charge, for the Crown rather than an absolute acquittal by the jury. Again we see the old approach in which the jury is "blamed" for an acquittal on the grounds of sympathetic lenience. In fact, jurors might well have been willing to issue a conviction for infanticide with its lesser punishment framework, but Crown prosecutors seemed unwilling to apply the charge.

13 Recall that jury trial judgments tend not to be reported except in certain circumstances. In this case there was a specific charge to the jury that required considerable judicial explanation.

14 *Marchello, supra* note 11, at 138-41.

15 The age limit for a newly born child was set at one year, following the 1953-54 amendments to the *Criminal Code,* S.C. 1954-55, c. 51, s. 2(27).

16 *R. v. O'Donoghue* (1927), 20 C.R. App. R. 132.

17 *Marchello, supra* note 11, at 158.

18 *Ibid.* at 141-42.

19 *R. v. Jacobs* (1952), 105 C.C.C. at 291.

20 The judge does not report his reason for acquittal on the charge of neglect and further fails to address how "wilful omission," as outlined in the infanticide provision, stands in relation to this acquittal.

21 *Hansard Parliamentary Debates,* vol. 3, 10 March 1954, 2865; and *Criminal Code,* S.C. 1953-54, c. 51, s. 570.

22 *Hansard Parliamentary Debates,* vol. 3, 10 March 1954, 2864-65.

23 *Ibid.* at 2864.

24 While nothing in the law itself creates a legal presumption of reproductive mental disturbance for a charge of infanticide to be laid, one might argue that such disturbance is "assumed" by the diminished punishment framework. This assumption explains why a man
cannot be charged with infanticide. Although judges and/or juries are not legally required
to consider reproductive mental disturbance, this does not solve the problem of the manner in which courts will construe it over time.

25 *Hansard, supra* note 22 at 2864.

26 *Ibid.* at 2865.

27 *Ibid.*

28 *Ibid.*

29 *Ibid.*

30 *Ibid.* at 2865-66.

31 See Chapter 6, where I argue that Knowles's fears were justified and that Nowlan's statement confirming that without "intent" there is no crime was overly optimistic. In the late
1990s, the federal Department of Justice commenced a broad consultation with child abuse
experts to consider introducing a new child homicide law in which the requirement to
prove intent is removed entirely from the *Criminal Code* framework. Such a provision would
undoubtedly be subject to a Charter challenge.

32 *Hansard, supra* note 22 at 2866.

33 *Ibid.*

34 *Ibid.*

35 *Ibid.*

36 *Ibid.*

37 *Ibid.*

38 *Ibid.*

39 *R. v. Bryan* (1959), 123 C.C.C. at 160.

40 *Ibid.* at 161.

41 *Ibid.* at 164.

42 *Ibid.* at 161.

43 *Ibid.* at 162.

44 *Ibid.* at 164.

45 *R. v. Smith* (1976), 32 C.C.C. (2d) 224.

46 *Ibid.* at 232.

47 *Ibid.* at 227.

48 *Ibid.* at 232.

49 *R. v. McHugh,* [1966] 1 C.C.C. 170, 50 C.R. 263, [1965-69] 5 N.S.R. 515 at 230.

50 *Smith, supra* note 45 at 231.

51 *Ibid.* at 233.

52 *R. v. Szola* (1977), 33 C.C.C. (2d) at 572.

53 *Ibid.*

54 *Ibid.* at 574.

55 *Ibid.*

56 *Ibid.*

57 *Ibid.* at 575-76.

58 *Ibid.* at 573.

59 See *infra* note 97 and accompanying text for *R. v. Gorrill* (1995), 139 N.S.R. (2d) 191; 397
A.P.R. 191.

60 *R. v. Del Rio* (1979), O.J. No. 16, on-line: QL (O.J.).

61 *Marchello, supra* note 11.

62 *Supra* note 22.

63 *Del Rio, supra* note 60 at para. 54.

64 *Ibid.* at para. 30 and 31.

65 *Ibid.* at para. 10.

66 *Ibid.*

67 *Ibid.* at para. 14.
68 *Ibid.* at para. 15.
69 *Ibid.* at para. 18.
70 *Ibid.* at para. 20 and 21.
71 *Ibid.* at para. 21.
72 *Ibid.* at para. 46.
73 *Ibid.* at para. 54.
74 *R. v. A.P.P.,* [1992] O.J. No. 1626, on-line: QL (O.J.R.E.).
75 It is also relevant to note here that this practice has the effect of placing maternal neonaticides in the crime category of second degree murder, according to the Canadian Criminal Justice Statistics practice of recording police laid charges. This practice results in the inflation of Canadian statistics on "infant murder," which is typically associated with much more extreme forms of violence and applies to older children.
76 *R. v. A.P.P., supra* note 74 at para. 1.
77 *Ibid.*
78 Recall the "discourse of virtue" that mitigates infanticide throughout the nineteenth century.
79 *R. v. A.P.P., supra* note 74 at para. 16.
80 *Ibid.*
81 *Ibid.*
82 *Ibid.*
83 *R. v. Lalli,* [1993] B.C.J. No. 2010, on-line: QL (B.C.J.R.).
84 See Appendix: Current Legal Framework Governing Maternal Neonaticide.
85 *R. v. Lalli, supra* note 83 at para. 11.
86 *Ibid.* at para. 12.
87 See discussion of the parliamentary debate to amend the *Criminal Code,* pp. 107-13 above.
88 *R. v. Lalli, supra* note 83 at paras. 3 and 4.
89 *Ibid.* at para. 26.
90 *Ibid.*
91 *R. v. Peters,* [1995] O.J. No. 4080, on-line: QL (O.J.R.E.).
92 *London Free Press,* 30 December 1993.
93 *R. v. Peters, supra* note 91 at para. 1.
94 *Ibid.* at para. 3.
95 *Ibid.* at para. 15.
96 *Ibid.* at para. 24.
97 *R. v. A.P.P., supra* note 74.
98 Recall the cases in Chapter 2, where strangulation, burning, stabbing, and manual suffocation are ordinary features in the deaths of neonates. This violence is of little or no concern in the responses/dispositions in these cases.
99 *R. v. Peters, supra* note 91 at para. 17.
100 *R. v. Gorrill* (1995), 139 N.S.R. (2d) 191; 397 A.P.R. 191.
101 *Ibid.* at 195.
102 *Ibid.* at 192.
103 *Ibid.* at 197.
104 *Ibid.* at 198.
105 *Ibid.* at 204.
106 *Ibid.*
107 *Ibid.* at 202, 204.
108 *Ibid.* at 199.
109 *Ibid.* at 203.
110 *Ibid.* at 203-4.
111 *R. v. Guimont* (1999), 141 C.C.C. (3d) 314-15.
112 *Ibid.* at 318.
113 *Ibid* at 317-18.
114 *Ibid.* at 320.

115 *R. c. Lucas* (1999-12-10) on-line source: http://www.canlii.org/qc/jug/qccq/1999/ 1999qccq199.html.

116 *Ibid.* at 6-7.

117 *Ibid.* at 5.

118 Recall how, in *R. v. Peters*, evidence that the accused considered having an abortion functioned to aggravate her intentionality because it was thought to suggest the baby was unwanted and, therefore, that she intended to kill it. In the *Lucas* case, the evidence is interpreted as a sign of maturity and lack of intent to kill.

119 *Guimont, supra* note 111 at 311.

120 Certain cases reveal that this shift is not yet complete. Some cases continue to be disposed of in the nineteenth-century manner. The determining factors for more punitive responses appear to be violence to the baby and single motherhood.

Chapter 5: Vengeance for the Innocents

1 In two cases children's aid societies in Ontario (in 1994 and 1995, respectively) have applied to the courts for Crown wardship on the grounds that a child was in need of protection on the basis of evidence of infanticide. In one case the society sought wardship of an infant on the grounds that her forty-one-year-old mother, described as developmentally handicapped and mentally ill, had been convicted of infanticide when she was twenty years old. According to the aid society's rationale, this woman's choice to become a mother was forfeited following her conviction for infanticide some twenty-one years earlier. The order was granted, mainly on the theory that the child was at serious risk of harm, without any evidence that mothers who commit infanticide are likely to repeat the offence decades later. In fact, most infanticide sentencing dispositions highlight the fact that these women *do not* pose any future threat (*CAS of the Durham Region v. J.R.,* [1995] O.J. No. 3419, on-line: QL). In the second case, the children's aid society sought guardianship appointment of a sixteen-year-old girl who gave birth unassisted and put the dead baby in a dumpster. The society argued that she was a child in need of protection and that she had suffered emotional harm due to her mother's lack of knowledge of her pregnancy and her failure to make legal arrangements for her daughter! This application was dismissed on the grounds that there was no evidence the teen's mother had failed in her duty as a parent (*CAS for the Districts of Sudbury and Manitoulin v. M.S.,* [1994] O.J. No. 2902, on-line: QL). I could find no evidence of such applications being made in other jurisdictions or during an earlier period.

2 See infant mortality data, World Health Organization Statistical Information System: http://www.who.int/whosis/.

3 Personal communication, Michael S. Pollanen, Department of Laboratory Medicine and Pathobiology, Office of the Chief Coroner for Ontario and Forensic Science Programme, University of Toronto, February 2000.

4 See, for example, Dorne (1989). There is a great deal of conceptual slippage between the use of the terms "infanticide" and "child abuse." American sociologists tend to keep the line fairly clear; however, they also attach the more severe descriptions of postpartum psychosis to the practice of infanticide. Any maternal neonaticides that fall outside of the strong psychiatric paradigm tend to be viewed as something other than infanticide. See, for example, Ewing (1997) on "dumpster babies," and for an overview of American research on postpartum illness, see Hamilton and Harberger (1992).

5 This book was first published in the United States in 1968 by the University of Chicago Press. The fifth edition was recently published in paperback (1997) as *The Battered Child* but without the editorial assistance of C. Henry Kempe, who died in 1984, or Ray Helfer, who died in 1992. This work was continued by M.E. Helfer and R.S. Kempe, the widows and colleagues of Ray Helfer and C. Henry Kempe, respectively. As a student and later colleague of both R. Helfer and C. Henry Kempe, R.D. Krugman provided editorial assistance on the fifth edition. Kempe himself was *the* key figure in the child abuse and neglect studies movement. Born in Germany, he spent most of his professional life in the United States and founded the International Society for the Prevention of Child Abuse and Neglect and its journal *Child Abuse and Neglect.* According to Jenkins (1992, 111), "these institutions

provided a forum for British specialists and activists and an opportunity to exchange ideas with their American and European counterparts."

6 This newspaper report is in fact not quite accurate. The Ontario Coroner's Office had been concerned about the deaths of children in the care of Child and Family Services for quite some time before the *Toronto Star* became involved and had identified the "trend" in the cases of infant deaths they had investigated over the years.

7 This represents 30 percent of those cases in which the deaths of "children" under the age of eighteen were investigated by the Ontario Coroner's Office over a five-year period.

8 According to Cyril Greenland (1973, 27), the province's child abuse registry has been in operation since 1966, and, in the first four years of its operation, over 1,600 cases were reported, with only 4 percent of those being cases of repeat battering. In these four years, 172 charges were laid, with forty-two convictions. Greenland's 1973 study identified many of the same problems with the registry identified in the 1990s by the Office of the Chief Coroner. One major problem identified by Greenland, but not by the Office of the Chief Coroner, is the registry's limited value for statistical purposes due to its lack of a standardized definition of "child abuse."

9 At the same time, a "super inquest" into domestic violence was announced. This announcement also came after a so-called "groundbreaking investigation of domestic violence by *The Star.*" Dr. Bonnie Porter, a deputy chief coroner for the Niagara region, stated simply: "The aim is to start a war against domestic abuse similar to the campaign now waged against drunk driving" ("Super Inquest to Probe Growing Family Violence," *Toronto Star,* 18 September 1996, A1).

10 Moira Welsh and Kevin Donovan, "Getting Away with Murder – of Children," *Toronto Star,* serial report, 18 May 1997, A6); Coroner's Investigation Case File no. 28183 (1993).

11 The definition of "children" includes anyone up to eighteen years of age.

12 A request for all inquests into the deaths of children (1980-98) in Ontario revealed only one case of maternal neonaticide in which an inquest was held. The inquest into the death of baby W in February 1981 made only vague recommendations about infanticide itself, as opposed to the law of infanticide. This jury recommended that "information regarding infanticide should be made available to those agencies where it would be helpful for them to track those people who have had previous offences" (Verdict of the Coroner's Jury, Office of the Chief Coroner for Ontario, case file no. 12164, 1981). In other words, it recommended, for the purposes of risk management, the enhanced regulation of women previously accused or convicted of infanticide.

13 Opening Statement, Verdict of the Coroner's Jury, case file no. 14936.

14 Recommendations 1 and 2, Verdict of the Coroner's Jury, case file no. 14936.

15 This comment is made in explanation of the paper's non-consideration of the defence of reasonable force as pertaining to correction applied toward a pupil or child.

Chapter 6: Retributive Justice

1 Office of the Chief Coroner for Ontario, the Ministry of Public Safety and Security, on-line at http://www.mpss.jus.gov.on.ca/english/pub_safety/office_coroner/about_coroner.html.

2 As defined in *R. v. McHugh,* [1966] 1 C.C.C. 170, 50 C.R. 263, [1965-69] 5 N.S.R. 515.

3 Personal communication, Office of the Chief Coroner, Toronto, Ontario, 29 October 1999.

4 Access to these files was obtained with the cooperation of the Office of the Chief Coroner for Ontario and by way of a court order granted by the Honourable Mr. Justice Brian Weagant. The court order was in compliance with the anonymity provision of the *Young Offenders Act* and is provided for under s. 44.1 of that act.

5 The coroner has the authority to investigate any death with the full cooperation of medical professionals and the police. An investigation is different from an inquest, which can only be called under certain circumstances, usually when an individual has died while in the care or control of a public institution such as a jail, mental health facility, or child welfare agency. See *Coroner's Act,* R.S.O. 1990, c. C-37.

6 Personal communication, Office of the Chief Coroner, Toronto, Ontario, 29 October 1999.

7 Personal communication, Manager, Coroner's Information System, Office of the Chief Coroner for Ontario, Toronto. Various telephone conversations and interviews, February and March 2000.

8 *Child and Family Services Act,* R.S.O. 1990, c. 11, s. 75(1)-(14).

9 Coroner's Investigation Case File no. 19733 (1987).

10 In all but two cases examined, Drs. Chitra Rao and Charles Smith performed the autopsies on the babies whose mothers were suspected of neonaticide. In each case they relied on the floating lung test and "other" social factors in their findings of live-birth.

11 Coroner's Investigation Case File nos. 11148 (1990), 26504 (1990), 30254 (1992).

12 *Toronto Sun, Peterborough Examiner,* and *The Toronto Star,* 10 November 1992, no page numbers; Coroner's Investigation File no. 30254 (1992).

13 *Toronto Sun,* 29 July 1994; Coroner's Investigation File no. 30254 (1992).

14 The *Star* report is likely referring to the provincial sentence of "two years less a day."

15 *London Free Press,* 5 January 1994; Coroner's Investigation File no. 28183 (1993).

16 Coroner's Investigation File no. 28183 (1993).

17 *R. v. McHugh,* [1966] 1 C.C.C. 170, 50 C.R. 263, [1965-69] 5 N.S.R. 515.

18 Recall, too, the babies burnt in ovens, trash incinerators, and strangled (see Chapter 2).

19 *London Free Press,* 11 October 1995; Coroner's Investigation Case File no. 28183 (1993).

20 Laura J. Miller, M.D. (2003, 81-91) describes three types of pregnancy denial – affective denial, pervasive denial, and psychotic denial – and their associated reasons and consequences. She concludes, in part, that "societies in which women are harshly punished or rejected for becoming pregnant, seeking abortion, or abandoning babies are more likely to give rise to pregnancy denial and resultant neonaticide" (101).

21 Robert H. Kirschner, M.D., former deputy chief medical examiner, Cook County, Illinois, is clinical associate in the Department of Pathology and the Department of Pediatrics at the University of Chicago and the LaRabida Children's Hospital and Research Center. He is also director of the International Forensic Program of Physicians for Human Rights. See Robert H. Kirschner, "The Pathology of Child Abuse" in M.E. Helfer, R.S. Kempe, and R.D. Krugman, eds., *The Battered Child,* 5th ed. (Chicago: University of Chicago Press, 1997).

22 These events are chronicled in Firstman and Talan (1997), a collaborative effort by a couple who worked for *Newsday* and whose work had earned them awards for investigative journalism and science writing. This book is well known to those in the forensic science community, including those members working in the Chief Coroner's Office for Ontario (personal communication with Jeff Mainland, Coordinator, Pediatric Death Review Committee, Office of the Chief Coroner for Ontario, February, 2000), who use it as a case in point.

23 See "Experts in Child Abuse Face Enquiry," *The Guardian,* 18 June 2004, on-line at http://www.guardian.co.uk/child/story/0,7369,1241541,00.html.

24 The *Yorkshire Post* of the UK reported on 12 June 2003 that the expert evidence given by Dr. Meadows against Mrs. Trupti Patel, on trial for murdering her three babies, was rejected by the jury. At the time, the courts were considering a review of at least six other cases of mothers convicted of murder in which Sir Roy was involved. In 1999 solicitor Sally Clark was wrongfully convicted of killing two of her babies after Meadows testified that the odds of her losing two of her babies to SIDS were one in 73 million. See http://www.nkmr.org/english/a_jury_gives_its_verdict_on_meadows_law.htm.

25 See "Mother Cleared of Killing Sons," on-line at <http://news.bbc.co.uk/1/hi/england/wiltshire/3306271.stm> and "Profile: Sir Roy Meadows," <http://news.bbc.co.uk/1/hi/health/3307427.stm>.

26 Coroner's Investigation Case File no. 2439 (1996).

27 *Ibid.*

28 Coroner's Investigation Case File no. 11103 (1993).

29 *Ibid.*

30 *London Free Press,* 3 June 1993; Coroner's Investigation Case File no. 11103 (1993).

31 *London Free Press,* 26 April 1994; Coroner's Investigation Case File no. 11103 (1993).

32 Coroner's Investigation Case File no. 11103 (1993).

33 *London Free Press,* 12 April 1994 (emphasis added); Coroner's Investigation Case File no. 11103 (1993).

34 *London Free Press,* 26 April 1994; Coroner's Investigation Case File no. 11103 (1993).

35 *Ibid.*

36 *Ibid.*
37 I have omitted one case from this discussion because the mother was never found. Coroner's Investigation Case File no. 6615 (1994).
38 Coroner's Investigation Case File no. 5451 (1993).
39 This case fits more comfortably within the parameters of infanticide cases in both the United States and Britain, where the homicide of babies who are more than a few hours old is still considered infanticide and where there is a stronger tradition of criminal law mitigation by reason of postpartum depression. This is likely a result of the manner in which postpartum depression operates as a defence of diminished responsibility with regard to manslaughter (Brockington 1999; Brockington and Kumar 1982; Kumar and Brockington 1988; Hamilton and Harberger 1992; Oberman 1996).
40 However, this is not surprising since the case sample was one in which all cases were considered homicide. The fact that every baby autopsied was deemed to have been born alive can be accounted for by the possible exclusion of certain cases in which the autopsy report indicated that the baby had been stillborn. There were no cases of stillbirth in the sample I looked at.
41 These two forensic pathologists performed autopsies in almost *all* cases of infant deaths, including those that were considered child abuse deaths and those in which child abuse was evident. Dr. Chitra Rao has provided expert testimony in cases involving child abuse, and Dr. Charles Smith autopsied all but a few cases where infanticide was suspected.
42 Coroner's Investigation Case File no. 14938 (1996/1997).
43 *Ibid.*
44 Coroner's Investigation Case File no. 3533 (1994).
45 *Ibid.*
46 Coroner's Investigation Case File no. 925 (1995).
47 *Ibid.*
48 *Ibid.*
49 *Ibid.*
50 *Ibid.*
51 *Hamilton Spectator,* 20, 21, and 26 January 1995, n.pp.; Coroner's Investigation Case File no. 925 (1995).
52 *Toronto Sun,* 17 September 1996; Coroner's Investigation Case File no. 925 (1995).
53 *Hamilton Spectator,* 17 September 1996; Coroner's Investigation Case File no. 925 (1995).
54 *Ibid.*
55 Letter from M.D. to regional coroner, Coroner's Investigation Case File no. 925 (1995).
56 Personal communication, Office of the Coroner for Ontario, Toronto, February 2000.
57 Coroner's Investigation Case File no. 5451 (1993).
58 According to the Office of the Coroner for Ontario, Crown prosecutors generally use the standard age of three months in determining whether an infanticide charge or plea is appropriate. Personal communication, February 2000.
59 US law does not include infanticide as a separate legal category; instead, infanticide operates as a defence to mitigate culpability for homicide (Oberman 1996).
60 See also Greenland (1987, 38-72), in particular his discussion of Ontario child abuse homicide cases, where he argues that "it is inappropriate to lump the twelve homicide cases in the BCS [Battered Child Syndrome] cases. This is because [except for one case] the other deaths were caused by a single physical assault" (61).
61 Coroners also appear to go to much greater lengths than previously to obtain evidence. For instance, the bodies of infants have been exhumed at the request of child death review teams to allow for forensic pathological investigation, something that does not appear to have occurred in the early part of the twentieth century.

Appendix: Current Legal Framework Governing Maternal Neonaticide
1 *Criminal Code,* R.S.C. 1985, c. C-46, and Amendments.
2 *Ibid.* s. 232(1).
3 *Ibid.* s. 235(1)(2).
4 *Ibid.* s. 236.

5 *Ibid.* s. 233. Under s. 2 a newly born child means a person under the age of one year.
6 *Ibid.* s. 237.
7 *Ibid.* s. 237, synopsis and annotations.
8 *Ibid.* s. 218, and synopsis.
9 *Ibid.* s. 242.
10 *Ibid.* s. 242, and synopsis (emphasis in original).
11 *Ibid.* s. 243.
12 *Ibid.* s. 243, and synopsis (emphasis in original).
13 *Ibid.* s. 238(1)(2), and synopsis (emphasis in original).
14 *Ibid.* s. 215(1)(a) (emphasis in original).
15 *Ibid.* s. 223(1)(2).
16 *Ibid.* s. 672.11.
17 *Ibid.* s. 663.
18 *Ibid.* s. 610(2)(4).
19 *Ibid.* s. 662(3)(4).

References

Allen, H. 1987. "Rendering Them Harmless: The Professional Portrayal of Women Charged with Serious Violent Crimes." In *Gender, Crime and Justice,* ed. Pat Carlen and Ann Worrall, 81-94. Milton Keynes: Open University Press.

Backhouse, Constance. 1984. "Desperate Women and Compassionate Courts: Infanticide in Nineteenth-Century Canada." *University of Toronto Law Journal* 34: 447-78.

–. 1991. *Petticoats and Prejudice: Women and Law in Nineteenth-Century Canada.* Toronto: The Osgoode Society.

–. 1994. "Prosecutions of Abortions under Canadian Law, 1900-1950." In *Essays in the History of Canadian Law.* Vol. 5: *Crime and Criminal Justice,* ed. Jim Phillips, Tina Loo, and Susan Lewthwaite, 252-92. Toronto: The Osgoode Society.

Bailey, M.J. 1991. "Servant Girls and Masters: The Tort of Seduction and the Support of Bastards." *Canadian Journal of Family Law* 10: 137-62.

Banks, Margaret. 1983. "The Evolution of the Ontario Courts, 1788-1981." In *Essays in the History of Canadian Law.* Vol. 2, ed. David H. Flaherty, 492-572. Toronto: The Osgoode Society.

Bauman, Carol-Ann. 1997. "Rethinking the Unthinkable: A Study of Child Homicides." *Criminal Reports* 8 (1): 139-49.

Beattie, J.M. 1986. *Crime and the Courts in England, 1660-1800.* Princeton: Princeton University Press.

Behlmer, George K. 1979. "Deadly Motherhood: Infanticide and Medical Opinion in Mid-Victorian England." *Journal of the History of Medicine and Allied Sciences* 4: 403-27.

Best, Joel. 1990. *Threatened Children: Rhetoric and Concern about Child-Victims.* Chicago: University of Chicago Press.

Blackstone, William Sir. 1966 [1769]. *Blackstone's Commentaries.* Vol. 4. Oxford: Clarendon Press.

Blugrass, Robert. 1990. "Infanticide and Filicide." In *Principles and Practices of Forensic Psychiatry,* ed. Robert Blugrass and Paul Bowden, 523-28. New York: Churchill Livingston.

Boyle, Christine, Isabel Grant, and Dorothy Chunn. 1994. *The Law of Homicide.* Toronto: Carswell Co.

Boys, William Fuller Alves. 1905. *A Practical Treatise on the Office and Duties of Coroners: Ontario and the Other Provinces and the Territories of Canada and in the Colony of Newfoundland.* Toronto: Carswell Co.

Brockington, Ian. 1999 [1996]. *Motherhood and Mental Health.* Oxford: Oxford University Press.

Brockington, I.F., and R. Kumar, eds. 1982. *Motherhood and Mental Illness.* London: Academic Press.

Busby, Karen. 1993. "LEAF and Pornography: Litigating on Equality and Sexual Representations." *Canadian Review of Law and Society* 9 (1): 165-92.

–. 1999. "'Not a Victim until a Conviction Is Entered': Sexual Violence Prosecutions and Legal 'Truth.'" In *Locating Law: Race/Class/Gender Connections*, ed. Elizabeth Comack, 260-88. Halifax: Fernwood Publishing.

Caffey, J. 1946. "Multiple Fractures in the Long Bones of Infants Suffering from Chronic Subdural Hematoma." *American Journal of Radiology* 56: 163-73.

Cellard, A. 1991. *Histoire de la folie au Québec: 1600-1850*. Montréal: Les Éditions du Boréal.

Cellard, A., and G. Pelletier. 1988. "Le code criminel canadien, 1892-1927: Etudes des acteurs sociaux," *Canadian Historical Review* 79 (2): 261-303.

Clark, Michael, and Catherine Crawford, eds. 1994. *Legal Medicine in History*. Cambridge: Cambridge University Press.

Clarke, Geoffrey. 1913. "The Forms of Mental Disorder Occurring in Connection with Child-Bearing." *Journal of Mental Science* 59: 67-74.

Coats, R.H. 1946. "Beginnings in Canadian Statistics." *Canadian Historical Review* 27 (2): 109-30.

Comacchio, Cynthia. 1993. *Nations Are Built of Babies: Saving Ontario's Mothers and Children, 1900-1940*. Montreal and Kingston: McGill-Queen's University Press.

Comack, Elizabeth. 1987. "Women Defendants and the 'Battered Wife Syndrome': A Plea for Sociological Imagination." *Crown Counsel's Review* 5: 11.

–. 1993. "Feminist Engagement with the Law: The Legal Recognition of the Battered Woman Syndrome." Paper no. 31. Ottawa: Canadian Research Institute for the Advancement of Women (CRIAW).

Davidson, G.M. 1941. "Medico-Legal Aspects of Infanticide." *Journal of Psychopathology* 2: 500-11.

Davies, Seaborne. 1968 [1937/38]. "Child Killing in English Law." In *Modern Approach to Criminal Law*. Vol. 4: *English Studies in Criminal Science*, ed. L. Radzinowicz and J.W.C. Turner, 301-43. Cambridge: Cambridge University Press.

Dorne, Clifford. 1989. *Crimes against Children*. New York: Harrow and Heston Publishers.

Dubinsky, Karen, and Franca Iocovetta. 1991. "Murder, Womanly Virtue, and Motherhood: The Case of Angelina Napolitano, 1911-1922." *Canadian Historical Review* 4: 505-31.

Duden, Barbara. 1993. *Disembodying Women: Perspectives on Pregnancy and the Unborn*. Massachusetts: Harvard University Press.

Edwards, Susan. 1984. *Women on Trial*. Manchester: Manchester University Press.

Ellis, Havelock. 1902. "Précis of 'Considerations on Infanticide [Quelques Considérations sur l'Infanticide].'" *Journal of Mental Science* 48 (2): 366.

Ewing, Charles P. 1997. *Fatal Families: The Dynamics of Intrafamilial Homicide*. London: Sage Publications.

Firstman, Richard, and Jamie Talan. 1997. *The Death of Innocents: A True Story of Murder, Medicine and High-Stakes Science*. New York: Bantam Books.

Fison, Lorimer, and Alfred Howitt. 1967 [1880]. *Kamilaroi and Kunai*. New York: Best Books.

Frigon, Sylvie. "L'homicide conjugal au feminine: D'hier à aujourd'hui." Montréal: Les editions du Remue-ménage.

Fudge, Judy, and Brenda Cossman. 1992. "Introduction: Privatization, Law and the Challenge of Feminism." In *Privatization, Law and the Challenge to Feminism*, ed. Brenda Cossman and Judy Fudge, 3-37. Toronto: University of Toronto Press.

Garland, David. 1985. "The Criminal and His Science." *British Journal of Criminology* 25 (2): 109-37.

–. 1988. "British Criminology before 1935." *British Journal of Criminology* 28 (2): 1-17.

–. 1990. *Punishment and Modern Society: A Study in Social Theory*. Chicago: University of Chicago Press.

Goldstein, Jan, ed. 1994. *Foucault and the Writing of History*. Oxford: Blackwell.

Greenland, Cyril. 1973. "Child Abuse in Ontario." Toronto: Ministry of Community and Social Services.

–. 1987. *Preventing CAN Deaths: An International Study of Deaths Due to Child Abuse and Neglect*. London: Tavistock Publications.

Guest, Dennis. 1980. *The Emergence of Social Security in Canada*. Vancouver: UBC Press.

Hacking, Ian. 1983. "Biopower and the Avalanche of Numbers." *Humanities and Society* 5: 279-95.

–. 1995. *Rewriting the Soul: Multiple Personality and the Sciences of Memory.* Princeton: Princeton University Press.

Haggerty, Kevin D. 2001. *Making Crime Count.* Toronto: University of Toronto Press.

Hamilton, James Alexander, and Particia Neel Harberger, eds. 1992. *Postpartum Psychiatric Illness: A Picture Puzzle.* Philadelphia: University of Pennsylvania Press.

Harder, T. 1967. "The Psychopathology of Infanticide." *Acta Psychiatrica Scandinavica* 43: 196-245.

Hay, D., P. Linebaugh, J.G. Rule, E.P. Thompson, and C. Winslow. 1975. *Albion's Fatal Tree.* Rev. ed. London: Harmondsworth.

Helfer, Mary Edna, Ruth S. Kempe, and Richard D. Krugman, eds. 1997. *The Battered Child.* 7th ed. Chicago: University of Chicago Press.

Hoffer, P.C., and N.E.H. Hull. 1981. *Murdering Mothers: Infanticide in England and New England, 1558-1803.* New York: New York University Press.

Hopwood, Joseph Stanley. 1927. "Child Murder and Insanity." *Journal of Mental Science* 73: 95-108.

Hunter, William. 1784. "On the Uncertainty of the Signs of Murder, in the Case of Bastard Children." In *Medical Observations and Inquiries By a Society of Physicians in London,* vol. 6, 266-90. London: T. Cadell.

Jackson, Mark. 1996. *New-Born Child Murder: Women, Illegitimacy and the Courts in Eighteenth-Century England.* Manchester: Manchester University Press.

–. 1997a. "Examining Bodies: Medical Evidence and the Coroner's Inquest." In *New-Born Child Murder: Women, Illegitimacy and the Courts in Eighteenth-Century England,* ed. Mark Jackson. New York: St. Martin's Press.

–, ed. 1997b. *New-Born Child Murder: Women, Illegitimacy and the Courts in Eighteenth-Century England.* New York: St. Martin's Press.

–, ed. 2002a. *Infanticide: Historical Perspectives on Child Murder and Concealment, 1550-2000.* Burlington and Aldershot: Ashgate Publishers.

–. 2002b. "The Trial of Harriet Vooght: Continuity and Change in the History of Infanticide." In *Infanticide: Historical Perspectives on Child Murder and Concealment, 1550-2000,* ed. Mark Jackson, 1-17. Burlington and Aldershot: Ashgate Publishers.

Jenkins, Philip. 1992. *Intimate Enemies: Moral Panics in Contemporary Great Britain.* New York: Aldine de Gruyter.

Jenks, Chris. *Childhood.* New York: Routledge, 1996.

Johnson, Kirsten, and Mary-Anne Kandrack. 1995. "On the Medico-Legal Appropriation of Menstrual Discourse: The Syndromization of Women's Experiences." *Resources for Feminist Research/Documentation sur la recherche féministe* 24 (1,2): 23-27.

Kains, John Alexander. 1893. *"How Say You?" A Review of the Movement for Abolishing the Grand Jury System in Canada.* St. Thomas: The Journal.

Kirschner, Robert H. 1997. "The Pathology of Child Abuse." In *The Battered Child,* 5th ed., ed. M.E. Helfer, R.S. Kempe, and R.D. Krugman, 248-95. Chicago: University of Chicago Press.

Kramar, Kirsten Johnson. 2000. *Unwilling Mothers and Unwanted Babies: Infanticide and Medico-legal Responsibility in 20th Century Canadian Legal Discourse.* PhD diss., University of Toronto.

Kumar, R., and I.F. Brockington, eds. 1988. *Motherhood and Mental Illness 2: Causes and Consequences.* London: Wright.

Kunzel, Regina. 1993. *Fallen Women, Problem Girls: Unmarried Mothers and the Professionalization of Social Work, 1890-1945.* New Haven: Yale University Press.

Ladd-Taylor, Molly, and Lauri Umansky, eds. 1998. *"Bad" Mothers: The Politics of Blame in Twentieth-Century America.* New York: New York University Press.

Laqueur, Thomas W. 1989. "Bodies, Details, and the Humanitarian Narrative." In *The New Cultural History,* ed. Linda Hunt, 176-204. California: University of California Press.

Laster, Kathy. 1989. "Infanticide: A Litmus Test for Feminist Criminological Theory." *Australian and New Zealand Journal of Criminology* 22 (3): 151-66.

Lewis, Jane. 1980. *The Politics of Motherhood: Child and Maternal Welfare in England, 1900-1939.* Montreal: McGill-Queen's University Press.

Light, Ruth, and Ruth Roach Pierson, eds. 1990. *No Easy Road: Women in Canada, 1920s to 1960s.* Toronto: New Hogtown Press.

Little, Margaret. 1998. *"No Car, No Radio, No Liquor Permit": The Moral Regulation of Single Mothers in Ontario, 1920-1997.* Toronto: Oxford University Press.

Lombroso-Ferrero, Gina. 1972. *Criminal Man, According to the Classification of Cesare Lombroso.* With an introduction by Cesare Lombroso. Montclair, NJ: Patterson Smith. (Orig. pub. 1911.)

Luhmann, Niklas. 1982. *The Differentiation of Society.* Trans. Stephen Holmes and Charles Larmore. New York: Columbia University Press.

–. 1985. *A Sociological Theory of Law.* 2nd ed. Trans. Elizabeth King and Martin Albrow, ed. Martin Albrow. London: Routledge and Kegan Paul.

–. 1988. "Closure and Openness: On Reality in the World of Law." In *Autopoietic Law: A New Approach to Law and Society,* ed. Gunther Teubner. Berlin: de Gruyter.

Mackay, R.D. 1993. "The Consequences of Killing Very Young Children." *Criminal Law Review:* 21-30.

McSherry, Bernadette. 1993. "The Return of the Raging Hormones Theory: Premenstrual Syndrome, Postpartum Disorders and Criminal Responsibility." *Sydney Law Review* 15: 292-316.

Maier-Katkin, D. 1991. "Postpartum Psychosis, Infanticide and the Law." *Crime Law and Social Change* 15: 109-23.

–. 1992. "Postpartum Psychosis, Infanticide, and Criminal Justice." In *Postpartum Psychiatric Picture Illness: A Picture Puzzle,* ed. James Alexander Hamilton and Patricia Neel Harberger, 275-95. Philadelphia: University of Pennsylvania Press.

Maier-Katkin, D., and R. Ogle. 1993. "A Rationale for Infanticide Laws." *Criminal Law Review:* 903-14.

–. 1997. "Policy Disparity: The Punishment of Infanticide in Britain and America." *International Journal of Comparative and Applied Criminal Justice* 21 (2): 305-16.

Malcolmson, R.W. 1977. "Infanticide in the Eighteenth Century." In *Crime in England, 1550-1800,* ed. J.S. Cockburn, 187-339. London: Methuen Press.

Malinowski, B. 1929. *The Sexual Life of Savages in North-Western Melanesia.* New York: Halcyon House.

Marcé, Louis Victor. 1858. *Traité de la Folie des Femmes Enceintes, des Nouvelles Accouchées et des Nourrices.* Paris: J.B. Ballière et Fils.

Martin, Sheilah, and Murray Coleman. 1995. "Judicial Intervention in Pregnancy." *McGill Law Journal/Revue de Droit de McGill* 40: 947-91.

Martin's Annual Criminal Code 2005. Aurora, ON: Canada Law Books.

May, A. 1995. "'She at First Denied It': Infanticide Trials at the Old Bailey." In *Women and History: Voices of Early Modern England,* ed. Valerie Frith. Toronto: Coach House Press.

Meyer, Cheryl M., and Michelle Oberman. 2001. *Mothers Who Kill Their Children: Understanding the Acts of Moms from Susan Smith to the "Prom Mom."* New York: New York University Press.

Miller, Laura J. 2003. "Denial of Pregnancy." In *Infanticide: Psychosocial and Legal Perspectives on Mothers who Kill,* ed. Margaret G. Spinelli. Washington: American Psychiatric Publishing.

Mitchinson, Wendy. 1991. *The Nature of Their Bodies: Women and Their Doctors in Victorian Canada.* Toronto: University of Toronto Press.

Morgan, Lynn. 1990. "When Does Life Begin? A Cross-Cultural Perspective on the Personhood of Fetuses and Young Children." In *Abortion Rights and Fetal Personhood,* ed. Edd Doer and James W. Prescott. Palo Alto, CA: Centerline Press.

Morton, J.H. 1934. "Female Homicides." *Journal of Mental Science* 80 (1): 64-74.

Naffine, Ngaire. 1987. *Female Crime: The Construction of Women in Criminology.* Sydney: Allen and Unwin.

–. 1990. *Law and the Sexes: Explorations in Feminist Jurisprudence.* Sydney: Allen and Unwin.

Oberman, Michelle. 1996. "Mothers Who Kill: Coming to Terms with Modern American Infanticide." *American Criminal Law Review* 34 (1): 1-110.

–. 2003. "A Brief History of Infanticide and the Law." In *Infanticide: Psychosocial and Legal Perspectives on Mothers Who Kill,* ed. Margaret G. Spinelli, 3-18. Washington: American Psychiatric Publishing, Inc.

O'Donovan, K. 1984. "The Medicalisation of Infanticide." *Criminal Law Review*: 259-64.

Osborne, Judith. 1987. "The Crime of Infanticide: Throwing the Baby Out with the Bathwater." *Canadian Journal of Family Law* 6: 47-59.

Pearson, Patricia. 1997. *When She Was Bad: Violent Women and the Myth of Innocence*. Toronto: Random House of Canada.

Petchesky, Rosalind. 1984. *Abortion and Woman's Choice: The State, Sexuality and Reproductive Freedom*. Boston: Northeastern University Press.

–. 1995. "The Body as Property: A Feminist Re-Vision." In *Conceiving The New World Order*, ed. F. Ginsburg and R. Rapp. Berkeley: University of California Press.

Petrie, Anne. 1998. *Gone to an Aunt's: Remembering Canada's Homes for Unwed Mothers*. Toronto: McClelland and Stewart.

Pfohl, Stephen. 1994. *Images of Deviance and Social Control: A Sociological History*. 2nd ed. New York: McGraw-Hill.

–. 1977. "The 'Discovery' of Child Abuse." *Social Problems* 24: 310-22.

Piers, Maria. 1978. *Infanticide*. New York: W.W. Norton and Company Inc.

Priest, Lisa. 1992. *Women Who Killed: Stories of Canadian Female Murders*. Toronto: McClelland and Stewart.

Reagan, Leslie. 1997. *When Abortion Was a Crime: Women, Medicine, and Law in the United States, 1967-1973*. Berkeley: University of California Press.

Reekie, Gail. 1998. *Measuring Immorality: Social Inquiry and the Problem of Illegitimacy*. Cambridge: Cambridge University Press.

Rich, Adrienne. 1976 (reissued 1995). *Of Woman Born: Motherhood as Experience and Institution*. New York: W.W. Norton and Co.

Roach, Kent. 1996. *Essentials of Canadian Criminal Law*. Toronto: Irwin Law.

–. 1999. *Due Process and Victims' Rights: The New Law and Politics of Criminal Justice*. Toronto: University of Toronto Press.

Rose, Lionel. 1986. *The Massacre of Innocents: Infanticide in Britain, 1800-1939*. London: Routledge and Kegan Paul.

Ryan, William Burke. 1858. "Child Murder in its Sanitary and Social Bearings." *Sanitary Review and Journal of Public Health* 4 (July): 165-84.

–. 1862. *Infanticide: Its Law, Prevalence, Prevention and History*. London: J. Churchill.

Said, Edward W. 1978. *Orientalism*. New York: Vintage Books.

Scheper-Hughes, Nancy. 1985. "Culture, Scarcity, and Maternal Thinking: Maternal Detachment and Infant Survival in a Brazilian Shantytown." *Ethos* 13 (4): 291-317.

–. 1987. "Introduction." In *Child Survival: Anthropological Perspectives on the Treatment and Maltreatment of Children*, ed. Nancy Scheper-Hughes, 1-29. Dortrecht, Holland: D. Reidel Publishing Company.

–. 1992. *Death without Weeping: The Violence of Everyday Life in Brazil*. Berkeley: University of California Press.

Scheper-Hughes, Nancy, and Carolyn Sargent. 1998. "Introduction: The Cultural Politics of Childhood." In *Small Wars: The Cultural Politics of Childhood*, ed. Nancy Scheper-Hughes and Carolyn Sargent, 1-33. Berkeley: University of California Press.

Scheper-Hughes, Nancy, and Howard F. Stein. 1987. "Child Abuse and the Unconscious in American Popular Culture." In *Child Survival: Anthropological Perspectives on the Treatment and Maltreatment of Children*, ed. Nancy Scheper-Hughes, 339-58. Dordrecht, The Netherlands: D. Reidel.

Scott, Walter. 1818. *The Heart of Midlothian* (Penguin Classics edition 1994.) New York and London: Penguin Books.

Scutt, J. 1981. "Sexism in Criminal Law." In *Women and Crime*, ed. S.K. Mukherjee and J.A. Scutt. Sydney/Boston: Australian Institute of Criminology/George Allen & Unwin.

Sharpe, J.A. 1983. *Crime in Seventeenth-Century England: A County Study*. Cambridge: Cambridge University Press.

–. 1984. *Crime in Early Modern England, 1550-1750*. London: Longman.

Showalter, E. 1985. *The Female Malady: Women, Madness, and English Culture, 1830-1980*. New York: Penguin Books.

Skottowe, Ian. 1942. "Mental Disorders in Pregnancy and the Puerperium." *Practitioner* 148 (3): 157-63.

Smart, Carol. 1976. *Women, Crime and Criminology: A Feminist Critique*. London: Routledge and Kegan Paul.

–. 1989. *Feminism and the Power of Law*. London: Routledge.

–. 1992. "Disruptive Bodies and Unruly Sex: The Regulation of Reproduction and Sexuality in the Nineteenth Century." In *Regulating Womanhood: Historical Essays on Marriage, Motherhood and Sexuality*, ed. Carol Smart, 7-32. New York: Routledge.

–. 1995. *Law, Crime and Sexuality: Essays in Feminism*. London: Sage Publications.

Smith, Roger. 1981. *Trial By Medicine: Insanity and Responsibility in Victorian Trials*. Edinburgh: Edinburgh University Press.

Sorenson, S.B., H. Shen, and J.F. Kraus. 1997. "Coroner-Reviewed Infant and Toddler Deaths: Many 'Undetermineds' Resemble Homicides." *Evaluation Review* 21 (1): 58-76.

Spinelli, Margaret G., ed. 2003. *Infanticide: Psychosocial and Legal Perspectives on Mothers Who Kill*. Washington: American Psychiatric Publishing, Inc.

Stange, C. 1995. *Toronto's Girl Problem: The Perils and Pleasures of the City, 1880-1930*. Toronto: University of Toronto Press.

Sullivan, W.C. 1911. "A Case of Infanticide with Mutilation," (Commentary). *Journal of Mental Science* 57: 401-2.

Teubner, Gunther. 1988. "Evolution of Autopoietic Law." In *Autopoietic Law: A New Approach to Law and Society*, ed. Gunther Teubner. Berlin: de Gruyter.

–. 1989. "How the Law Thinks: Toward A Contructivist Epistemology of Law." *Law and Society Review* 23 (5): 727-57.

–. 1990. "Social Order from Legislative Noise? Autopoietic Closure as a Problem for Legal Regulation." In *State, Law, and Economy as Autopoietic Systems*, ed. Gunther Teubner and Alberto Febbrajo. Milano: Giuffrè.

–. 1993. *Law as an Autopoietic System*. Oxford: Basil Blackwell.

Tooley, Michael. 1983. *Abortion and Infanticide*. Oxford: Clarendon Press.

Valverde, Mariana. 1991. *The Age of Light, Soap and Water: Social Purity and Philanthropy in Canada, 1885-1925*. Toronto: McClelland and Stewart.

Walker, Nigel. 1968. *Crime and Insanity in England*. Vol. 1: *The Historical Perspective*. Edinburgh: Oxford University Press.

–. 1987. "Infanticide." *Crime and Criminology: A Critical Introduction*. New York: Oxford University Press.

Walkowitz, Judith R. 1992. *City of Dreadful Delight: Narratives of Sexual Danger in Late Nineteenth-Century London*. Chicago: University of Chicago Press.

Ward, Tony. 1999. "The Sad Subject of Infanticide: Law, Medicine and Child Murder, 1860-1938." *Social and Legal Studies* 8 (2): 163-80.

–. 2002. "Legislating for Human Nature: Legal Responses to Infanticide, 1860-1938." In *Infanticide: Historical Perspectives on Child Murder and Concealment, 1550-2000*, ed. Mark Jackson, 249-69. Burlington and Aldershot: Ashgate.

Weiler, Karen M., and Katherine Cantton. 1976. "The Unborn Child in Canadian Law." *Osgoode Hall Law Journal* 14 (3): 643-59.

Wilczynksi, Ania. 1991. "Images of Women Who Kill Their Infants: The Mad and the Bad." *Women and Criminal Justice* 2 (2): 71-88.

–. 1997a. *Child Homicide*. London: Greenwich Medical Media Ltd.

–. 1997b. "Mad or Bad? Child Killers, Gender and the Courts." *British Journal of Criminology* 37 (3): 419-36.

Williams, Glanville. 1978. "The Legal Evaluation of Infanticide." In *Infanticide and the Value of Life*, ed. Marvin Kohl. Buffalo: Prometheus Books.

Wilson, Robert F. 1976. "A Brief Introduction to Sepsis: Its Importance and Some Historical Notes." *Heart and Lung* 5 (3): 393-96.

Wright, Mary Ellen. 1987. "Unnatural Mothers: Infanticide in Halifax, 1850-1875." *Nova Scotia Historical Review* 7 (2): 13-29.

Zay, Nicolas. 1965. "Section Y: Justice." In *Historical Statistics of Canada*, ed. M.C. Urquhart and K.A.H. Buckley (asst. ed.), 634-36. Toronto: Macmillan Company of Canada Ltd.

Zelizer, Vivian. 1985. *Pricing the Priceless Child: The Changing Social Value of Children*. New York: Basic Books.

Legislation
Criminal Code, S.C. 1953-54, c. 51.
Criminal Code, R.S.C. 1985, c. C-46.

Reported and Unreported Cases
CAS for the Districts of Sudbury and Manitoulin v. M.S. (1994), O.J. No. 2902, on-line: QL.
CAS of The Durham Region v. J.R. (1995), O.J. No. 3419, on-line: QL.
R. v. A.P.P., [1992] O.J. No. 1626, on-line: QL (O.J.R.E.).
R. v. Bryan (1959), 123 C.C.C. at 160 [1959] 103 O.W.N. (C.A.) (2:1).
R. v. Del Rio (1979), O.J. No. 16, on-line: QL (O.J.).
R. v. Drummond (1996), 143 D.L.R. (4th) at 368.
R. v. Gorrill (1995), 139 N.S.R. (2d) 191; 377 A.P.R. 191.
R. v. Guimont (1999), 141 C.C.C. (3d) 314.
R. v. Jacobs (1952), 105 C.C.C. at 291.
R. v. Lalli, [1993] B.C.J. No. 2010, on-line: QL (B.C.J.R.).
R. c. Lucas, (1999-12-10) QCCQ 110-01-002768-989, http://www.canlii.org/qc/jug/qccq/1999/1999/qccq199.html.
R. v. McHugh, [1966] 1 C.C.C. 170, 50 C.R. 263, [1965-69] 5 N.S.R. 515.
R. v. Marchello (1951), 100 C.C.C. 137, [1957] 4 D.L.R. 751, 12 C.R. 7.
R. v. O'Donoghue (1927), 20 C.R. App. R. 132.
R. v. Peters [1995], O.J. No. 4080, on-line: QL (O.J.R.E.).
R. v. Pichè, [1879] C.P. Michaelmas Term, 52 Vol. 30, 43 Vic. 409.
R. v. Smith (1976), 32 C.C.C. (2d) 224.
R. v. Szola (1977), 33 C.C.C. (2d) at 572.
Re: Sloan Estate, [1937] 3 W.W.R. 455 (B.C.S.C.).
Rex v. Krueger (1948), 93 C.C. at 247.

Ontario Provincial Coroner's Inquest by Verdict, 1980-98
Verdict of the Coroner's Jury (Baby Girl Waldron), Office of the Chief Coroner for Ontario, Case File no. 12164. 1981.
Verdict of the Coroner's Jury (Edward Maglicic), Office of the Chief Coroner for Ontario, Case File no. 12803. 1984.
Verdict of the Coroner's Jury (Thomas Michael Davies), Office of the Chief Coroner for Ontario, Case File no. 13221. 1985.
Verdict of the Coroner's Jury (Malcolm Bruce McArthur and Jody Lynn McArthur), Office of the Chief Coroner for Ontario, Case File no. 13440. 1986.
Verdict of the Coroner's Jury (Kasandra Hislop (aka) Shepherd), Office of the Chief Coroner for Ontario, Case File no. 14952. 1997.
Verdict of the Coroner's Jury (Margaret Kasonde), Office of the Chief Coroner for Ontario, Case File no. n/a. 1997.
Verdict of the Coroner's Jury (Angela Dombroskie; David Dombroskie; Jamie Lee Burns; Devon Burns), Office of the Chief Coroner for Ontario, Case File no. n/a. 1997.
Verdict of the Coroner's Jury (Shanay Johnson), Office of the Chief Coroner for Ontario, Case File no. 14936. 1997.
Verdict of the Coroner's Jury (Jennifer Koval's'kyj-England and Marion Johnson), Office of the Chief Coroner for Ontario, Case File no. n/a. 1998.

Coroner's Investigation Case Files, 1986-1998 (Closed Cases)
Coroner's Investigation Case File no. 19733 (6920), Office of the Chief Coroner for Ontario, Toronto, Ontario. 1987.
Coroner's Investigation Case File no. 11148, Office of the Chief Coroner for Ontario, Toronto, Ontario. 1990.
Coroner's Investigation Case File no. 26504, Office of the Chief Coroner for Ontario, Toronto, Ontario. 1990.
Coroner's Investigation Case File no. 30254, Office of the Chief Coroner for Ontario, Toronto, Ontario. 1992.

Coroner's Investigation Case File no. 5451, Office of the Chief Coroner for Ontario, Toronto, Ontario. 1993.

Coroner's Investigation Case File no. 11103, Office of the Chief Coroner for Ontario, Toronto, Ontario. 1993.

Coroner's Investigation Case File no. 28183, Office of the Chief Coroner for Ontario, Toronto, Ontario. 1993.

Coroner's Investigation Case File no. 3533, Office of the Chief Coroner for Ontario, Toronto, Ontario. 1994.

Coroner's Investigation Case File no. 6615, Office of the Chief Coroner for Ontario, Toronto, Ontario. 1994.

Coroner's Investigation Case File no. 925, Office of the Chief Coroner for Ontario, Toronto, Ontario. 1995.

Coroner's Investigation Case File no. 2439, Office of the Chief Coroner for Ontario, Toronto, Ontario. 1996.

Coroner's Investigation Case File no. 14938, Office of the Chief Coroner for Ontario, Toronto, Ontario. 1996/97.

Archival Sources

Library and Archives Canada
RG 13-1419, no. 174A, Maria McCabe (1889)
RG 13-1627, no. CC522, Annie Rubletz (1940)
RG 13-1637 (1,2,3), no. CC544, Rose Stasiuk (1942)
RG 13-2700, no. CC124, Lovica (Viola) Thompson (1919)

Archives of Ontario
RG-22-392-3617, no. 86, Catherine Graham (1858)
RG 22-392-5598, no. 144, Josephine Flaro (1892)
RG 22-392-4451, no. 105, Charlotte Saunders (1897)
RG 22-392-2821, no. 67, Annie Humeston (1897)
RG 22-392-3826, no. 91, Mary McGraw (1897)
RG 22-392-2388, no. 56, Helen Darrah (1898)
RG 22-392-3296, no. 80, Edith O'Donoghue (1898)
RG 22-392-8749, no. 262, Annie Flavelle (1900)
RG 22-392-495, no. 13, Lucy Nadgwan (1901)
RG 22-392-5519, no. 140, Eliza Logan (1902)
RG 22-392-4890, no. 116, Rachel Boakes (1904)
RG 22-392-4891, no. 116, Louisa Kalkhorst (1904)
RG 22-392-5673, no. 147, Alma Barry (1906)
RG 22-392-3610, no. 86, Hannah Pearson (1906)
RG 22-392-5752, no. 151, Annie Robinson (1909)
RG 22-392-4006, no. 95, Norah Purcell (1910)
RG 22-392, no. 95, Eva Suter (1910)
RG 22-392-5535, no. 140, Pearl Smith (alias Anderson) (1911)
RG 22-392-8976, no. 270, Matilda Samilli (1912)
RG 22-392-8957, no. 269, May Clayton (1912)
RG 22-392-5703, no. 149, Iva Bigford (1912)
RG 22-392-3025, 3026, no. 72, Vina Lucas (1914)
RG 22-392-5776, no. 152, Frances Chapeski (1914)
RG 22-392-5710, no. 149, Julia Taylor (1914)
RG 22-392-75, no. 3, Florence James (1915)
RG 22-392-5204, no. 124, Phoebe Lindsay (1916)
RG 22-392-5209, no. 124, Alice Douglas and Annie Douglas (1917)
RG 22-392-3407, no. 83, Lena and Charles McCabe (1918)
RG 22-392-3144, no. 76, Christina MacKay (1918)
RG 22-392-9138, no. 278, Grace Henderson (1919)

RG 22-392-4511, no. 107, Mabel Huggins (1920)
RG 22-392-2603, no. 62, Gladys Naebel (1923)
RG 22-392-9311, no. 285, Jean Fraser (1926)
RG 22-392-2884, no. 69, Nellie Oliver (1926)
RG 22-392-9312, no. 285, Grace Hamilton (1926)
RG 22-392-2210, no. 51, Vera Fish (1926)
RG 22-392-6807, no. 186, Josephine Lamandio (1927)
RG 22-517, no. 51, Kathleen Whalon (1932)
RG 22-517, no. 51, Dora Chase (1932)
RG 22-517, no. 51, Agnes Fox (alias Fairfield) (1934)
RG 22-517, no. 51, Jean Gruintel (1935)
RG 22-517, no. 51, Edna Damonde (1935)
RG 22-517, no. 51, Leslie Sheardown (1935)
RG 22-517, no. 52, Edna May Atkinson (1936)
RG 22-517, no. 52, Claire Sneath (1936)
RG 22-517, no. 52, Linnie Bessant (1937)
RG 22-517, no. 53, Emma Passarello (1941)
RG 22-517, no. 53, Edna Damonde (1945)
RG 22-517, no. 53, Lucy Hawley (1945)
RG 22-517, no. 53, Vivian Hodge (1945)
RG 22-517, no. 54, Mary-Ellen Thatcher (1949)
RG 22-517, no. 55, Rose Welkie (1951)
RG 22-517, no. 55, Marion Ellison (1952)
RG 22-517, no. 55, Edna LeBlanc (1953)
RG 22-517, no. 56, Dorothy Joan Bryan (1958)
RG 22-517, no. 57, Georgia Manta (1961) *restricted*

Government Documents

Canada. 1912-16. *Criminal Statistics*. Ottawa: Minister of Trade and Commerce.
–. 1917-48. *Statistics of Criminal and Other Offences*. Ottawa: Dominion Bureau of Statistics.
–. 1999. "Child Victims and the Criminal Justice System: Technical Background Paper."
    Ottawa: Department of Justice, Family, Children and Youth Division. (November).
–. 1867-1955. Parliament. House of Commons. *Hansard Parliamentary Debates*. Ottawa.
New South Wales. 1993. "Provocation, Diminished Responsibility and Infanticide." Aus-
    tralia: Law Reform Commission Publication.
Ontario. 1968. *Royal Commission Inquiry into Civil Rights* (McRuer Report). Report no. 1, vol.
    2. Toronto: Queen's Printer, 1968-71.
–. 1996. *Terms of Reference for the Pediatric Review Committee*. Toronto: Office of the Chief
    Coroner.
–. 1998a. *Inquest Recommendations by Topic*. Toronto: Ontario Association of Children's Aid
    Societies (OACAS), February.
–. 1998b. *Ontario Child Mortality Task Force Recommendations*. Toronto: Ontario Association
    of Children's Aid Societies (OACAS), April.
–. Office of the Chief Coroner for Ontario, the Ministry of Public Safety and Security. http://
    www.mpss.jus.gov.on.ca/english/pub_safety/office_coroner/about_coroner.html.

Index

LAW AND
SOCIETY

Gerald Kernerman
Multicultural Nationalism: Civilizing Difference, Constituting Community (2005)

Pamela A. Jordan
Defending Rights in Russia: Lawyers, the State, and Legal Reform in the Post-Soviet Era (2005)

Anna Pratt
Securing Borders: Detention and Deportation in Canada (2005)

Kirsten Johnson Kramar
Unwilling Mothers, Unwanted Babies: Infanticide in Canada (2005)

W.A. Bogart
Good Government? Good Citizens? Courts, Politics, and Markets in a Changing Canada (2005)

Catherine Dauvergne
Humanitarianism, Identity, Nation: Migration Laws of Australia and Canada (2005)

Michael Lee Ross
First Nations Sacred Sites in Canada's Courts (2005)

Andrew Woolford
Between Justice and Certainty: Treaty Making in British Columbia (2005)

John McLaren, Andrew Buck, and Nancy Wright (eds.)
Despotic Dominion: Property Rights in British Settler Societies (2004)

Georges Campeau
From UI to EI: Waging War on the Welfare State (2004)

Alvin J. Esau
The Courts and the Colonies: The Litigation of Hutterite Church Disputes (2004)

Christopher N. Kendall
Gay Male Pornography: An Issue of Sex Discrimination (2004)

Roy B. Flemming
Tournament of Appeals: Granting Judicial Review in Canada (2004)

Constance Backhouse and Nancy L. Backhouse
The Heiress vs the Establishment: Mrs. Campbell's Campaign for Legal Justice (2004)

Christopher P. Manfredi
Feminist Activism in the Supreme Court: Legal Mobilization and the Women's Legal Education and Action Fund (2004)

Annalise Acorn
Compulsory Compassion: A Critique of Restorative Justice (2004)

Jonathan Swainger and Constance Backhouse (eds.)
People and Place: Historical Influences on Legal Culture (2003)

Jim Phillips and Rosemary Gartner
Murdering Holiness: The Trials of Franz Creffield and George Mitchell (2003)

David R. Boyd
Unnatural Law: Rethinking Canadian Environmental Law and Policy (2003)

Ikechi Mgbeoji
Collective Insecurity: The Liberian Crisis, Unilateralism, and Global Order (2003)

Rebecca Johnson
Taxing Choices: The Intersection of Class, Gender, Parenthood,
and the Law (2002)

John McLaren, Robert Menzies, and Dorothy E. Chunn (eds.)
Regulating Lives: Historical Essays on the State, Society, the Individual,
and the Law (2002)

Joan Brockman
Gender in the Legal Profession: Fitting or Breaking the Mould (2001)

Learning Resources
Centre